AMERICA'S
TEST KITCHEN

ALSO BY AMERICA'S TEST KITCHEN

The New Essentials Cookbook

Dinner Illustrated

Cook's Illustrated Revolutionary Recipes

Tasting Italy: A Culinary Journey

Cooking at Home with Bridget and Julia

The Complete Diabetes Cookbook

The Complete Slow Cooker

The Complete Make-Ahead Cookbook

The Complete Mediterranean Cookbook

The Complete Vegetarian Cookbook

The Complete Cooking for Two Cookbook

Just Add Sauce

How to Roast Everything

Nutritious Delicious

What Good Cooks Know

Cook's Science

The Science of Good Cooking

The Perfect Cake

The Perfect Cookie

Bread Illustrated

Master of the Grill

Kitchen Smarts

Kitchen Hacks

100 Recipes: The Absolute Best Ways to Make the True Essentials

The New Family Cookbook

The America's Test Kitchen Cooking School Cookbook

The Cook's Illustrated Meat Book

The Cook's Illustrated Baking Book

The Cook's Illustrated Cookbook

The America's Test Kitchen Family Baking Book

The Best of America's Test Kitchen (2007–2019 Editions)

The Complete America's Test Kitchen TV Show Cookbook 2001–2019

Sous Vide for Everybody

Multicooker Perfection

Food Processor Perfection

Pressure Cooker Perfection

Vegan for Everybody

Naturally Sweet

Foolproof Preserving

Paleo Perfected

The How Can It Be Gluten-Free Cookbook: Volume 2

The How Can It Be Gluten-Free Cookbook

The Best Mexican Recipes

Slow Cooker Revolution Volume 2: The Easy-Prep Edition

Slow Cooker Revolution

The Six-Ingredient Solution

The America's Test Kitchen D.I.Y. Cookbook

THE COOK'S ILLUSTRATED ALL-TIME BEST SERIES

All-Time Best Brunch

All-Time Best Dinners for Two

All-Time Best Sunday Suppers

All-Time Best Holiday Entertaining

All-Time Best Appetizers

All-Time Best Soups

COOK'S COUNTRY TITLES

One-Pan Wonders

Cook It in Cast Iron

Cook's Country Eats Local

The Complete Cook's Country TV Show Cookbook

FOR A FULL LISTING OF ALL OUR BOOKS

CooksIllustrated.com

AmericasTestKitchen.com

PRAISE FOR OTHER AMERICA'S TEST KITCHEN TITLES

"This impressive installment from America's Test Kitchen equips readers with dozens of repertoire-worthy recipes. . . . This is a must-have for beginner cooks and more experienced ones who wish to sharpen their skills."
PUBLISHERS WEEKLY (STARRED REVIEW) ON *THE NEW ESSENTIALS COOKBOOK*

Selected as one of the 10 Best New Cookbooks of 2017
THE LA TIMES ON *THE PERFECT COOKIE*

"*The Perfect Cookie*. . . is, in a word, perfect. This is an important and substantial cookbook. . . . If you love cookies, but have been a tad shy to bake on your own, all your fears will be dissipated. This is one book you can use for years with magnificently happy results."
THE HUFFINGTON POST ON *THE PERFECT COOKIE*

Selected as the Cookbook Award Winner of 2017 in the Baking category
INTERNATIONAL ASSOCIATION OF CULINARY PROFESSIONALS (IACP) ON *BREAD ILLUSTRATED*

"This cookbook from the staff at America's Test Kitchen deserves a place on the bookshelf of every cake baker. More than 200 recipes, all written in the confident voice of the Test Kitchen, will inspire home cooks and offer a master class in baking and decorating."
PUBLISHERS WEEKLY (STARRED REVIEW) ON *THE PERFECT CAKE*

Selected as one of Amazon's Best Books of 2015 in the Cookbooks and Food Writing category
AMAZON ON *THE COMPLETE VEGETARIAN COOKBOOK*

"Another winning cookbook from ATK. . . . The folks at America's Test Kitchen apply their rigorous experiments to determine the facts about these pans."
BOOKLIST ON *COOK IT IN CAST IRON*

"This encyclopedia of meat cookery would feel completely overwhelming if it weren't so meticulously organized and artfully designed. This is Cook's Illustrated at its finest."
THE KITCHN ON THE *COOK'S ILLUSTRATED MEAT BOOK*

"The 21st-century *Fannie Farmer Cookbook* or *The Joy of Cooking*. If you had to have one cookbook and that's all you could have, this one would do it."
CBS SAN FRANCISCO ON *THE NEW FAMILY COOKBOOK*

"This book upgrades slow cooking for discriminating, 21st-century palates—that is indeed revolutionary."
THE DALLAS MORNING NEWS ON *SLOW COOKER REVOLUTION*

"The go-to gift book for newlyweds, small families, or empty nesters."
ORLANDO SENTINEL ON *THE COMPLETE COOKING FOR TWO COOKBOOK*

"The sum total of exhaustive experimentation . . . anyone interested in gluten-free cookery simply shouldn't be without it."
NIGELLA LAWSON ON *THE HOW CAN IT BE GLUTEN-FREE COOKBOOK*

"A one-volume kitchen seminar, addressing in one smart chapter after another the sometimes surprising whys behind a cook's best practices. . . . You get the myth, the theory, the science, and the proof, all rigorously interrogated as only America's Test Kitchen can do."
NPR ON *THE SCIENCE OF GOOD COOKING*

"Some 2,500 photos walk readers through 600 painstakingly tested recipes, leaving little room for error."
ASSOCIATED PRESS ON *THE AMERICA'S TEST KITCHEN COOKING SCHOOL COOKBOOK*

"Some books impress by the sheer audacity of their ambition. Backed up by the magazine's famed mission to test every recipe relentlessly until it is the best it can be, this nearly 900-page volume lands with an authoritative wallop."
CHICAGO TRIBUNE ON *THE COOK'S ILLUSTRATED COOKBOOK*

"This book is a comprehensive, no-nonsense guide. . . a well-thought-out, clearly explained primer for every aspect of home baking."
THE WALL STREET JOURNAL ON *THE COOK'S ILLUSTRATED BAKING BOOK*

COOK IT IN YOUR
DUTCH OVEN

150 Foolproof Recipes Tailor-Made for Your Kitchen's Most Versatile Pot

AMERICA'S TEST KITCHEN

Library of Congress Cataloging-in-Publication Data
Names: America's Test Kitchen (Firm), publisher.
Title: Cook it in your Dutch oven : 150 foolproof recipes tailor-made
    for your kitchen's most versatile pot / America's Test Kitchen.
Description: Boston, MA : America's Test Kitchen, [2018] |
    Includes index.
Identifiers: LCCN 2018024993 | ISBN 9781945256561 (pbk.)
Subjects: LCSH: Dutch oven cooking. | One-dish meals. |
    LCGFT: Cookbooks.
Classification: LCC TX840.D88 C66 2018 | DDC 641.5/89—dc23
LC record available at https://lccn.loc.gov/2018024993

America's Test Kitchen
21 Drydock Avenue, Boston, MA 02210
Manufactured in the United States of America

10 9 8 7 6 5 4 3 2 1

Distributed by Penguin Random House Publisher Services
Tel: 800.733.3000

PICTURED ON FRONT COVER Weeknight Pasta Bolognese (page 63)

PICTURED ON BACK COVER Chicken Pot Pie with Spring
Vegetables (page 28), Coconut Shrimp with Mango Dipping
Sauce (page 209), Roasted Pork Loin with Barley, Butternut
Squash, and Swiss Chard (page 172), Oatmeal-Raisin Bread
(page 274), Blueberry Grunt (page 290)

EDITORIAL DIRECTOR, BOOKS Elizabeth Carduff

EXECUTIVE EDITOR Adam Kowit

EXECUTIVE FOOD EDITOR Dan Zuccarello

DEPUTY FOOD EDITOR Anne Wolf

ASSOCIATE EDITORS Melissa Drumm, Joseph Gitter, and
    Russell Selander

EDITORIAL ASSISTANTS Kelly Gauthier and Alyssa Langer

DESIGN DIRECTOR, BOOKS Carole Goodman

ART DIRECTOR, BOOKS Lindsey Chandler

DEPUTY ART DIRECTORS Allison Boales and Jen Kanavos Hoffman

ASSOCIATE ART DIRECTOR Katie Barranger

PRODUCTION DESIGNER Reinaldo Cruz

PHOTOGRAPHY DIRECTOR Julie Bozzo Cote

PHOTOGRAPHY PRODUCER Meredith Mulcahy

CONTRIBUTING PHOTOGRAPHY DIRECTION Greg Galvan

SENIOR STAFF PHOTOGRAPHER Daniel J. van Ackere

STAFF PHOTOGRAPHERS Steve Klise and Kevin White

ADDITIONAL PHOTOGRAPHY Keller + Keller and Carl Tremblay

FOOD STYLING Catrine Kelty, Chantel Lambeth, Kendra McKnight,
    Marie Piraino, Elle Simone Scott, and Sally Staub

PHOTOSHOOT KITCHEN TEAM

   MANAGER Timothy McQuinn

   LEAD TEST COOK Daniel Cellucci

   TEST COOK Jessica Rudolph

   ASSISTANT TEST COOKS Sarah Ewald, Eric Haessler, and
   Devon Shatkin

PRODUCTION MANAGER Christine Spanger

IMAGING MANAGER Lauren Robbins

PRODUCTION AND IMAGING SPECIALISTS Heather Dube, Dennis Noble,
    and Jessica Voas

COPY EDITOR Jeff Schier

PROOFREADER Karen Wise

INDEXER Elizabeth Parson

CHIEF CREATIVE OFFICER Jack Bishop

EXECUTIVE EDITORIAL DIRECTORS Julia Collin Davison and
    Bridget Lancaster

CONTENTS

WELCOME TO AMERICA'S TEST KITCHEN

This book has been tested, written, and edited by the folks at America's Test Kitchen. Located in Boston's Seaport District in the historic Innovation and Design Building, it features 15,000 square feet of kitchen space, including multiple photography and video studios. It is the home of *Cook's Illustrated* magazine and *Cook's Country* magazine and is the workday destination for more than 60 test cooks, editors, and cookware specialists. Our mission is to test recipes over and over again until we understand how and why they work and until we arrive at the best version.

We start the process of testing a recipe with a complete lack of preconceptions, which means that we accept no claim, no technique, and no recipe at face value. We simply assemble as many variations as possible, test a half-dozen of the most promising, and taste the results blind. We then construct our own recipe and continue to test it, varying ingredients, techniques, and cooking times until we reach a consensus. As we like to say in the test kitchen, "We make the mistakes so you don't have to." The result, we hope, is the best version of a particular recipe, but we realize that only you can be the final judge of our success (or failure). We use the same rigorous approach when we test equipment and taste ingredients.

All of this would not be possible without a belief that good cooking, much like good music, is based on a foundation of objective technique. Some people like spicy foods and others don't, but there is a right way to sauté, there is a best way to cook a pot roast, and there are measurable scientific principles involved in producing perfectly beaten, stable egg whites. Our ultimate goal is to investigate the fundamental principles of cooking to give you the techniques, tools, and ingredients you need to become a better cook. It is as simple as that.

To see what goes on behind the scenes at America's Test Kitchen, check out our social media channels for kitchen snapshots, exclusive content, video tips, and much more. You can watch us work (in our actual test kitchen) by tuning in to America's Test Kitchen or Cook's Country on public television or on our websites. Listen in to test kitchen experts on public radio (SplendidTable.org) to hear insights that illuminate the truth about real home cooking. Want to hone your cooking skills or finally learn how to bake—with an America's Test Kitchen test cook? Enroll in one of our online cooking classes. However you choose to visit us, we welcome you into our kitchen, where you can stand by our side as we test our way to the best recipes in America.

facebook.com/AmericasTestKitchen
twitter.com/TestKitchen
youtube.com/AmericasTestKitchen
instagram.com/TestKitchen
pinterest.com/TestKitchen
google.com/+AmericasTestKitchen

AmericasTestKitchen.com
CooksIllustrated.com
CooksCountry.com
OnlineCookingSchool.com

GETTING STARTED

INTRODUCTION

It may sound bold to declare that an enameled Dutch oven is very nearly the only pot you'll ever need in your kitchen. But the more we use these pots in our own cooking, the more convinced we are that it's true.

Many home cooks relegate their Dutch oven to the back of the cabinet, to be pulled out just for cold-weather soups and braises, or the occasional large batch of beans or grains. But that big, beautiful pot is also a true kitchen workhorse: You can use it to make one-pot weeknight meals (complete with side dishes), fried foods, and even breads and desserts. Plus, if you have an enameled version (and we think you should), it's probably a showpiece to boot. So make room in the front of your cabinet, because with this book you'll reach for your Dutch oven again and again.

These ultraversatile pots aren't new—they've been around for centuries. Dutch ovens were originally made of uncoated cast iron that had to be seasoned; more modern iterations often have enameled coatings that don't require seasoning and are a bit easier to use and clean. These classic pieces of cookware have never gone away, but they are currently experiencing a renewed popularity as more people realize how multipurpose they really are.

In this book we unlocked the full potential of the Dutch oven by creating recipes that not only can be made in a Dutch oven, but should be. We took advantage of the pot's unique features, such as the heavy cast-iron construction, the enameled surface, the high sides, and the tight-fitting lid (read more about these in the pages that follow) to make each and every recipe foolproof. Of course we captured the classics—Ultimate French Onion Soup, Simple Pot Roast, Creamy Mashed Potatoes. But we also found plenty of international inspiration (cooking in heavy, covered pots is a worldwide tradition, from Moroccan tagines to French cocottes) for one-pot dinners like Thai Green Curry with Shrimp, Snow Peas, and Shiitakes, and Latin American Pork and Rice. And did you know you can even use your Dutch oven to make artisanstyle breads, including a showstopping Braided Chocolate Babka, and impressive desserts such as Chocolate-Orange Lava Cake for a Crowd?

When developing recipes, we also took into account that not everyone owns the same-size Dutch oven. A survey of our readers revealed that most own round Dutch ovens with a capacity between 5½ and 7 quarts. Knowing this, we designed all our recipes to work in pots of this shape and size, even testing recipes multiple times in different-size pots to make sure they were foolproof. If your Dutch oven is oval-shaped, or is much smaller or much larger than this range, you may need to adjust cooking times and be more diligent about following visual cues.

Our hope is not only that this book will prove to you how invaluable your Dutch oven is, but that it will cement the Dutch oven's place in your daily cooking routine.

TESTING DUTCH OVENS

Is there anything you can't do with a Dutch oven? We use these large, heavy-duty pots for boiling, searing, frying, braising, baking, and more. They might just be the busiest pots in our kitchen.

Our longtime favorite from Le Creuset works perfectly, but at $367.99 it costs a pretty penny. At the other end of the spectrum is a classic cast-iron model that costs one-seventh as much—and there's a pot in every price bracket in between. So how much do you need to spend to get a Dutch oven that lasts for years, is capable of cooking everything you throw at it, and makes said cooking as easy as possible?

To find out, we chose 11 widely available models priced from $54.31 to $367.99, including the Le Creuset and our longtime favorite inexpensive option from Cuisinart ($83.70). Each holds at least 6.5 quarts, a capacity that works well for all our recipes. We put them through a litany of tests, rating each pot on the quality of its food, how easy it was to use and clean, and how durable it was. We concluded that all the pots are capable of making good food, but some were much easier to use. Here's what mattered.

MATERIAL DIFFERENCES

Lighter, thinner Dutch ovens tend to scorch food because the heat zips right through them, so we focused on heavier ceramic and cast-iron models. The only ceramic model we tested weighed 9.75 pounds; the cast-iron pots ranged from 13.7 to 18.15 pounds. We had hoped that the ceramic might provide a lighter alternative to cast iron, but it proved too fragile for such a workhorse pot. We were nervous handling it, and the lid cracked when we firmly set it on the base from a mere 2 inches up. This left us with the cast-iron models and our next question: coated or uncoated?

All but one of the cast-iron pots were coated with enamel, a type of glass; we tested one uncoated Dutch oven from Lodge, the maker of our winning traditional cast-iron skillet. Like the skillet, it arrived fully seasoned but required extra care, as it has to be dried and oiled immediately after washing.

In the past, when we tested the uncoated Lodge Dutch oven, we found that food cooked in it sometimes tasted metallic. This time around, though, tasters didn't notice any off-flavors, even after we simmered an acidic tomato sauce

OUR FAVORITE DUTCH OVEN ACCESSORIES

WOODEN SPOON An enameled pot can withstand metal utensils, but wooden spoons are best used when possible. The **SCI Bamboo Wood Cooking Spoon** is broad enough to churn bulky stews, yet small enough to rotate a single piece of beef, with an easy-to-grasp rectangular handle.

SILICONE SPATULA This is a helpful tool for scraping down thick sauces or braising liquids from the sides of the Dutch oven before transferring it to the oven. The **Di Oro Living Seamless Silicone Spatula—Large** is firm enough to scrape and scoop, and it fits neatly into tight corners.

TONGS A sturdy pair of tongs makes it easy to transfer pieces of beef, pork, or chicken to and from the Dutch oven, and it's invaluable when deep-frying. Our favorite pair, the **OXO Good Grips 12-Inch Tongs**, has scalloped edges and a comfortable silicone-padded handle. If you prefer silicone-coated tongs, our runner-up is the **OXO Good Grips 12-Inch Tongs with Silicone Heads**.

POTHOLDERS AND OVEN MITTS A Dutch oven's handles get hot, so a good pair of oven mitts or potholders is essential for moving the pot around. We like the **Ritz Basic Potholder** and the **San Jamar Cool Touch Flame Oven Mitt**.

(acid can strip the pot's seasoning) and then cooked fairly neutral white rice and French fries in it. A Lodge representative said that the company is constantly improving its equipment, so newer pots may have more-durable seasoning.

SEEING THE LIGHT

Like the uncoated model, four of the enameled Dutch ovens had dark interiors. This made it difficult to monitor browning and to see how dark our fond got as we seared beef. It also made it more challenging to use our remote thermometer to track the temperature of oil during frying; the dark interior prevented us from easily spotting the tip of the probe to ensure that it wasn't touching the pot, which can cause it to give a false reading. Overall, lighter interiors provided better visibility and were easier to cook in.

Some pots were tall and narrow; others were short and broad. We preferred those with generous cooking surfaces, at least 9 inches across. More usable surface area meant we could work faster, particularly when browning in batches. We also preferred low, straight sides, as tall or curved sides tended to partially block our view into the pot.

Handle style was another important factor, especially since we prefer heavier Dutch ovens. Our lineup included two styles: flat (like little tabs) and looped (semicircles). We much preferred the latter style because the loops allowed for a fuller, more secure grip; bigger loops were even better, especially when we were wearing oven mitts.

A light-colored enameled surface (left) lets you know just how brown your fond is getting so you can avoid scorching.

A POT FOR EVERY KITCHEN

In the end we were able to recommend all but two models; however, the Le Creuset ($367.99) is the best. It is heavy enough to conduct heat well yet is still the lightest of the cast-iron models. It has a broad, light-colored cooking surface; low, straight sides; and large looped handles that make it easy to use.

We recommend the Cuisinart Chef's Classic Enameled Cast Iron Covered Casserole ($83.70) as our Best Buy. It is shaped very similar to the Le Creuset. It's 3 pounds heavier and has smaller handles but costs almost $300.00 less. Like most of the models in our lineup, both of these pots come with a limited lifetime warranty. But the Le Creuset held up better to the kind of everyday wear and tear not covered by the warranty; the Cuisinart pot chipped during our durability tests, while our winner emerged from testing looking as good as new.

RATING DUTCH OVENS

We tested 11 Dutch ovens priced from $54.31 to $367.99. Prices shown are what we paid online. Pots are listed in order of preference.

KEY   Good ★ ★ ★   Fair ★ ★   Poor ★

HIGHLY RECOMMENDED

WINNER LE CREUSET 7¼ Quart Round Dutch Oven
Model: LS2501-28 **Price:** $367.99
Materials: Enameled cast iron, phenolic knob
Weight: 13.7 lbs
Interior Height: 4.5 in
Cooking Surface Diameter: 9 in
Interior Color: Light

Cooking ★ ★ ★
Ease of Use ★ ★ ★
Durability ★ ★ ★

This perfect, pricy pot bested the competition again. It was substantial enough to hold and distribute heat evenly without being unbearably heavy. The light-colored interior and low, straight sides combined to give us good visibility and made it easy to monitor browning and thermometer position. The broad cooking surface saved us time since we could cook more food at once. The lid was smooth and easy to clean. This pot is expensive, but it was exceptionally resistant to damage.

RECOMMENDED

BEST BUY CUISINART Chef's Classic Enameled Cast Iron Covered Casserole
Model: CI670-30CR **Price:** $83.70
Materials: Enameled cast iron
Weight: 16.7 lbs
Interior Height: 4.38 in
Cooking Surface Diameter: 10 in
Interior Color: Light

Cooking ★ ★ ★
Ease of Use ★ ★ ½
Durability ★ ★ ½

With an exceptionally broad cooking surface and low, straight sides, this 7-quart pot shared the same advantageous shape as the Le Creuset. It was heavier, but not prohibitively so. The looped handles were comfortable to hold, though slightly smaller than ideal. The rim and lid chipped cosmetically when we repeatedly slammed the lid onto the pot, so it's slightly less durable than our winner.

CROCK-POT 7 Quart Round Cast Iron Dutch Oven With Lid
Model: 69144.02 **Price:** $79.99
Materials: Enameled cast iron, stainless steel knob
Weight: 14.35 lbs
Interior Height: 5.19 in
Cooking Surface Diameter: 8.88 in
Interior Color: Light

Cooking ★ ★ ★
Ease of Use ★ ★
Durability ★ ★ ★

This pot's large looped handles were easy to grab even with oven mitts on. It also had a light interior so we could ensure our fond didn't burn. The medium weight was hefty enough to conduct heat nicely without being burdensome. It had taller sides and a slightly smaller cooking surface, which at times made it harder to maneuver in and slowed us down, as we had to sear beef in three batches instead of two. But it made great food and was resistant to chipping.

LAVA SIGNATURE 7 Qt. Enameled Cast Iron Round Dutch Oven
Model: LV Y TC 28 K2 BLU **Price:** $134.95
Materials: Enameled cast iron, stainless steel knob
Weight: 14.9 lbs
Interior Height: 4.31 in
Cooking Surface Diameter: 9.75 in
Interior Color: Dark

Cooking ★ ★ ★
Ease of Use ★ ½
Durability ★ ★ ★

With an especially broad cooking surface, this pot got through its searing stages faster than other models. We liked the looped handles (though they weren't as roomy as some) and the low, straight sides. However, the dark interior made it hard to monitor browning. The lid's inner spikes, designed to drip moisture back into the pot (we didn't notice a difference in the food), and ridged design made it harder to clean. This model was very resistant to damage.

STAUB Cast Iron 7 qt Round Cocotte
Model: 1102806 **Price:** $279.99
Materials: Enameled cast iron, stainless steel knob
Weight: 14.95 lbs
Interior Height: 5.13 in
Cooking Surface Diameter: 9.38 in
Interior Color: Dark

Cooking ★ ★ ★
Ease of Use ★ ½
Durability ★ ★ ★

This very durable pot conducted heat well and had a broad cooking surface, which saved time when browning, but the dark interior made it hard to see what was going on. The knob frequently became wiggly, though it was easy to tighten. The handles were looped but a little small. The lid had spikes designed to cycle moisture back into the food (we saw no measurable benefit) and a deep ridge; both made it harder to clean.

LODGE Porcelain Enamel on Cast Iron Dutch Oven
Model: EC7D33 **Price:** $73.99
Materials: Enameled cast iron, stainless steel knob
Weight: 18.15 lbs
Interior Height: 4.38 in
Cooking Surface Diameter: 8 in
Interior Color: Light

Cooking ★★★
Ease of Use ★½
Durability ★★★

This 7.5-quart pot had a light interior and large looped handles that were easy to grab, even with clumsy oven mitts. It was the heaviest pot we tested, and we found that extra weight trying when hauling it out of the oven full of beef stew or flipping it during cleaning. But for all that heft, it had a comparatively small cooking surface, thanks to sloped sides; this meant additional batches when searing beef or meatballs. It passed our durability test handily.

TRAMONTINA 6.5 Qt Enameled Cast-Iron Round Dutch Oven
Model: 80131/621DS **Price:** $58.81
Materials: Enameled cast iron, phenolic knob
Weight: 15.1 lbs
Interior Height: 4.75 in
Cooking Surface Diameter: 8.5 in
Interior Color: Light

Cooking ★★★
Ease of Use ★½
Durability ★★★

With taller sides and a narrower cooking surface, this pot was harder to see into and maneuver. Searing often required an additional batch. Its handles were looped, which we liked, but they were fatter, robbing them of some usable space. The smooth lid made it easy to clean. This model is not recommended for use over 400 degrees because of the knob's material; we cooked a single loaf of bread at 425 degrees and didn't encounter any issues.

LODGE 7-quart Cast Iron Dutch Oven
Model: L10DOL3 Price: $54.31
Materials: Cast iron
Weight: 16.9 lbs
Interior Height: 4.38 in
Cooking Surface Diameter: 8.63 in
Interior Color: Dark

Cooking ★★★
Ease of Use ★½
Durability ★★★

This uncoated cast-iron pot came preseasoned, but we had to dry and oil it immediately after each use. The cast iron never made our food taste metallic, but its manual says to avoid acidic foods "until the seasoning is well-established." We liked the broad cooking surface and low sides, but the dark interior made it hard to see browning, and the handles were a bit small. Breads turned out exceptionally crusty.

RECOMMENDED WITH RESERVATIONS

LA CUISINE 6.5 Qt. Cast Iron Round Casserole
Model: LC 5250MB **Price:** $90.50
Materials: Enameled cast iron, stainless steel knob
Weight: 14.65 lbs
Interior Height: 4.5 in
Cooking Surface Diameter: 8 in
Interior Color: Light

Cooking ★★★
Ease of Use ★
Durability ★★★

This pot's light interior made it easy to position our thermometer and to monitor browning. The pot was heavy enough to hold heat well but not so heavy that it was a bear to use. The smaller cooking surface limited the amount of beef or meatballs it could accommodate at once, which added to our cooking time. Its handles were looped, but they tapered to a point that dug into our hands; this was particularly painful when cleaning the pot or transporting it laden with food.

NOT RECOMMENDED

ANOLON VESTA Cast Iron 7 Qt. Covered Round Dutch Oven
Model: 51822 **Price:** $121.17
Materials: Enameled cast iron, stainless steel loop on lid
Weight: 15.3 lbs
Interior Height: 4.63 in
Cooking Surface Diameter: 8.5 in
Interior Color: Dark

Cooking ★★★
Ease of Use ½
Durability ★★★

This pot's slightly smaller cooking surface meant we had to sear in more batches than ideal. The flat handles were small and dicey to hold, particularly when the pot was full and the handles were greasy from frying or searing. At 5.35 pounds, the lid was notably heavy and stressed our wrists when we lifted it. The interior was dark, which limited our visibility.

EMILE HENRY Flame Top Round Dutch Oven
Model: 794570 **Price:** $200.00
Materials: Ceramic
Weight: 9.75 lbs
Interior Height: 4.63 in
Cooking Surface Diameter: 8.5 in
Interior Color: Dark

Cooking ★★★
Ease of Use ½
Durability ★

The only ceramic pot we tested was comparably light. It cooked a bit slower and had a slightly smaller cooking surface, a dark interior, and flat handles that were hard to grasp. Our major gripe: Ceramic is just too fragile for a workhorse pot. We were always nervous when washing it, plus the lid cracked when we firmly plopped it on the base from a mere 2 inches above.

DON'T JUST STEW—MAKE THE MOST OF YOUR DUTCH OVEN

You already know that you can use your Dutch oven for soups and stews, and you'll find plenty of those recipes in this book. But what you may not know is how much more your Dutch oven can do. We use it in all kinds of applications, both straightforward and unexpected.

MAKE ONE-POT MEALS

Nowhere is the Dutch oven's do-it-all power more apparent than in one-pot meals. Its capacity to hold large amounts of food, along with its ability to handle nearly any cooking method, make preparing a recipe an easy task from start to finish—without reaching for a second pan.

A Real Multitasker Casseroles typically require one pan for preparing a filling and a second for baking. But the Dutch oven does it all; we even use it to toast tortillas for our Beef Enchilada Casserole (page 34) before simmering the sauce and then layering everything in the pot to bake.

Cook Pasta Right in the Sauce Few cooking methods are more delightfully hands-off than pastas that cook in the sauce—no extra pots or draining boiling water necessary. Our one-pot Weeknight Pasta Bolognese (page 63) is the most convenient path to this hearty, rustic dish we know.

BRAISE ANYTHING

The Dutch oven's tight-fitting lid and heavy construction are key to the even, gentle cooking that results in beautifully tender meat, poultry, fish, beans, and vegetables.

Go From Stovetop to Oven With a Dutch oven, we can brown meat and vegetables on the stovetop, then simply cover the pot and move it to the oven to finish cooking. This ensures that none of the flavorful fond is lost.

Cook en Cocotte This classic French method relies on a heavy covered pot to trap moisture released by the food itself, thereby creating a concentrated jus as the meat essentially braises in its own juices, becoming supertender in the process, such as our Leg of Lamb with Garlic and Rosemary Jus (page 182).

FRY YOUR FAVORITE FOODS

Chances are you don't own a deep-fryer—but that doesn't mean you can't make plenty of fried foods, from pub-style fish and chips to doughnuts. Even shallow-fried foods like our Extra-Crunchy Fried Chicken (page 195) are worth making in a Dutch oven, as the pot's high sides alleviate splattering.

Whether you're deep- or shallow-frying, the Dutch oven's heat retention ensures foods fry up crisp, not greasy or soggy. For more information on frying, see page 8.

ROAST MEAT WITH SIDES

The idea may not immediately spring to mind, but a Dutch oven is excellent for roasting. As it does with braising, the pot makes it easy to brown meat on the stovetop before going into the oven (uncovered, in this case) to finish.

Concentrate Liquids Compared with a roasting pan, the Dutch oven's more-enclosed space means that any liquid can concentrate without fully evaporating. For our Chicken in a Pot with Red Potatoes, Carrots, and Shallots (page 148), a cup of liquid helped the vegetables turn tender while reducing just enough to become an intense jus. The pot's shape also lets us place a roast directly atop vegetables so that its juices can baste and flavor them as they cook.

Cover, or Don't Unlike a roasting pan, a Dutch oven comes with a lid. This feature proved especially beneficial in recipes such as Braised Short Ribs with Wild Mushroom Farrotto (page 156), in which we roasted the meat uncovered to brown it and render fat, before covering the pot to allow the ribs and farro to finish cooking by braising gently.

BAKE ARTISAN-STYLE BREADS

Using a Dutch oven is hands-down the easiest way to re-create the loaves you find at a bakery. The pot mimics the steamy environment of a professional bread oven to create open interiors and crisp crusts, and it also helps enriched doughs rise high as they bake. For more information on baking bread in a Dutch oven, see page 10.

MAKE "ONE-BOWL" DESSERTS

For many of the desserts in this book, the Dutch oven acts not only as a baking dish, but also as an extra-large mixing bowl. This saves on dishes and also makes it easy to combine large volumes of ingredients. In our Pear-Ginger Crisp (page 286) and Apple Pandowdy (page 284), for example, we mix a generous 5 pounds of fruit with the sugar and other filling ingredients right in the pot.

FRY WITHOUT FEAR IN YOUR DUTCH OVEN

Many cooks shy away from frying at home, but it's easy and largely foolproof with a Dutch oven and a good thermometer. Why? The cast-iron construction of our preferred Dutch oven means it has an uncanny ability to retain and regain heat—key when frying, since fried foods need to be cooked at a consistently hot oil temperature to turn out browned and crispy. The Dutch oven's high sides cut down on splattering, while the roomy interior gives food plenty of space to cook, preventing items from sticking to one another as they fry in the oil. And finally, a light-colored enamel surface makes it easier to position a temperature probe successfully in the pot (if the probe is sitting directly on the surface of the pot, it may give an inaccurate reading). With your Dutch oven by your side and by following the tips below, you'll be able to turn out great fried food every time.

1 **Use the right amount of oil** There are two ways to fry: shallow-frying, where the oil comes partway up the food, which therefore must be flipped partway through cooking; and deep-frying, which means that the food is completely submerged in the oil. When shallow-frying, make sure the oil reaches halfway up the sides of the food; otherwise, you'll end up with a pale band around the exterior. When deep-frying, make sure not to fill the pot more than half full with oil to avoid splattering once food is added. Follow the guidelines in the recipes for how high the oil level in the pot should be.

2 **Monitor the temperature** When deep-frying, use a clip-on candy/deep-fry thermometer to guarantee that the oil reaches—and remains at—the target temperature (generally between 325 and 375 degrees). Don't let the thermometer touch the bottom or sides of the pot; if it does, you may get a false reading. Our favorite clip-on probe thermometer is the **ThermoWorks ChefAlarm**, which is intuitive and easy to use. Keep in mind that you may need to adjust the burner to keep the oil at a constant temperature, turning it up slightly when food is added, then gradually down again as the oil regains heat.

3 **Include some "recycled" oil when deep-frying** The first batch is often paler and less crispy than those that follow. But by mixing strained, previously used frying oil into fresh oil, you can get golden, crispy results from the start. Why? Oil that's already been exposed to heat produces surfactants that can penetrate the water barrier that surrounds food as it fries. This increased contact promotes browning and a nice crust. We like to use a 1:5 ratio of used oil to fresh. A few rules to follow when reusing oil: Let the oil cool completely, then strain it through at least two layers of cheesecloth or coffee filters. Store used oil in the refrigerator, and discard it after three uses; at that point it will have degraded too much. Don't reuse oil that smoked or that was used to fry fish.

4 **Fry in batches** Add food to the hot oil in small portions. Even in a cast iron pot, adding too much food at once will make the temperature drop too much and will result in soggy—rather than crisp—fried food.

5 **Let the fried food drain** Use a spider skimmer or a slotted spoon to remove food from the oil; the gaps will help drain oil away immediately. Our favorite spider skimmer is the **Rösle Wire Skimmer**, which has a long handle to keep hands safely away from the hot oil. For larger, less delicate items like our Extra-Crunchy Fried Chicken (page 195) or Texas Chicken-Fried Steaks (page 201), you can also use tongs to fish the food from the oil. Let the finished food drain on paper towels or a wire rack to minimize greasiness.

WHY IS THE OIL TEMPERATURE IMPORTANT?

In order to create a crisp crust on fried foods, moisture (in the form of steam) must be quickly driven from the food's surface. As the steam flees the frying food, it leaves tiny craters in its wake, and a small amount of oil moves in to take its place. As the food cooks, its outermost coating of starch (we generally fry starchy food, or nonstarchy food battered in starch) dries out, becoming porous and crispy, with lots of oil clinging to the newly formed crust. If the oil isn't hot enough, the moisture will not turn to steam, the outer edge will not dry out, and the trademark brown and crispy crust will not form.

BRING THE BAKERY HOME WITH DUTCH OVEN BREADS

One of the most impressive feats you can pull off in your Dutch oven is producing artisan-style breads. The covered pot's steamy interior gives loaves a dramatic open crumb and a crisp crust that otherwise can be difficult to achieve at home. That's not all: Heavy cast-iron Dutch ovens can do the work of a baking stone, transferring heat evenly and steadily to bread, encouraging the development of a thick, crisp bottom crust. A baking stone also provides an initial blast of heat that causes a loaf to rise high—what we call "oven spring"—which gives the bread an airier crumb. We use a Dutch oven to similar effect in our Fig and Fennel Bread (page 270), lowering the dough into a preheated pot, which gives the bread superior lift and a crispier crust. The Dutch oven's round shape and high sides also help bread—which can seem to have a mind of its own—hold its shape while proofing and baking. Even soft, dairy-enriched doughs like Braided Chocolate Babka (page 280) and Pull-Apart Dinner Rolls (page 276) rise tall and beautiful. These tips and tidbits will also help you to produce perfect loaves.

1 Measure everything (even liquids) by weight The ratio of flour to water in your recipe greatly impacts the end result, so accuracy in measuring is crucial. We highly recommend buying a digital kitchen scale (our favorite is the **OXO Good Grips 11 lb Food Scale with Pull Out Display**).

2 Use a stand mixer Although you can knead most doughs by hand, we recommend using a stand mixer with a dough hook attachment. Not only is this easier and faster—the mixer does all the work—but you're more likely to get good results because you won't be tempted to add extra flour to a sticky dough, which can compromise the texture of the baked loaf. (You want a mixer with a strong motor that can knead stiff dough with ease; our favorite is the **KitchenAid Pro Line Series 7-Qt Bowl Lift Stand Mixer**.) With a dough hook, kneading takes about 8 minutes. The dough will at first stick to the bowl's sides. After 4 minutes, it will start to pull away from the bowl. Fully kneaded dough will clear the bowl's sides and feel elastic enough that it can be pulled like a rubber band without snapping.

3 Slash before baking Slashing a loaf creates designated weak spots in the dough's gluten sheath that is formed during shaping. The slashes allow the loaf to expand in the right direction in the oven. Without the slashes, the loaf will expand in an odd shape. You can make slashes with a sharp paring knife or a single-edge razor blade. In this book, we slash our breads in a ½-inch-deep X shape. Act decisively when slashing; otherwise, the implement will drag, creating messy lines.

4 Know when it's done For our breads, we give both an internal temperature and a visual cue for doneness. It's important to pay attention to both: If you pull a loaf as soon as it comes to temperature, it could have a pale, soft crust and a gummy interior. Waiting until the crust reaches the indicated color will ensure more flavor and a perfectly baked crumb. Why? Bread contains moisture, so the temperature of a loaf plateaus because it cannot rise above the boiling point of water (212 degrees). This means that bread registering 210 degrees won't overbake if you leave it in the oven until the exterior is properly browned. We take a bread's temperature with an instant-read thermometer to avoid keeping our hand in the oven any long than necessary; our favorite is the **ThermoWorks Thermapen Mk4**.

5 Cool it completely The hard work is done, and your reward is a beautifully browned loaf. But that cast-iron Dutch oven is still hot! That's why we initially lower our dough into the pot using a parchment sling, which facilitates quick removal after baking. The next step is a challenge—resisting the urge to slice into warm bread! As the loaf cools to room temperature, its starches continue to gelatinize, excess moisture evaporates, and the true flavor of the loaf comes to the fore. This can take 3 hours for most large loaves. For perfect cooling, place your loaf or rolls on a wire cooling rack so that air can circulate, preventing escaping moisture from softening the crust. When your loaf is finally ready, be sure to use a serrated knife (not a chef's knife), which preserves the loaf's crust and interior holes as it slices back and forth through the bread.

WHY IS STEAM IMPORTANT IN BREAD BAKING?

Professional bread bakers use steam-injected ovens. The moist environment transfers heat more rapidly to the dough than dry heat does, allowing the gases inside the loaf to expand quickly in the first few minutes of baking, to ensure maximum volume. Steam prevents the bread's exterior from drying out too quickly, which would limit rise, and converts the exterior starches into a thin coating of gel that eventually results in a glossy, crackly crust. For this reason, we bake breads such as Almost No-Knead Bread in a covered Dutch oven. The moisture escaping from the dough creates a steamy environment similar to that of professional ovens—only on a smaller scale. Uncovering the pot for the last part of baking allows the crust to dry out and brown.

HACK YOUR DUTCH OVEN

Braising and baking are all well and good—but your Dutch oven can do even more with these fun tricks.

Heavyweight champ Dutch ovens are heavy—probably one of the heaviest pots in your kitchen. Their solid construction is key to their ability to retain heat well, but it's also handy in a number of other ways, too. Try using it to weigh down tofu to rid it of extra moisture before stir-frying. You can also use it to press a butterflied chicken during cooking, as in classic chicken-under-a-brick (just wrap foil around the bottom of the pot to make cleanup a breeze). No panini press? No problem: Place your sandwiches on a hot skillet, then gently place the Dutch oven on top of them to get near-perfect paninis.

Think outside the pot In our Chicken Pot Pie with Spring Vegetables (page 28), we flip the lid upside down to cover the filling and bake a puff pastry crust on top of the inverted lid. This trick saves having to fit a separate rimmed baking sheet in the oven (and having to wash it later): The lid emulates a baking sheet, allowing heat to circulate around the crust and encouraging it to crisp evenly, and prevents the crust from turning soggy, as it would if baked directly on top of the filling. The lid has other uses, too (beyond simply covering the pot). Invert it and use it to keep your counters clean by resting greasy utensils on it while you're cooking, or place browned pieces of chicken, beef, or pork on it when cooking in batches.

Pull double duty In our Smothered Pork Chops with Broccoli (page 167), we place a steamer basket of broccoli on top of the pork partway through cooking. This way we don't have to wait for an additional pot of water to come to a simmer, we don't have to wash that second pot, and we don't have to coat our broccoli in gravy to cook it. This trick could easily be applied in a number of braises, as long as you have a steamer basket that will lift vegetables above the level of the liquid. Try it with asparagus, green beans, carrots, or peas.

Cool down Dutch ovens' cast-iron material is great for maintaining a consistent temperature. But this feature doesn't apply just to heat—it works with cold as well. The next time you need to keep a dish such as a salad cold for company, or if you need a punch bowl, try placing your Dutch oven in the refrigerator until the pot is thoroughly chilled (you can also fill it with ice water and let it stand for 5 minutes). Then transfer chilled food into the pot for serving. The pot will retain the cold temperature much longer than would a glass or plastic serving bowl.

SHOW IT OFF: KEEPING YOUR DUTCH OVEN PRISTINE

Now that you know which Dutch oven to buy and how to put it to work, you might be wondering how to preserve that investment. We know these pots aren't cheap, but with a little care and a few tricks, you can ensure that this showpiece always remains the pride of your kitchen.

A CHIP OFF THE OLD POT

Enamel is a glass-like coating that is fired onto the cast-iron pot, similar to a glaze that is painted and fired onto pottery. If it's sharply struck with something harder, it can crack or chip. While you don't need to avoid metal utensils entirely, just be sure to take care when you do use them: Try not to bang them against the edge of the pot or strike the inside too hard. Other good practices to keep your pot in tip-top shape: Don't subject it to dramatic temperature changes, especially near moisture; don't heat an empty pot; and reserve high heat for boiling water or for cooking dishes with plenty of liquid.

If your enameled cookware does crack or chip, it's not the end of the world: There's just plain cast iron under the enamel, which is perfectly safe to cook with.

STUBBORN MESS? DON'T WORRY.

We've created our share of messes in the test kitchen and have had a few cooking snafus that required tons of cleanup. Here's how to clean your enameled cookware.

1 Boil Water Fill it halfway with tap water and put the pan on the stovetop, uncovered. Bring to a boil and boil briskly for 2 or 3 minutes, then turn off the burner.

2 Scrape Off Residue Scrape the pan with a wooden spatula, pour off the water, and let the pan sit briefly. Residue will start to flake off as the pan dries. Wash the cookware with hot water and dishwashing liquid, and then dry.

A LITTLE BLEACH TO THE RESCUE

Our favorite Dutch ovens have light-colored enameled interiors, which allow us to monitor browning. But the downside is that the surfaces easily become discolored and stained with use. To solve this, we soak them in a solution of 1 part bleach to 3 parts water. After standing overnight, a lightly stained pot was just as good as new. A heavily stained one required an additional night of soaking before it, too, was stain-free.

SAFE HANDLING

Our favorite Dutch oven is made almost entirely of cast iron, except for its phenolic lid handle. While in newer pots this knob is ovensafe up to 500 degrees, knobs on older pots are ovensafe only to 390 degrees (check the owner's manual for more information). So if you plan to put the covered pot in the oven at higher temps, you may need to replace the handle. You can also simply remove it and cover the pot with foil before putting the lid on to get a good seal.

Chicken Pot Pie with Spring Vegetables

ONE-POT DINNERS

EASY WEEKNIGHT CHICKEN TACOS

SERVES 4   TOTAL TIME 45 MINUTES

WHY THIS RECIPE WORKS Braising in a Dutch oven is often used for long, slow cooking, but it's also well suited for quick weeknight-friendly dinners like this flavor-packed chicken taco filling. We built a savory, well-balanced braising base with smoky chipotle in adobo, aromatic garlic and cilantro, bright and acidic orange juice, and savory Worcestershire sauce. Nestling chicken breasts right into the pot imbued both the braising liquid and the chicken with bold flavor; covering the pot during the brief cook time ensured that the chicken cooked evenly. Once the chicken was done, we reduced the braising liquid into an easy sauce right in the Dutch oven. A little mustard thickened the sauce and provided a sharp counterpoint to the sweet orange juice. Finally, we shredded and sauced the chicken; warm tortillas and a few basic toppings completed our tacos. To warm the tortillas, stack them on a plate, cover with a damp dish towel, and microwave for 60 to 90 seconds. Serve with shredded cheese, shredded lettuce, chopped tomatoes, diced avocado, and sour cream.

3 tablespoons unsalted butter

4 garlic cloves, minced

2 teaspoons minced canned chipotle chile in adobo sauce

¾ cup chopped fresh cilantro

½ cup orange juice

1 tablespoon Worcestershire sauce

1½ pounds boneless, skinless chicken breasts, trimmed

1 teaspoon yellow mustard
  Salt and pepper

12 (6-inch) flour tortillas, warmed
  Lime wedges

1 Melt butter in Dutch oven over medium-high heat. Add garlic and chipotle and cook until fragrant, about 30 seconds. Stir in ½ cup cilantro, orange juice, and Worcestershire and bring to simmer. Nestle chicken into pot. Reduce heat to medium-low, cover, and cook until chicken registers 160 degrees, about 15 minutes, flipping chicken halfway through cooking.

2 Transfer chicken to cutting board, let cool slightly, then shred into bite-size pieces using 2 forks.

3 Meanwhile, increase heat to medium-high and cook liquid left in pot until reduced to ¼ cup, about 5 minutes. Off heat, whisk in mustard. Add chicken and remaining ¼ cup cilantro and toss to combine. Season with salt and pepper to taste. Serve with tortillas and lime wedges.

MEDITERRANEAN CHICKEN WITH EGGPLANT AND SPINACH

SERVES 4   TOTAL TIME 1 HOUR

WHY THIS RECIPE WORKS This Mediterranean-inspired meal of chicken with eggplant, spinach, and bulgur is healthy, delicious, and simple to make. Our roomy Dutch oven allowed us to cook both the chicken and the vegetables at once. We started by browning boneless, skinless chicken breasts to give them more flavor. We then set the chicken aside while we sautéed the eggplant with some aromatics—onion, garlic, coriander, and fenugreek—which gave the dish layers of flavor and cut down on excess moisture. Next, we stirred in canned diced tomatoes and returned our chicken to the pot. After about 15 minutes, we simply removed the perfectly cooked chicken from the pot and stirred some baby spinach into the warm vegetables so it could wilt slightly. To complete our meal, we microwaved quick-cooking bulgur with some chicken broth and curry powder for a simple but flavor-packed accompaniment—no additional pots or pans required. Adding cilantro to the bulgur and sprinkling more over the chicken and vegetables provided freshness, and a squeeze of lime delivered instant brightness. When shopping, do not confuse bulgur with cracked wheat, which has a much longer cooking time and will not work in this recipe.

4 (6- to 8-ounce) boneless, skinless chicken breasts, trimmed
  Salt and pepper
2 tablespoons extra-virgin olive oil
1 pound eggplant, cut into ½-inch pieces
1 onion, chopped
3 garlic cloves, minced
2 teaspoons ground coriander
1 teaspoon ground fenugreek
1 (14.5-ounce) can diced tomatoes, drained
1½ cups chicken broth
1 cup fine-grind bulgur
2 teaspoons curry powder
¼ cup minced fresh cilantro
4 ounces (4 cups) baby spinach
  Lime wedges

1 Pat chicken dry with paper towels and season with salt and pepper. Heat 1 tablespoon oil in Dutch oven over medium-high heat until just smoking. Brown chicken on both sides, 8 to 10 minutes; transfer to plate.

2 Add remaining 1 tablespoon oil, eggplant, onion, ½ teaspoon salt, and ½ teaspoon pepper to now-empty pot; cook over medium heat until vegetables are softened and lightly browned, 5 to 7 minutes. Stir in garlic, coriander, and fenugreek and cook until fragrant, about 30 seconds. Stir in tomatoes and bring to simmer. Nestle chicken into pot, adding any accumulated juices. Reduce heat to low, cover, and cook until chicken registers 160 degrees, about 15 minutes, flipping chicken halfway through cooking.

3 Meanwhile, combine broth, bulgur, curry powder, and ½ teaspoon salt in large bowl. Microwave, covered, until bulgur is tender and all liquid has been absorbed, about 5 minutes. Add 2 tablespoons cilantro and fluff with fork to combine; cover to keep warm.

4 Transfer chicken to serving platter and tent with aluminum foil. Add spinach to eggplant mixture and cook over medium heat, stirring occasionally, until spinach is wilted and tender, about 3 minutes. Season with salt and pepper to taste and sprinkle with remaining 2 tablespoons cilantro. Serve with lime wedges.

COUSCOUS RISOTTO WITH CHICKEN AND SPINACH

SERVES 4   TOTAL TIME 50 MINUTES

WHY THIS RECIPE WORKS This ultrasimple and appealing recipe transforms pearl couscous into a creamy, risotto-like dish using just a few humble ingredients. We used the Dutch oven first to brown bite-size pieces of chicken, then we set the chicken aside so it wouldn't overcook while the couscous simmered. Leeks gave our dish aromatic backbone, and toasting the couscous while softening the leeks brought out its nutty flavor. Chicken broth offered more depth than water. Finally, we stirred the chicken back into the pot so it could finish cooking through, then stirred in baby spinach and peas for spring-y flavor and Parmesan for nutty depth. To give the dish a texture and richness reminiscent of risotto, we stirred in 1/3 cup of cream. Pearl couscous is often labeled Israeli couscous in the supermarket. Do not substitute regular couscous, as it requires a different cooking method and will not work in this recipe. Depending on the size of your Dutch oven, you may need to brown the chicken in two batches rather than one.

2   pounds boneless, skinless chicken breasts, trimmed and cut into 1-inch pieces
    Salt and pepper
3   tablespoons unsalted butter
2   leeks, white and light green parts only, halved lengthwise, sliced thin, and washed thoroughly
1½ cups pearl couscous
3   cups chicken broth
2   ounces (2 cups) baby spinach, chopped coarse
1½ ounces Parmesan cheese, grated (¾ cup)
½   cup frozen peas
⅓   cup heavy cream

1 Season chicken with salt and pepper. Melt 1 tablespoon butter in Dutch oven over medium-high heat. Brown chicken on all sides, about 6 minutes; transfer to bowl.

2 Melt remaining 2 tablespoons butter in now-empty pot over medium heat. Add leeks and couscous and cook until leeks have softened and couscous is lightly toasted, 4 to 6 minutes. Stir in broth and 1 teaspoon salt and bring to simmer. Reduce heat to medium-low, cover, and cook, stirring occasionally, until couscous is tender, about 12 minutes.

3 Stir in chicken and any accumulated juices and cook, covered, until chicken is cooked through, about 5 minutes. Off heat, stir in spinach, Parmesan, peas, and cream and let sit until heated through, about 5 minutes. Serve.

CLEANING LEEKS

1 Lay trimmed, halved leeks cut side down on cutting board and cut to desired size.

2 Transfer leeks to bowl of cold water and rub together until layers separate. Set aside for 1 minute to allow grit to settle to bottom of bowl.

3 Lift leeks from water and transfer to colander to drain. (Do not pour leeks from bowl into colander, or you'll pour dirt over them again.)

CLASSIC CHICKEN CURRY

SERVES 4   TOTAL TIME 1 HOUR 30 MINUTES

WHY THIS RECIPE WORKS The complex flavor of fragrant and rich Indian curry elevates even simple chicken breasts and potatoes in this classic, warming dish. To keep our recipe approachable, we bypassed the laundry list of spices and simply bloomed store-bought curry powder in butter to maximize its flavor. We then created a flavorful base with aromatics like onion, jalapeño, garlic, and ginger. Staggering the addition of each ingredient was key to getting each element cooked perfectly: We first added two bone-in split chicken breasts to the pot and simmered them, covered, until they were tender enough to shred. We removed the chicken, added the potatoes, and let the potatoes cook for a few minutes before adding the cauliflower. When the chicken was cool enough, we shredded it and added it back to the pot along with peas, allowing them to just warm through but not overcook. Whole-milk yogurt offered creaminess and tang, and a sprinkle of bright, fresh cilantro made for a nice finishing touch. Do not substitute low-fat or nonfat yogurt for the whole-milk yogurt called for in this recipe, or the finished dish will be much less creamy. Serve with rice.

3 tablespoons unsalted butter

2 tablespoons curry powder

2 onions, chopped

1 jalapeño chile, stemmed, seeded, and minced
  Salt and pepper

3 garlic cloves, minced

1 tablespoon grated fresh ginger

2 (12-ounce) bone-in split chicken breasts, trimmed

1½ cups water

8 ounces Yukon Gold potatoes, peeled and cut into ½-inch pieces

½ head cauliflower (1 pound), cored and cut into 1-inch florets

1 cup frozen peas

¾ cup plain whole-milk yogurt

¼ cup minced fresh cilantro

1 Melt butter in Dutch oven over medium heat. Add curry powder and cook until fragrant, about 10 seconds. Stir in onions, jalapeño, 1¼ teaspoons salt, and ¼ teaspoon pepper and cook until vegetables are softened, about 5 minutes. Stir in garlic and ginger and cook until fragrant, about 30 seconds.

2 Add chicken and water to pot and bring to simmer. Reduce heat to low, cover, and cook until chicken registers 160 degrees, 22 to 24 minutes, flipping chicken halfway through cooking. Transfer chicken to cutting board, let cool slightly, then shred into rough 2-inch pieces using 2 forks; discard skin and bones.

3 Meanwhile, stir potatoes and ¼ teaspoon salt into curry, cover, and cook over low heat until potatoes are slightly tender, about 8 minutes. Stir in cauliflower and cook, covered, until potatoes are fully cooked and cauliflower is tender, about 15 minutes, stirring occasionally. Stir in chicken and peas and cook until heated through, about 1 minute. Off heat, stir in yogurt and cilantro. Season with salt and pepper to taste. Serve.

PAELLA

SERVES 6   TOTAL TIME 1 HOUR 45 MINUTES

WHY THIS RECIPE WORKS Named for the broad steel pan in which it is traditionally prepared, Spain's most famous rice dish, paella, is a showstopping one-pot meal. But most American cooks don't own a paella pan. Luckily, our Dutch oven's ability to retain heat, along with its broad base, made it a perfect stand-in for the traditional pan. For proteins, tasters liked a combination of chorizo, chicken thighs, shrimp, and mussels because of their varying flavors and textures. Browning the chicken and chorizo deepened their flavor, and cooking the garlic, onions, and tomatoes (canned diced tomatoes, which are consistent in quality year-round) in the rendered fat further boosted the dish's savory depth. Chicken broth, white wine, saffron, and a bay leaf were the perfect choices for liquid and seasoning, adding the right amount of flavor without overcomplicating our recipe. Moving the pot to the oven allowed everything to cook through gently and evenly, and adding the shrimp and mussels partway through ensured that these delicate items didn't overcook. However, the oven's even heat and the Dutch oven's excellent insulation meant that the traditional layer of crunchy rice, known as *socarrat*, didn't naturally form on the bottom of the pot. This was easy to fix; we could simply move the pot back to the direct heat of the stovetop to crisp up the bottom layer of rice. A final drizzle of decadent aïoli on each serving brought extra richness to this company-worthy dish. Dry-cured Spanish chorizo is the sausage of choice for paella, but fresh chorizo or linguiça sausage is an acceptable substitute. We have included directions for how to make socarrat in step 7, but if you prefer you can skip this step and go directly from step 6 to step 8. Serve with Aïoli (recipe follows).

1 pound extra-large shrimp (21 to 25 per pound), peeled and deveined

2 tablespoons extra-virgin olive oil, plus extra as needed

8 garlic cloves, minced
   Salt and pepper

1 pound boneless, skinless chicken thighs, trimmed and halved crosswise

1 red bell pepper, stemmed, seeded, and cut into ½-inch-wide strips

8 ounces Spanish-style chorizo sausage, sliced on bias ½ inch thick

1 onion, chopped fine

1 (14.5-ounce) can diced tomatoes, drained, minced, and drained again

2 cups Valencia or Arborio rice

3 cups chicken broth

⅓ cup dry white wine

½ teaspoon saffron threads, crumbled

1 bay leaf

12 mussels, scrubbed and debearded

½ cup frozen peas, thawed

2 teaspoons chopped fresh parsley
   Lemon wedges

1 Adjust oven rack to lower-middle position and heat oven to 350 degrees. Toss shrimp with 1 tablespoon oil, 1 teaspoon minced garlic, ¼ teaspoon salt, and ¼ teaspoon pepper in bowl; cover and refrigerate until needed. Pat chicken dry with paper towels and season with salt and pepper.

2 Heat 2 teaspoons oil in Dutch oven over medium-high heat until shimmering. Add bell pepper and cook, stirring occasionally, until skin begins to blister and turn spotty black, about 4 minutes; transfer to bowl.

3 Heat remaining 1 teaspoon oil in now-empty pot until shimmering. Add chicken in single layer and cook, undisturbed, until browned, about 3 minutes. Turn pieces and cook until browned on second side, about 3 minutes; transfer to separate bowl. Add chorizo to now-empty pot and cook over medium heat, stirring frequently, until deeply browned and fat begins to render, about 5 minutes; transfer to bowl with chicken.

4 Add extra oil to fat left in pot to equal 2 tablespoons and heat over medium heat until shimmering. Add onion and cook until softened, about 3 minutes. Stir in remaining garlic and cook until fragrant, about 1 minute. Stir in tomatoes and cook until mixture begins to darken and thicken slightly, about 3 minutes. Stir in rice and cook until grains are well coated with tomato mixture, about 2 minutes.

5 Stir in broth, wine, saffron, bay leaf, and ½ teaspoon salt. Return chicken and chorizo to pot, increase heat to medium-high, and bring to boil, stirring occasionally. Cover, transfer pot to oven, and bake until almost all liquid is absorbed, 15 to 20 minutes.

6 Remove pot from oven. Scatter shrimp and mussels evenly over rice and push hinge side of mussels into rice so they stand up. Cover, return pot to oven, and bake until shrimp are opaque throughout and mussels have opened, 10 to 15 minutes.

7 For optional socarrat, transfer pot to stovetop and remove lid. Cook over medium-high heat for about 5 minutes, rotating pot as needed, until bottom layer of rice is well browned and crisp.

8 Discard any mussels that refuse to open and bay leaf, if it can be easily removed. Arrange bell pepper strips in pinwheel pattern over rice and sprinkle peas over top. Cover and let paella sit for 5 minutes. Sprinkle with parsley and serve with lemon wedges.

AÏOLI
MAKES ABOUT 1 CUP
The egg yolks in this recipe are not cooked. If you prefer, ¼ cup Egg Beaters may be substituted.

- 2 large egg yolks
- 4 teaspoons lemon juice
- 2 garlic cloves, peeled and smashed
- 1 tablespoon water, plus extra as needed
- ¼ teaspoon Dijon mustard
- ⅛ teaspoon sugar
-    Salt and pepper
- ¾ cup vegetable oil

Process egg yolks, lemon juice, garlic, water, mustard, sugar, and ¼ teaspoon salt in blender until combined, about 10 seconds, scraping down sides of blender jar as needed. With blender running, slowly add oil and process until aïoli is emulsified, about 2 minutes. Adjust consistency with water as needed. Season with salt and pepper to taste. (Aïoli can be refrigerated for up to 3 days.)

DEBEARDING MUSSELS

Occasionally, mussels will have a weedy but harmless piece, called a beard, protruding from their shells. To remove it, grasp the beard between your thumb and the flat side of a paring knife and tug.

Paella

Chicken Pot Pie with Spring Vegetables

CHICKEN POT PIE WITH SPRING VEGETABLES

SERVES 6   TOTAL TIME 1 HOUR 30 MINUTES

WHY THIS RECIPE WORKS The delights of classic chicken pot pie are many—from the burnished, flaky crust to the luscious, savory filling. But putting it together can be a chore: Between making pie dough (which often requires pulling out a food processor), poaching chicken in one pot and building a gravy in another, and then transferring the filling and crust to a pie plate to bake, this comfort food requires a major time commitment, not to mention a battery of pots and pans. We wanted an easier way and found our trusty Dutch oven to be just the ticket to get us there using only one pot. Boneless, skinless chicken thighs, cut into pieces, were easy to work with and stayed moist through cooking. While tasters liked the deeper flavor provided by browning the chicken, they weren't keen on the crusty, browned exterior on the pieces—it didn't jive with the luxurious, creamy filling. Instead, we simply stirred bite-size pieces of chicken right into the gravy and turned to two powerhouse ingredients—tomato paste and soy sauce—to boost savoriness without being distinguishable in their own right. To give our pot pie fresh spring flavor we swapped in leeks for onions and stirred in some fresh asparagus, peas, and tarragon after pulling the pot from the oven. With our one-pot filling perfected, we turned to the crust. Instead of labor-intensive home-made pastry, we decided to use buttery store-bought puff pastry and wove it into a simple but stunning lattice. But no matter what we tried, baking the crust on top of the filling inevitably led to sorry, soggy results. In the past we skirted this problem by baking the crust separately on a baking sheet, but we were hesitant to add more dishes to our recipe. We realized, however, that the lid of the Dutch oven could act as a stand-in baking sheet: We simply turned the lid upside down before covering the pot and baked the pastry on top. A simple egg wash turned the crust a deep golden. Once we slid the baked crust onto the filling, our simplified centerpiece was complete. To thaw frozen puff pastry, let it sit either in the refrigerator for 24 hours or on the counter for 30 minutes to 1 hour. We prefer to place the baked pastry on top of the filling in the pot just before serving for an impressive presentation; however, you can also cut the pastry into wedges and place them over individual portions of the filling.

1 (9½ by 9-inch) sheet puff pastry, thawed
4 tablespoons unsalted butter
1 pound leeks, white and light green parts only, halved lengthwise, cut into ½-inch pieces, and washed thoroughly
4 carrots, peeled and cut into ½-inch pieces
Salt and pepper
½ cup all-purpose flour
4 garlic cloves, minced
1 teaspoon tomato paste
3 cups chicken broth, plus extra as needed

¼ cup heavy cream
1 teaspoon soy sauce
2 bay leaves
2 pounds boneless, skinless chicken thighs, trimmed and cut into 1-inch pieces
1 large egg, lightly beaten
1 pound asparagus, trimmed and cut on bias into 1-inch lengths
1 cup frozen peas
2 tablespoons chopped fresh tarragon or parsley
1 tablespoon grated lemon zest plus 2 teaspoons juice

1 Cut sheet of parchment paper to match outline of Dutch oven lid and place on large plate or upturned rimmed baking sheet. Roll puff pastry sheet into 15 by 11-inch rectangle on lightly floured counter. Using pizza cutter or sharp knife, cut pastry widthwise into ten 1½-inch-wide strips.

2 Space 5 pastry strips parallel and evenly across parchment circle. Fold back first, third, and fifth strips almost completely. Lay additional pastry strip perpendicular to second and fourth strips, keeping it snug to folded edges of pastry, then unfold strips. Repeat laying remaining 4 pastry strips evenly across parchment circle, alternating between folding back second and fourth strips and first, third, and fifth strips to create lattice pattern. Using pizza cutter, trim edges of pastry following outline of parchment circle. Cover loosely with plastic wrap and refrigerate while preparing filling.

3 Adjust oven rack to lower-middle position and heat oven to 400 degrees. Melt butter in Dutch oven over medium heat. Add leeks, carrots, and 1 teaspoon salt and cook until vegetables are softened, about 5 minutes. Stir in flour, garlic, and tomato paste and cook for 1 minute.

4 Slowly stir in broth, scraping up any browned bits and smoothing out any lumps. Stir in cream, soy sauce, and bay leaves. Bring to simmer and cook until mixture is thickened, about 3 minutes. Stir in chicken and return to simmer.

5 Off heat, cover pot with inverted lid and carefully place parchment with pastry on lid. Brush pastry with egg and sprinkle with salt. Transfer pot to oven and bake until pastry is puffed and golden brown, 25 to 30 minutes, rotating pot halfway through baking.

6 Remove pot from oven. Transfer parchment with pastry to wire rack; discard parchment. Remove lid and discard bay leaves. Stir asparagus into filling and cook over medium heat until crisp-tender, 3 to 5 minutes. Off heat, stir in peas and let sit until heated through, about 5 minutes. Adjust filling consistency with extra hot broth as needed. Stir in tarragon and lemon zest and juice. Season with salt and pepper to taste. Set pastry on top of filling and serve.

MAKING A LATTICE TOP

 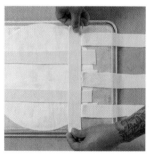  

1 Space 5 pastry strips parallel and evenly across parchment circle. Fold back first, third, and fifth strips almost completely.

2 Lay pastry strip perpendicular to second and fourth strips, keeping it snug to folded edges of pastry, then unfold strips.

3 Repeat laying remaining 4 pastry strips evenly across parchment circle, alternating between folding back second and fourth strips and first, third, and fifth strips to create lattice pattern.

4 Using pizza cutter, trim edges of pastry following outline of parchment circle.

STEAK TIPS AND HORSERADISH POTATO SALAD

SERVES 4 TO 6   TOTAL TIME 45 MINUTES

WHY THIS RECIPE WORKS Steak and potatoes are a classic duo for a satisfying weeknight meal, and using our Dutch oven allowed us to streamline cooking and cleanup to a single pot. We decided to pair simple steak tips with a horseradish-spiked potato salad. Small, low-starch fingerlings were perfect since they cooked up creamy and didn't require much prep. Starting the potatoes in just an inch of cold salted water and then bringing them to a simmer ensured that they cooked evenly; meanwhile, we marinated the meat. Once we had drained the potatoes, we seared our steak tips in the Dutch oven and removed them to rest while we made the potato salad. A combination of sour cream and mayonnaise kept the dressing light and tangy, and including celery leaves as well as chopped celery added dimension. Horseradish nicely accented the meat and the potatoes. Sirloin steak tips, also known as flap meat, can be sold as whole steaks, cubes, and strips; we prefer to purchase whole steaks and cut them ourselves. Look for potatoes that are about 2 inches long. Small red potatoes measuring 1 to 2 inches in diameter can be substituted for the fingerling potatoes. If celery leaves are not available, increase the parsley to ½ cup. The strength of prepared horseradish can vary greatly; start with 1 tablespoon and add more according to taste. Buy refrigerated prepared horseradish, not the shelf-stable kind, which contains preservatives and additives.

2 teaspoons Worcestershire sauce
  Salt and pepper
1 teaspoon garlic powder
1½ pounds sirloin steak tips, trimmed and cut into 2-inch pieces
1½ pounds fingerling potatoes, unpeeled, halved lengthwise
3 tablespoons white wine vinegar
2 tablespoons vegetable oil
¼ cup mayonnaise
¼ cup sour cream
2 celery ribs, minced, plus ½ cup celery leaves
¼ cup finely chopped red onion
1–3 tablespoons prepared horseradish
¼ cup fresh parsley leaves

1 Combine Worcestershire, ¾ teaspoon salt, and garlic powder in medium bowl. Add steak tips and toss until evenly coated; set aside.

2 Place potatoes and 1 teaspoon salt in Dutch oven and cover with cold water by 1 inch. Bring to simmer over medium-high heat and cook until potatoes are tender, 10 to 15 minutes.

3 Drain potatoes and spread into single layer on rimmed baking sheet. Drizzle with 2 tablespoons vinegar and gently toss to coat. Refrigerate potatoes until slightly cooled, about 15 minutes.

4 Meanwhile, wipe pot clean with paper towels. Pat steak tips dry with paper towels and season with pepper. Heat oil in now-empty pot over medium-high heat until just smoking. Add steak tips and cook until well browned on all sides and meat registers 120 to 125 degrees (for medium-rare) or 130 to 135 degrees (for medium), 6 to 10 minutes. Transfer steak tips to serving platter and let rest while finishing salad.

5 Whisk mayonnaise, sour cream, celery, onion, horseradish, ½ teaspoon salt, ¼ teaspoon pepper, and remaining 1 tablespoon vinegar together in large bowl. Add potatoes, celery leaves, and parsley and gently toss to combine. Serve with steak tips.

THICK-CUT STEAKS WITH GLAZED MUSHROOMS, PEPPERS, AND TOMATOES

SERVES 4   TOTAL TIME 50 MINUTES

WHY THIS RECIPE WORKS Inspired by steak *pizzaiola*—tender steaks topped with a chunky, long-simmered sauce of tomatoes and mushrooms—we set out to create a weeknight-friendly version of the restaurant classic. A Dutch oven allowed us to get a great sear on the steaks and was then roomy enough to build our sauce; the vegetables benefited from picking up the flavorful fond left behind by the meat. We used thick-cut strip steaks for their intense flavor. Since the thick steaks needed to spend some time in the hot pot, we minimized the band of overcooked meat on the surface of the steaks by flipping them every couple of minutes, ensuring more even cooking. Starting the steaks over medium-high heat and finishing them on medium ensured that their interiors didn't overcook. While the steaks rested, we sautéed mushrooms and onions in the flavorful rendered fat, then added garlic and oregano for aromatic backbone. Roasted red peppers and sun-dried tomatoes offered great depth of flavor with minimal effort, and balsamic vinegar added another dimension of richness and complexity to this simple dish.

2   (1-pound) boneless strip steaks, about 1½ inches thick, trimmed and halved crosswise
    Salt and pepper
¼   cup extra-virgin olive oil
8   ounces cremini mushrooms, trimmed and quartered
1   onion, chopped fine
3   garlic cloves, minced
2   teaspoons minced fresh oregano or ½ teaspoon dried
1½ cups jarred roasted red peppers, patted dry and chopped
¼   cup oil-packed sun-dried tomatoes, chopped
3   tablespoons balsamic vinegar
3   tablespoons chopped fresh basil

1 Pat steaks dry with paper towels and season with salt and pepper; gently press sides of steaks until uniform 1½ inches thick. Heat 2 tablespoons oil in Dutch oven over medium-high heat until just smoking. Brown steaks, about 2 minutes per side.

2 Flip steaks again, reduce heat to medium, and continue to cook, flipping every 2 minutes, until steaks are well browned and meat registers 120 to 125 degrees (for medium-rare) or 130 to 135 degrees (for medium), 7 to 10 minutes. Transfer steaks to serving platter and let rest while making sauce.

3 Add mushrooms, onion, 1 tablespoon oil, and ¼ teaspoon salt to fat left in pot. Cover and cook over medium heat until mushrooms have released their liquid, about 3 minutes. Uncover and continue to cook until mushrooms are dry, about 5 minutes. Stir in garlic and oregano and cook until fragrant, about 30 seconds. Stir in red peppers, tomatoes, and vinegar, scraping up any browned bits. Cook until vinegar is reduced slightly and begins to coat vegetables, about 1 minute. Off heat, stir in basil and season with salt and pepper to taste. Spoon vegetables over steaks and drizzle with remaining 1 tablespoon oil. Serve.

BEEF ENCHILADA CASSEROLE

SERVES 8 TO 10   TOTAL TIME 1 HOUR 45 MINUTES

WHY THIS RECIPE WORKS We love beef enchiladas, but making enough for a crowd can be a challenge, so we set out to create an uncomplicated layered casserole with all the flavor of true enchiladas. To keep things streamlined, we did all the cooking in our Dutch oven, which was large enough to hold the whole assembly. Ground beef was easier and faster than traditional braised meat to cook; stirring some of our homemade enchilada sauce right into the beef gave it great flavor. The tortillas pulled double duty in our recipe: Blending some with a can of Ro-tel tomatoes and some broth, and then stirring the mixture into the beef, created a nice, thick consistency, while layering the rest of the tortillas (toasted in the dry Dutch oven to bring out their corn flavor and prevent them from disintegrating) into the pot was easier than making individual rolled enchiladas. Baking the casserole uncovered produced an irresistibly golden-brown top. If you can't find Ro-tel tomatoes, substitute 1¼ cups of canned diced tomatoes plus an additional minced jalapeño. Serve with sour cream, chopped scallions, and lime wedges.

18 (6-inch) corn tortillas
1 (10-ounce) can Ro-tel Original Diced Tomatoes & Green Chilies
1½ cups beef broth
3 tablespoons vegetable oil
2 pounds 85 percent lean ground beef
2 onions, chopped fine
8 garlic cloves, minced
2 tablespoons chili powder
1 teaspoon ground cumin
3 (15-ounce) cans tomato sauce
12 ounces Monterey Jack cheese, shredded (3 cups)
3 jalapeño chiles, stemmed, seeded, and minced
½ cup chopped fresh cilantro
1 tablespoon hot sauce

1 Adjust oven rack to middle position and heat oven to 450 degrees. Working in batches, toast tortillas in Dutch oven over medium-high heat until lightly browned, about 20 seconds per side; transfer to plate and cover with dish towel.

2 Tear 8 tortillas into rough 2-inch pieces and transfer to food processor. Add tomatoes and their juice and ¾ cup broth and process until finely ground, about 2 minutes; transfer to large bowl.

3 Heat 1 tablespoon oil in now-empty pot over medium-high heat until shimmering. Add ground beef and cook, breaking up meat with wooden spoon, until no longer pink, about 5 minutes. Drain beef in colander, then stir into processed tortilla mixture.

4 Add remaining 2 tablespoons oil and onions to now-empty pot and cook over medium heat until onions are softened, about 5 minutes. Stir in garlic, chili powder, and cumin and cook until fragrant, about 30 seconds. Stir in tomato sauce and remaining ¾ cup broth, bring to simmer, and cook until slightly thickened, 5 to 7 minutes; transfer to separate bowl.

5 Stir half of tomato sauce mixture, 1½ cups Monterey Jack, half of jalapeños, cilantro, and hot sauce into beef mixture. Spread half of beef mixture over bottom of now-empty pot. Shingle 5 tortillas around edge of pot in pinwheel pattern. Repeat with remaining beef mixture and remaining 5 tortillas. Spread remaining tomato sauce mixture over tortillas and sprinkle with remaining 1½ cups Monterey Jack and jalapeños.

6 Scrape down exposed sides of pot, then transfer to oven. Bake, uncovered, until cheese is browned and casserole is bubbling around edges, 25 to 30 minutes. Let casserole cool for 15 minutes before serving.

STEAMED CHEESEBURGERS

SERVES 4   TOTAL TIME 40 MINUTES

WHY THIS RECIPE WORKS Steamed cheeseburgers, a Connecticut diner specialty, stay juicy even when cooked to medium-well or beyond. They're made by pressing the meat and cheese into separate shallow molds, placing the molds in custom-made steam cabinets, and then smothering the cooked burgers with the gooey, melted cheese before serving. We wanted to re-create this unusual comfort food at home, without the need for any special equipment. The answer lay in our Dutch oven and a steamer basket; the Dutch oven was wide enough to hold four burgers, and the steamer basket held the burgers just above the water. To make up for the savory flavor that other burgers get from browning, we mixed soy sauce, tomato paste, and onion powder into the meat. Making a shallow indentation in the center of each burger ensured that they didn't puff in the steam. For a flavorful, evenly melted layer of cheese, we used shredded cheddar and added it off heat so it didn't slide off the burgers. Thirty seconds before serving, we added the buns to the steamer too, giving them just enough time to soften and warm through. You will need a collapsible steamer basket for this recipe. The water should not touch the bottom of the steamer basket; adjust the water depth as needed. We prefer these burgers cooked medium-well, but for medium burgers, steam them for 7 minutes before removing them from the heat and adding the cheese. Serve these burgers with the usual array of garnishes and condiments: lettuce, tomato, onion, ketchup, mayonnaise, and mustard.

1½ pounds 85 percent lean ground beef
 2 teaspoons soy sauce
 1 teaspoon onion powder
 1 teaspoon tomato paste
 ¾ teaspoon salt
 ¾ teaspoon pepper
 4 ounces sharp cheddar cheese, shredded (1 cup)
 4 hamburger buns

1 Using your hands, combine ground beef, soy sauce, onion powder, tomato paste, salt, and pepper in bowl. Divide beef mixture into 4 lightly packed balls, then gently flatten each ball into ¾-inch-thick patty. Press shallow indentation in center of each patty.

2 Bring 1 inch water to boil in covered Dutch oven over medium-high heat. Arrange patties in steamer basket, then transfer basket to pot. Cover and cook for 8 minutes. Off heat, top burgers with cheddar, cover, and let sit until cheese has melted, about 2 minutes. Place top buns on burgers and bottom buns, cut side up, on top of top buns. Cover and let sit until buns soften, about 30 seconds. Transfer bottom buns to cutting board, add condiments, and top with burgers and top buns. Serve.

LATIN AMERICAN PORK AND RICE

SERVES 4 TO 6   TOTAL TIME 2 HOURS 30 MINUTES

WHY THIS RECIPE WORKS *Arroz con puerco*, a one-pot dish often made in Cuba and Puerto Rico, is a cousin of *arroz con pollo* but gets its uniquely alluring and ultrasavory profile from pork. We chose pork butt for its deep flavor and good marbling; cutting it into chunks and braising it in water with a quartered onion, smashed garlic cloves, and bay leaves tenderized this tough cut while simultaneously yielding a rich pork broth in which to cook the rice. We then set the pork and broth aside so we could sauté our *sofrito* of red bell pepper, onion, garlic, cumin and dried oregano. We added medium-grain rice (which turns creamy once cooked), *sazón* (a Latin seasoning blend), and the pork and broth. Letting the pot sit for 20 minutes after cooking allowed the flavors to meld and the rice to absorb any extra moisture. Chopped green olives, peas, cilantro, and a little red wine vinegar stirred in at the end brightened up this satisfying dish. Goya Sazón with Coriander and Annatto (or con Culantro y Achiote) can be found in the international aisle of most supermarkets; 1 packet equals about 1½ teaspoons. If you can't find it, you can make your own with ½ teaspoon garlic powder, ¼ teaspoon salt, ¼ teaspoon paprika, ¼ teaspoon ground coriander, and ⅛ teaspoon ground cumin. Let the rice rest for the full 20 minutes before lifting the lid to check it. Long-grain rice may be used, but it will be slightly less creamy. Pork butt roast is often labeled Boston butt in the supermarket.

1¾ pounds boneless pork butt roast, trimmed and cut into 1-inch pieces

6 cups water

2 onions (1 peeled and quartered through root end, 1 chopped)

5 garlic cloves (3 peeled and smashed, 2 minced)

2 bay leaves
  Salt and pepper

2 tablespoons vegetable oil

1 red bell pepper, stemmed, seeded, and chopped

1½ teaspoons ground cumin

1½ teaspoons dried oregano

2 cups medium-grain rice, rinsed

1½ teaspoons Goya Sazón with Coriander and Annatto

½ cup frozen peas

½ cup pimento-stuffed green olives, chopped

¼ cup chopped fresh cilantro

1 tablespoon red wine vinegar

1 Combine pork, water, onion quarters, smashed garlic, bay leaves, and 1 tablespoon salt in Dutch oven and bring to boil over medium-high heat, skimming off any foam that rises to surface. Reduce heat to low, partially cover, and cook until pork is tender, about 1 hour.

2 Set colander in large bowl and drain pork, reserving cooking liquid (you should have at least 4 cups; if not, add enough water to equal 4 cups). Discard onion, garlic, and bay leaves.

3 Wipe pot clean with paper towels. Heat oil in now-empty pot over medium heat until shimmering. Add bell pepper, chopped onion, minced garlic, cumin, oregano, ½ teaspoon pepper, and ¼ teaspoon salt and cook until vegetables are tender, 5 to 7 minutes.

4 Stir in rice and sazón and cook until edges of rice begin to turn translucent, about 2 minutes. Add pork and 4 cups reserved broth and bring to boil. Reduce heat to low, scrape sides of pot clean of any rice, cover, and cook, undisturbed, for 20 minutes.

5 Remove pot from heat and let sit, covered, for 20 minutes. Fluff rice with fork. Stir in peas, olives, cilantro, and vinegar. Serve.

ITALIAN SAUSAGES WITH WHITE BEANS AND KALE

SERVES 4   TOTAL TIME 1 HOUR

WHY THIS RECIPE WORKS Nothing is more comforting on a cool night than a flavorful bowl of hearty beans and sausage. For a new take on this simple dish, we paired creamy, tender white beans and robust kale with meaty Italian sausage. We wanted the sausages to be napped in a velvety sauce, so we started by pureeing some of the cannellini beans and canned diced tomatoes. The canned tomatoes' juices and some chicken broth deepened the flavor of the puree and gave it just the right consistency. Next, we ensured that the sausages held their shape by pricking the casings with a fork before cooking. After browning them to build some fond, we removed the sausages, softened chopped onion in the meaty renderings, and added garlic and the bean-tomato puree to the pot. The remaining intact diced tomatoes created some textural contrast, and wilting a whole pound of chopped kale was as easy as stirring it in and then covering the pot and letting it simmer away. We returned the browned sausages to the pot along with more cannellinis during the last 10 minutes of cooking, allowing the sausages to cook through and the beans to absorb some of the flavorful broth before serving. Serve with crusty bread.

2 (15-ounce) cans cannellini beans, rinsed

1 (28-ounce) can diced tomatoes, drained with juice reserved

1 cup chicken broth

2 tablespoons extra-virgin olive oil

1 pound sweet or hot Italian sausage, pricked all over with fork

1 onion, chopped fine

3 garlic cloves, minced

1 pound kale, stemmed and chopped
  Salt and pepper

1 Puree ½ cup beans, ½ cup tomatoes, reserved tomato juice, and chicken broth in food processor until smooth, about 30 seconds.

2 Heat oil in Dutch oven over medium heat until shimmering. Add sausages and brown on all sides, about 5 minutes; transfer to plate.

3 Add onion to fat left in pot and cook until softened, about 5 minutes. Stir in garlic and cook until fragrant, about 30 seconds. Stir in pureed bean mixture, kale, remaining tomatoes, and ¼ teaspoon salt, scraping up any browned bits, and bring to simmer. Reduce heat to medium-low, cover, and cook, stirring occasionally, until kale is wilted and tender, about 15 minutes.

4 Stir in remaining beans, then nestle sausages into pot, adding any accumulated juices. Cover and cook until sausages register 160 degrees and sauce is thickened slightly, about 10 minutes. Season with salt and pepper to taste and serve.

LAMB MEATBALLS WITH ORZO, TOMATOES, AND FETA

SERVES 4 TOTAL TIME 1 HOUR 15 MINUTES

WHY THIS RECIPE WORKS Pasta and meatballs are a perfect match, but for a unique spin on this classic duo we turned to lamb instead of beef or pork, and to orzo instead of spaghetti, and we enhanced the dish with fresh, bold Greek flavors like mint, oregano, and cinnamon. A panade—a simple paste made from Greek yogurt and panko—kept the meatballs moist and lent the dish welcome tangy flavor. We used our Dutch oven to deeply brown the meatballs and create lots of flavorful fond in the pot. Using some of the rendered fat to cook our aromatics gave our orzo pilaf a supersavory base. After toasting the orzo to golden brown, we added a combination of white wine and chicken broth and cooked the orzo until it was nearly tender. We were then able to simply nestle our seared meatballs back into the pot to cook them through. We finished the dish with a bright topping of cherry tomatoes, more fresh mint, and feta, which cut through the richness for a highly satisfying one-pot meal. Depending on the size of your Dutch oven, you may need to brown the meatballs in two batches rather than one.

½ cup plain whole-milk Greek yogurt

¼ cup panko bread crumbs

3 tablespoons water

1 large egg

2 tablespoons minced fresh mint, plus 2 tablespoons torn leaves

4 garlic cloves, minced

2 teaspoons minced fresh oregano or ½ teaspoon dried

Salt and pepper

¾ teaspoon ground cinnamon

1½ pounds ground lamb

2 tablespoons extra-virgin olive oil

1 onion, chopped fine

2 cups orzo

3 cups chicken broth

½ cup dry white wine

8 ounces cherry tomatoes, halved

2 ounces feta cheese, crumbled (½ cup)

1 Mash yogurt, panko, and water together with fork in large bowl to form paste. Stir in egg, minced mint, half of garlic, oregano, 1 teaspoon salt, ⅛ teaspoon pepper, and cinnamon until combined. Add ground lamb and knead with your hands until thoroughly combined. Pinch off and roll mixture into eighteen 1½-inch meatballs.

2 Heat oil in Dutch oven over medium-high heat until just smoking. Brown meatballs on all sides, 7 to 10 minutes; transfer to plate. Pour off all but 2 tablespoons fat from pot.

3 Add onion and ½ teaspoon salt to fat left in pot and cook over medium heat until onion is softened and lightly browned, 5 to 7 minutes. Stir in remaining garlic and cook until fragrant, about 30 seconds. Add orzo and cook, stirring frequently, until lightly browned and golden, about 5 minutes.

4 Stir in broth and wine, scraping up any browned bits. Bring to simmer and cook, stirring occasionally, until most of liquid has been absorbed and orzo is almost tender, 7 to 10 minutes.

5 Reduce heat to medium-low and nestle meatballs into orzo. Cover and cook until orzo is tender and meatballs are fully cooked through, 5 to 10 minutes. Sprinkle with tomatoes, feta, and torn mint. Serve.

HALIBUT WITH ROASTED GARLIC AND CHERRY TOMATOES

SERVES 4   TOTAL TIME 1 HOUR

WHY THIS RECIPE WORKS Cooking fish at a low temperature in a covered pot is a nearly foolproof way to achieve perfectly cooked fish, since the heavy Dutch oven holds in moisture and allows the fish to cook through gently and evenly. This method is also a wonderful way to concentrate flavor, meaning that a minimum of ingredients can make a big impact. We started by browning sliced garlic in oil, which mellowed its flavor and infused the dish with warm aromatic notes. Cherry tomatoes, which are of reliable quality year-round, became soft and sweet with the gentle cooking. Capers provided briny bites, and thyme gave the dish an herbal base note. Browning the halibut was unnecessary; it didn't contribute much to the flavor, and the fish's texture was better without it. While the halibut rested, we finished the sauce by cooking off some of the excess liquid on the stovetop. Sea bass and swordfish steaks are good substitutes for the halibut.

¼ cup extra-virgin olive oil

2 garlic cloves, sliced thin

⅛ teaspoon red pepper flakes
   Salt and pepper

12 ounces cherry tomatoes, quartered

1 tablespoon capers, rinsed

1 teaspoon minced fresh thyme or ¼ teaspoon dried

2 (1¼-pound) skin-on full halibut steaks, about
   1¼ inches thick and 10 to 12 inches long, trimmed

1 Adjust oven rack to lowest position and heat oven to 250 degrees. Heat 2 tablespoons oil in Dutch oven over medium-low heat until shimmering. Add garlic, pepper flakes, and pinch of salt and cook until garlic is light golden, 2 to 4 minutes. Off heat, stir in tomatoes, capers, and thyme.

2 Season steaks with salt and pepper and lay on top of tomatoes. Cover, transfer pot to oven, and cook until halibut flakes apart when gently prodded with paring knife and registers 140 degrees, 35 to 40 minutes.

3 Remove pot from oven. Using 2 thin spatulas, transfer steaks to cutting board, tent with aluminum foil, and let rest while finishing sauce. Bring tomato mixture to simmer over medium-high heat and cook until slightly thickened, about 2 minutes. Off heat, stir in remaining 2 tablespoons oil and season with salt and pepper to taste.

4 Remove skin from steaks and separate quadrants of meat from bone by slipping spatula gently between them. Serve halibut with sauce.

TRIMMING HALIBUT STEAKS

Cut off cartilage at each end of steaks to remove small bones and ensure that steaks will fit neatly in pot.

THAI GREEN CURRY WITH SHRIMP, SNOW PEAS, AND SHIITAKES

SERVES 4   TOTAL TIME 1 HOUR

WHY THIS RECIPE WORKS Thai curries embrace a delicate balance of tastes, textures, temperatures, and colors that come together to create a harmonious whole. Green curry, one of the spiciest and most intense varieties, gets it verdant, aromatic flavor from curry paste. Making the paste from scratch can require a laundry list of ingredients, not to mention a fair amount of time; using jarred paste was convenient and made our curry weeknight-friendly. Browning the paste with the cream from a can of coconut milk concentrated and bloomed its flavor. A slug of fish sauce offered complexity, and coconut milk gave the sauce richness and a silky texture. A couple tablespoons of brown sugar balanced out the heat and pungency. With our sauce completed, we continued cooking right in the Dutch oven: We poached shrimp and meaty shiitake mushrooms in the sauce before adding snow peas and a red bell pepper for color and contrasting texture. Some fresh herbs and lime juice stirred in at the very end perfectly balanced the rich, spicy flavors of the dish. To make scooping the cream from a can of coconut milk easier, refrigerate the can for 24 hours and do not shake it.

2 (14-ounce) cans coconut milk
2 tablespoons Thai green curry paste
2 tablespoons fish sauce
2 tablespoons packed brown sugar
1½ pounds extra-large shrimp (21 to 25 per pound), peeled, deveined, and tails removed
5 ounces shiitake mushrooms, stemmed and halved if small or quartered if large
4 ounces snow peas, strings removed
1 red bell pepper, stemmed, seeded, and cut into ¼-inch-wide strips
1 Thai chile, stemmed, seeded, and quartered lengthwise (optional)
¼ cup coarsely chopped fresh basil leaves
¼ cup coarsely chopped fresh mint leaves
1 tablespoon lime juice
  Salt

1 Carefully spoon off about 1 cup of top layer of cream from 1 can of coconut milk. Whisk coconut cream and curry paste together in Dutch oven. Bring to simmer over high heat and cook until almost all of liquid has evaporated, 5 to 7 minutes. Reduce heat to medium-high and continue to cook, whisking constantly, until oil separates from solids and mixture is darkened and aromatic, 4 to 8 minutes.

2 Whisk in remaining coconut milk, fish sauce, and sugar. Bring to simmer and cook until flavors meld and sauce is thickened, about 5 minutes. Stir in shrimp and mushrooms and cook for 5 minutes. Stir in snow peas, bell pepper, and Thai chile, if using, and cook until vegetables are crisp-tender and shrimp are opaque throughout, about 2 minutes. Off heat, stir in basil, mint, and lime juice. Season with salt to taste. Serve.

SEARED SCALLOPS WITH WARM BARLEY SALAD

SERVES 4 TOTAL TIME 1 HOUR

WHY THIS RECIPE WORKS Perfectly cooked scallops can be difficult to achieve at home, but the appeal of their delicate, almost creamy centers encased in golden, nutty exteriors is undeniable. We wanted to bring this luxury to our weeknight dinner table; we also wanted to make our scallops into a complete meal by pairing them with a fresh, satisfying salad. First, we cooked hearty, nutty barley in the Dutch oven in plenty of water for an easy salad base. The keys to perfect scallops are speed and heat—the quicker a good sear develops, the less likely the centers are to overcook. Since moisture prevents browning, we blotted the scallops with dish towels and let them drain for a few minutes so they were as dry as possible. Meanwhile, we crisped a few slices of chopped bacon in the pot; the rendered fat was a perfect cooking medium for the scallops. We then seared the scallops in two batches to prevent crowding and steaming. The Dutch oven's even, intense heat produced gorgeously browned crusts on the scallops in just a few minutes. We finished the salad with sweet apple, crunchy fennel, lightly bitter frisée, and a bright cider vinegar–based dressing. We recommend buying "dry" scallops, which don't have chemical additives and taste better than "wet." Dry scallops will look ivory or pinkish; wet scallops are bright white. Do not substitute hulled, hull-less, quick-cooking, or presteamed barley (read the ingredient list on the package to determine this) in this recipe.

1 cup pearled barley
  Salt and pepper
6 slices bacon, cut into ½-inch pieces
1½ pounds large sea scallops, tendons removed
3 tablespoons extra-virgin olive oil
2 tablespoons cider vinegar
1 fennel bulb, 3 tablespoons fronds chopped coarse, stalks discarded, bulb halved, cored, and sliced thin
1 Fuji or Honeycrisp apple, cored and cut into ½-inch pieces
1 head frisée (6 ounces), torn into bite-size pieces
  Lemon wedges

1 Bring 4 quarts water to boil in Dutch oven. Add barley and 1 tablespoon salt, return to boil, and cook until barley is tender, 20 to 40 minutes. Drain barley and set aside. Wipe pot clean with paper towels.

2 Cook bacon in now-empty pot over medium-high heat until crisp, about 5 minutes. Using slotted spoon, transfer bacon to paper towel–lined plate; set aside for serving.

3 Meanwhile, place scallops in rimmed baking sheet lined with clean dish towel. Place second clean dish towel on top of scallops and press gently on towel to blot liquid. Let scallops sit at room temperature, covered with towel, for 10 minutes.

4 Season scallops with salt and pepper. Heat fat left in pot over high heat until just smoking. Add half of scallops in single layer and cook, undisturbed, until well browned on first side, about 2 minutes. Flip scallops and continue to cook, undisturbed, until well browned on second side, about 2 minutes. Transfer scallops to serving platter and tent with aluminum foil. Repeat with remaining scallops; transfer to platter.

5 Whisk oil, vinegar, and ¼ teaspoon salt together in large bowl. Add barley, fennel and fennel fronds, apple, and frisée and gently toss to combine. Season with salt and pepper to taste and sprinkle with reserved bacon. Serve scallops with salad and lemon wedges.

GREEN SHAKSHUKA

SERVES 4   TOTAL TIME 50 MINUTES

WHY THIS RECIPE WORKS The classic Tunisian dish *shakshuka* is a humble yet satisfying one-pot meal, usually consisting of eggs cooked in a long-simmered, spiced tomato and pepper sauce. We wanted to use this as a template for a version that swapped out the long-cooked red sauce for a fresh, vibrant mix of greens that would be transformed into a quick any-night meal. For the greens, we settled on savory Swiss chard and easy-to-prep baby spinach. We cooked a cup of the sliced chard stems (any more and their vegetal flavors overwhelmed the dish) with onion to create an aromatic base. We eschewed the traditional strong flavors of cumin and paprika in favor of coriander and mild Aleppo pepper—their citrusy notes allowed the greens' flavors to stay center stage. The roomy Dutch oven allowed us to wilt a large volume of raw greens easily. We blended a cup of the greens mixture with broth to give the sauce a creamy, cohesive texture, then added frozen peas for contrasting pops of sweetness. To finish, we poached eight eggs directly in the sauce, covering the pot to contain the heat for efficient, even cooking. We served our green shakshuka with a sprinkling of bright herbs and salty, creamy feta cheese. If you can't find Aleppo pepper, you can substitute ⅛ teaspoon paprika and ⅛ teaspoon finely chopped red pepper flakes. The Dutch oven will seem crowded when you first add the greens, but they will quickly wilt down. Serve with toasted pita or crusty bread to mop up the sauce. Avoid removing the lid during the first 5 minutes of cooking in step 3; it will increase the total cooking time of the eggs.

2 pounds Swiss chard, stems removed and reserved, leaves chopped

¼ cup extra-virgin olive oil

1 large onion, chopped fine

Salt

4 garlic cloves, minced

2 teaspoons ground coriander

11 ounces (11 cups) baby spinach, chopped

½ cup chicken or vegetable broth

1 cup frozen peas

1½ tablespoons lemon juice

8 large eggs

½ teaspoon ground dried Aleppo pepper

2 ounces feta cheese, crumbled (½ cup)

2 tablespoons chopped fresh dill

2 tablespoons chopped fresh mint

1 Slice chard stems thin to yield 1 cup; discard remaining stems or reserve for another use. Heat 2 tablespoons oil in Dutch oven over medium heat until shimmering. Add chard stems, onion, and ¾ teaspoon salt and cook until vegetables are softened and lightly browned, 5 to 7 minutes. Stir in garlic and coriander and cook until fragrant, about 1 minute.

2 Add chard leaves and spinach. Increase heat to medium-high, cover, and cook, stirring occasionally, until wilted but still bright green, 3 to 5 minutes. Off heat, transfer 1 cup chard mixture to blender. Add broth and process until smooth, about 45 seconds, scraping down sides of blender jar as needed. Stir chard mixture, peas, and lemon juice into pot.

3 Make 4 shallow indentations (about 2 inches wide) in surface of greens using back of spoon. Crack 2 eggs into each indentation, sprinkle with Aleppo pepper, and season with salt. Cover and cook over medium-low heat until edges of egg whites are just set, 5 to 10 minutes. Off heat, let sit, covered, until whites are fully set and yolks are still runny, 2 to 4 minutes. Sprinkle with feta, dill, and mint and drizzle with remaining 2 tablespoons oil. Serve immediately.

LENTILS AND RICE WITH YOGURT SAUCE AND TOASTED ALMONDS

SERVES 4 TO 6 TOTAL TIME 1 HOUR 30 MINUTES

WHY THIS RECIPE WORKS This vegetarian dish is a textbook example of how a few humble ingredients can add up to something satisfying and complex. We used a pilaf method to cook the rice and lentils, blooming warm spices (coriander, cumin, cinnamon, and black pepper) and toasting the rice in shallot-infused oil to deepen the flavor and enhance the rice's nuttiness. Giving the lentils a 15-minute head start ensured that they finished cooking along with the rice. We found that soaking the rice in hot water and then rinsing it gave it a fluffy, not sticky, texture. To make our dish more of a complete meal, we added baby spinach. A sprinkle of toasted almonds provided needed textural contrast, and a bracing garlicky yogurt sauce made the perfect finishing touch. We prefer the richer flavor of whole-milk yogurt in this recipe, but low-fat or nonfat yogurt can be substituted. Large green or brown lentils work well in this recipe; do not substitute French green lentils (*lentilles du Puy*).

Yogurt Sauce
- 1 cup plain whole-milk yogurt
- 2 tablespoons lemon juice
- ½ teaspoon minced garlic
- ½ teaspoon salt

Lentils and Rice
- 8½ ounces (1¼ cups) large green or brown lentils, picked over and rinsed
- Salt and pepper
- 1¼ cups basmati rice
- 3 tablespoons vegetable oil
- 2 shallots, minced
- 3 garlic cloves, minced
- 1½ teaspoons ground coriander
- 1½ teaspoons ground cumin
- ¾ teaspoon ground cinnamon
- 6 ounces (6 cups) baby spinach
- ¼ cup slivered almonds, toasted

1 For the yogurt sauce Whisk all ingredients together in bowl; cover and refrigerate until ready to serve.

2 For the lentils and rice Bring lentils, 4 cups water, and 1 teaspoon salt to boil in Dutch oven. Reduce heat to low and cook until lentils are tender, 15 to 17 minutes. Drain lentils and transfer to large bowl. Wipe pot clean with paper towels.

3 Meanwhile, place rice in medium bowl, add hot tap water to cover by 2 inches, and let sit for 15 minutes. Using hands, gently swish rice to release excess starch, then carefully pour off water. Continue to add cold tap water to bowl of rice, swish gently, and pour off starchy water 4 or 5 more times until water runs almost clear. Drain rice in fine-mesh strainer.

4 Add oil and shallots to now-empty pot and cook over medium heat until shallots are softened, 3 to 5 minutes. Stir in garlic, coriander, cumin, cinnamon, and ¼ teaspoon pepper and cook until fragrant, about 30 seconds. Stir in drained rice and cook, stirring occasionally, until edges of rice begin to turn translucent, about 3 minutes. Stir in 2½ cups water and 1 teaspoon salt and bring to boil. Stir in lentils, reduce heat to low, cover, and cook until rice is tender and liquid has been absorbed, about 12 minutes.

5 Remove pot from heat and place spinach on top of lentils and rice. Lay clean dish towel over pot, cover with lid, and let sit for 10 minutes. Using fork, fluff lentils and rice and incorporate wilted spinach. Season with salt and pepper to taste, sprinkle with almonds, and serve with yogurt sauce.

UDON NOODLES WITH MUSTARD GREENS AND SHIITAKE-GINGER SAUCE

SERVES 4 TO 6   TOTAL TIME 1 HOUR 15 MINUTES

WHY THIS RECIPE WORKS Noodles and greens are a common pairing in many Asian cuisines. We thought this partnership was a great way to create a delicate yet filling noodle dish, and we set out to develop a recipe that married the spicy bite of mustard greens with rustic udon noodles. Udon are fat, chewy noodles made of wheat flour; because they're starchy and a bit sweet, they stand up well to savory sauces. We made a highly aromatic broth from Asian pantry staples, first browning meaty shiitake mushrooms for flavor and then adding water and mirin along with rice vinegar, soy sauce, cloves of garlic, and a chunk of fresh ginger. Dried shiitake mushrooms, sesame oil, and chili-garlic sauce rounded out the flavors. After this mixture simmered and reduced, we had a sauce that was light and brothy but supersavory—and we could use the Dutch oven again to cook our noodles and greens together. Because fresh noodles cook so quickly, we made sure to add the greens to the pot before the noodles. Do not substitute other types of noodles for the udon noodles here.

1 tablespoon vegetable oil

8 ounces fresh shiitake mushrooms, stemmed and sliced thin

¼ cup mirin

3 tablespoons rice vinegar

3 tablespoons soy sauce

2 garlic cloves, peeled and smashed

1 (1-inch) piece ginger, peeled, halved, and smashed

½ ounce dried shiitake mushrooms, rinsed and minced

1 teaspoon toasted sesame oil

1 teaspoon Asian chili-garlic sauce

1 pound mustard greens, stemmed and cut into 2-inch pieces
  Salt and pepper

1 pound fresh udon noodles

1 Heat vegetable oil in Dutch oven over medium-high heat until shimmering. Add fresh mushrooms and cook, stirring occasionally, until softened and lightly browned, about 5 minutes. Stir in 2 cups water, mirin, vinegar, soy sauce, garlic, ginger, dried mushrooms, sesame oil, and chili-garlic sauce and bring to simmer. Reduce heat to medium-low and simmer until liquid has reduced by half, 8 to 10 minutes. Off heat, discard garlic and ginger. Transfer mixture to bowl and cover to keep warm.

2 Bring 4 quarts water to boil in now-empty pot. Add mustard greens and 1 tablespoon salt and cook until greens are nearly tender, about 5 minutes. Add noodles and cook until greens and noodles are tender, about 2 minutes. Reserve ⅓ cup cooking water, drain noodles and greens, and return them to pot. Add sauce and reserved cooking water and toss to combine. Cook over medium-low heat, tossing constantly, until sauce clings to noodles, about 1 minute. Season with salt and pepper to taste and serve.

RIGATONI WITH TOMATOES, BACON, AND FENNEL

SERVES 4 TO 6   TOTAL TIME 1 HOUR

WHY THIS RECIPE WORKS Often, making even a simple pasta dish requires at least two large pots: one to boil the pasta, and another to make the sauce. We wanted to streamline prep for an easy, one-pot pasta dinner with a tomato sauce bolstered with smoky bacon and fragrant fennel seeds. The Dutch oven was essential here for its large capacity. We first rendered some chopped bacon, then removed the pieces to keep them crisp for serving and used the flavorful fat to soften some onion and garlic. A couple of minced anchovies—an umami powerhouse—dramatically amped up the savoriness of the sauce without lending any distinctive flavor. We found that adding diced tomatoes straight from the can gave the sauce a raw, metallic flavor because of the short cook time, so we opted to brown the tomatoes to deepen their flavor, reserving the juice to use as part of the pasta cooking liquid. A bit of broth and water made up the rest of the liquid; we added the pasta straight to the pot and used the absorption method to cook it to al dente perfection. The pasta absorbed tons of flavor from the sauce as it cooked, and in turn the pasta's starch nicely thickened the sauce. To finish, we simply stirred in some tangy, salty Pecorino Romano and fresh parsley. With a sprinkle of crisp bacon on top, our one-pot pasta was complete. You can substitute 1 pound of ziti or penne for the rigatoni, if desired.

6 slices bacon, cut into ½-inch pieces

1 onion, chopped fine
  Salt and pepper

3 garlic cloves, minced

2 anchovy fillets, rinsed, patted dry, and minced

2 teaspoons fennel seeds, lightly cracked

¼ teaspoon red pepper flakes

1 (28-ounce) can diced tomatoes, drained with juice reserved

2½ cups chicken broth

2 cups water, plus extra as needed

1 pound rigatoni

¼ cup grated Pecorino Romano cheese, plus extra for serving

2 tablespoons minced fresh parsley

1 Cook bacon in Dutch oven over medium-high heat until crisp, about 5 minutes. Using slotted spoon, transfer bacon to paper towel–lined plate; set aside for serving. Pour off all but 2 tablespoons of fat from pot.

2 Add onion and ¼ teaspoon salt to fat left in pot and cook over medium heat until onion is softened, about 5 minutes. Stir in garlic, anchovies, fennel seeds, and pepper flakes and cook until fragrant, about 1 minute. Stir in tomatoes and cook until dry and slightly darkened, about 5 minutes.

3 Stir in broth, water, and reserved tomato juice, scraping up any browned bits, and bring to boil. Stir in pasta, return to vigorous simmer, and cook, stirring often, until pasta is tender, 15 to 20 minutes. Off heat, stir in Pecorino and parsley and adjust sauce consistency with extra hot water as needed. Season with salt and pepper to taste. Serve, sprinkling individual portions with reserved bacon and extra Pecorino.

BUCATINI WITH PEAS, KALE, AND PANCETTA

SERVES 4 TO 6   TOTAL TIME 1 HOUR

WHY THIS RECIPE WORKS Salty pancetta and fresh, sweet peas are a classic combination and pair well with pasta, which eagerly takes up the pancetta's rich flavors. Add in hearty but quick-cooking baby kale and you have a simple, fresh pasta dish with a meaty backbone. To start, we rendered the pancetta, reserving the crispy pieces for garnish and using the fat to bloom lemon zest and garlic. Then we added white wine, chicken broth, and water to build a savory cooking liquid for our pasta. As our pasta approached doneness, we stirred in baby kale and peas. A quick, vigorous stir with the addition of some Parmesan at the end of cooking released more of the pasta's starch and bound the reduced liquid in a cheesy, cohesive sauce. For crunchy contrast, we topped off each serving with a bold panko mixture as well as the crisped pancetta. You can substitute 1 pound of spaghetti for the bucatini, if desired. Depending on the size of your Dutch oven, you may need to break the bucatini in half before adding it to the pot.

½ cup panko bread crumbs, toasted

1½ ounces Parmesan cheese, grated (¾ cup)

1 tablespoon extra-virgin olive oil

1 tablespoon grated lemon zest

Salt and pepper

2 ounces pancetta, cut into ½-inch pieces

2 garlic cloves, minced

½ cup dry white wine

2½ cups water, plus extra as needed

2 cups chicken broth

1 pound bucatini

5 ounces (5 cups) baby kale

1 cup frozen peas

1 Combine panko, ¼ cup Parmesan, oil, 1 teaspoon lemon zest, ¼ teaspoon salt, and ¼ teaspoon pepper in bowl; set aside for serving. Cook pancetta in Dutch oven over medium heat until crisp, 6 to 8 minutes. Using slotted spoon, transfer pancetta to paper towel–lined plate; set aside for serving.

2 Add garlic and remaining 2 teaspoons zest to fat left in pot and cook until fragrant, about 30 seconds. Stir in wine, scraping up any browned bits, and cook until nearly evaporated, about 3 minutes.

3 Stir in water and broth and bring to boil. Stir in pasta, return to vigorous simmer, and cook, stirring often, until pasta is nearly tender, 8 to 10 minutes.

4 Stir in kale and peas and continue to cook until pasta and kale are tender, about 4 minutes. Add remaining ½ cup Parmesan and stir vigorously until pasta is creamy and well coated, about 30 seconds. Adjust sauce consistency with extra hot water as needed. Season with salt and pepper to taste. Serve, sprinkling individual portions with bread-crumb mixture and pancetta.

BREAKING LONG-STRAND PASTA IN HALF

1 Loosely fold pasta in clean dish towel, keeping pasta flat, not bunched.

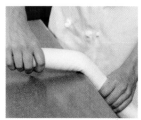

2 Position bundle so that half of pasta rests on counter and remainder hangs off edge. Firmly press bundle against counter edge to break strands in half.

CREAMY RIGATONI WITH MUSHROOMS, BUTTERNUT SQUASH, AND PINE NUTS

SERVES 4 TO 6   TOTAL TIME 1 HOUR 15 MINUTES

WHY THIS RECIPE WORKS We wanted to create a pasta dish that brought out the delicate, earthy flavor hiding in supermarket mushrooms. We selected cremini mushrooms, which have a meatier texture and a more intense, woodsy flavor than button mushrooms but are still readily available. Butternut squash heightened the dish's wintertime appeal and gave it heft and a subtle sweetness that perfectly complemented the mushrooms. To start, we sautéed the mushrooms with shallots, garlic, thyme, and a small amount of salt to help the cremini release their liquid, then added the squash. The liquid released by the mushrooms was just enough to steam the squash, and cooking both together gave the smaller mushroom pieces time to brown and create fond. We removed the vegetables, and then poured in chicken broth and water to cook our pasta. Adding heavy cream toward the end of cooking, and then stirring vigorously while mixing in Parmesan cheese, drew out the pasta's starches and created a thick, creamy sauce, into which we folded our meaty cooked vegetables. A splash of lemon juice, a sprinkling of fresh chives, and some toasted pine nuts were the perfect finishes to the dish. You can substitute 1 pound of ziti or penne for the rigatoni, if desired.

1 tablespoon extra-virgin olive oil

2 large shallots, minced

3 garlic cloves, minced

4 teaspoons minced fresh thyme or 1½ teaspoons dried

12 ounces cremini mushrooms, trimmed and sliced thin
  Salt and pepper

1½ pounds butternut squash, peeled, seeded, and cut into ½-inch pieces (4 cups)

2½ cups water, plus extra as needed

2 cups chicken or vegetable broth

1 pound rigatoni

½ cup heavy cream

2 ounces Parmesan cheese, grated (1 cup)

1 tablespoon lemon juice

2 tablespoons minced fresh chives

¼ cup pine nuts, toasted

1 Heat oil in Dutch oven over medium heat until shimmering. Add shallots and cook until softened, about 3 minutes. Stir in garlic and thyme and cook until fragrant, about 30 seconds. Stir in mushrooms and ½ teaspoon salt and cook until mushrooms begin to release their liquid, about 4 minutes. Stir in squash, cover, and cook, stirring occasionally, until squash is tender and lightly browned, about 12 minutes. Transfer vegetables to bowl and cover to keep warm.

2 Add water, broth, and ¼ teaspoon salt to now-empty pot, scraping up any browned bits, and bring to boil. Stir in pasta, return to vigorous simmer, and cook, stirring often, until pasta is nearly tender, about 10 minutes.

3 Stir in cream and continue to cook until pasta is tender and has absorbed most of liquid, about 4 minutes.

4 Add Parmesan and stir vigorously until sauce is creamy and pasta is well coated, about 30 seconds. Stir in reserved vegetables and lemon juice and cook until heated through, about 1 minute. Off heat, adjust sauce consistency with extra hot water as needed. Stir in chives and season with salt and pepper to taste. Serve, sprinkling individual portions with pine nuts.

WEEKNIGHT PASTA BOLOGNESE

SERVES 4 TO 6   TOTAL TIME 1 HOUR 30 MINUTES

WHY THIS RECIPE WORKS Making Bolognese is often an all-day affair, but its depth and richness can't be beat. We wanted a quicker, weeknight-friendly version that wouldn't sacrifice flavor. Our first move was to use our Dutch oven to deeply brown the aromatics and some pancetta (but not the ground beef, which would dry out and toughen if seared) to develop a flavorful fond; we also treated the ground beef with a baking soda solution to ensure that it stayed tender. Tomato paste and red wine added brightness. Some grated Parmesan thickened the sauce and offered savory depth. To save on dishes, we found that we could cook the pasta right in the pot by thinning out the sauce and stirring in the dried pappardelle. The pasta absorbed the flavorful liquid, and the sauce ended up with just the right noodle-coating consistency. Do not substitute fresh pappardelle here; it is too delicate and will break apart. You can substitute 1 pound dried fettuccine for the pappardelle, if desired; break the pasta in half before adding it to the pot and increase the cooking time to 16 to 18 minutes in step 5.

1 pound 93 percent lean ground beef

2 tablespoons plus 1½ cups water, plus extra as needed

¼ teaspoon baking soda

Salt and pepper

6 ounces pancetta, chopped coarse

1 onion, chopped coarse

1 large carrot, peeled and chopped coarse

1 celery rib, chopped coarse

1 tablespoon unsalted butter

1 tablespoon extra-virgin olive oil

3 tablespoons tomato paste

1 cup dry red wine

4 cups beef broth

1 ounce Parmesan cheese, grated (½ cup), plus extra for serving

1 pound dried pappardelle

1 Toss beef with 2 tablespoons water, baking soda, and ¼ teaspoon pepper in bowl until thoroughly combined; set aside.

2 Pulse pancetta in food processor until finely chopped, 15 to 20 pulses. Add onion, carrot, and celery and pulse until vegetables are finely chopped and mixture has paste-like consistency, 12 to 15 pulses, scraping down sides of bowl as needed.

3 Heat butter and oil in Dutch oven over medium-high heat until shimmering. Add pancetta-vegetable mixture and ¼ teaspoon pepper and cook, stirring occasionally, until liquid has evaporated, about 8 minutes. Spread mixture in even layer in bottom of pot and continue to cook, stirring every couple of minutes, until very dark browned bits form on bottom of pot, 7 to 12 minutes. Stir in tomato paste and cook until paste is rust-colored and bottom of pot is dark brown, 1 to 2 minutes.

4 Reduce heat to medium, add beef mixture, and cook, using wooden spoon to break meat into pieces no larger than ¼ inch, until beef has just lost its raw pink color, 4 to 7 minutes. Stir in wine, scraping up any browned bits, and bring to simmer. Cook until wine has evaporated and sauce has thickened, about 5 minutes. Stir in broth, Parmesan, and remaining 1½ cups water and bring to simmer. Reduce heat to low, cover, and cook for 20 minutes.

5 Increase heat to medium-high and bring sauce to boil. Gently nestle pasta into sauce and return to vigorous simmer. Cover and cook, stirring often, until pasta is tender, 10 to 12 minutes. Adjust sauce consistency with hot water as needed. Season with salt and pepper to taste. Serve, passing extra Parmesan separately.

CHEESE AND TOMATO LASAGNA

SERVES 6   **TOTAL TIME** 1 HOUR 30 MINUTES

WHY THIS RECIPE WORKS A cheesy, bubbling lasagna is the pinnacle of comfort food. We wanted a rich and appealing version that could be made with minimal effort (and minimal dishes), and decided to do everything in our Dutch oven—from simmering the sauce to assembling and baking the casserole. We started building a flavorful sauce by sautéing onion, garlic, and red pepper flakes. We then briefly simmered a combination of canned crushed tomatoes and canned diced tomatoes, which gave our sauce just the right consistency. Adding a little bit of extra water to the sauce ensured that the noodles could fully hydrate in the sauce. After cooking the sauce, we emptied the pot and layered the lasagna as we would in a casserole dish, with the tomato sauce, a ricotta-egg mixture, no-boil lasagna noodles, and plenty of Parmesan and mozzarella. Once our lasagna was assembled, we topped it with more cheese and transferred the pot to the oven. In 30 minutes we had the bubbly, cheesy top and perfectly cooked pasta we were looking for, all made in a single pot. Do not substitute nonfat ricotta or fat-free mozzarella here. We find it best to use the edge of the counter to break the lasagna noodles in half. Don't worry if a few noodles break unevenly or into more than two pieces; just be sure to create a uniform layer when shingling the pieces in step 3.

2 tablespoons extra-virgin olive oil
1 onion, chopped fine
    Salt and pepper
3 garlic cloves, minced
¼ teaspoon red pepper flakes
1 (28-ounce) can crushed tomatoes
1 (14.5-ounce) can diced tomatoes
1 cup water
12 ounces (1½ cups) whole-milk ricotta cheese
1 large egg
2 teaspoons minced fresh oregano
8 ounces mozzarella cheese, shredded (2 cups)
¼ cup grated Parmesan cheese
12 no-boil lasagna noodles, broken in half crosswise
3 tablespoons chopped fresh basil

1 Adjust oven rack to middle position and heat oven to 400 degrees. Heat oil in Dutch oven over medium heat until shimmering. Add onion and ½ teaspoon salt and cook until onion is softened and lightly browned, 5 to 7 minutes. Stir in garlic and pepper flakes and cook until fragrant, about 30 seconds. Stir in crushed tomatoes and diced tomatoes and their juice, bring to simmer, and cook until sauce is thickened and reduced to 4 cups, 10 to 15 minutes. Transfer sauce to bowl and stir in water.

2 Combine ricotta, egg, oregano, ½ teaspoon salt, and ½ teaspoon pepper in separate bowl. Combine mozzarella and Parmesan in third bowl.

3 Spread ¾ cup sauce over bottom of now-empty pot. Shingle 7 noodle halves around edge of pot and place 1 noodle half in center. Dollop one-third of ricotta mixture over noodles, then top with one-quarter of mozzarella mixture and one-third of remaining sauce (in that order). Repeat layering twice, beginning with noodles and ending with sauce. Sprinkle with remaining mozzarella mixture.

4 Scrape down exposed sides of pot, then transfer to oven. Bake, uncovered, until lasagna is bubbling around edges and cheese is spotty brown, 25 to 30 minutes. Let lasagna cool for 10 minutes, then sprinkle with basil and serve.

CLASSIC SOUPS

Mexican Beef and Vegetable Soup

CLASSIC CHICKEN NOODLE SOUP

SERVES 8 TO 10   TOTAL TIME 2 HOURS 15 MINUTES

WHY THIS RECIPE WORKS A Dutch oven is the perfect vessel for making soups that serve a crowd: The wide bottom is great for creating a flavorful base right in the pot, and the generous capacity means you can make a large volume of soup at once. For our classic chicken noodle, we made a streamlined from-scratch broth using chicken thighs instead of a whole bird. Our tasters liked the richness that the thighs added to the broth but preferred white meat in their soup, so we also poached breasts in the broth to shred and stir in. Cooking the noodles right in the broth intensified their flavor. Note that the thighs are used just to flavor the broth; the meat can be used for chicken salad or pot pie. If you prefer dark meat in your soup, omit the chicken breasts and add the shredded thigh meat to the soup instead. Depending on the size of your Dutch oven, you may need to brown the chicken thighs in three batches.

Broth

- 4 pounds bone-in chicken thighs, trimmed
  Salt and pepper
- 1 tablespoon vegetable oil
- 1 onion, chopped
- 12 cups water
- 2 bay leaves
- 1 pound boneless, skinless chicken breasts, trimmed

Soup

- 1 tablespoon vegetable oil
- 1 onion, chopped fine
- 1 carrot, peeled and sliced thin
- 1 celery rib, halved lengthwise and sliced thin
- 2 teaspoons minced fresh thyme or ½ teaspoon dried
- 6 ounces wide egg noodles
- ¼ cup minced fresh parsley
  Salt and pepper

1 For the broth Pat chicken thighs dry with paper towels and season with salt and pepper. Heat oil in Dutch oven over medium-high heat until just smoking. Cook half of thighs, skin side down, in pot until deep golden brown, about 6 minutes. Turn thighs and cook until lightly browned on second side, about 2 minutes; transfer to large plate and discard skin. Repeat with remaining thighs; transfer to plate and discard skin.

2 Pour off all but 1 tablespoon fat from pot. Add onion and cook over medium heat until softened, about 5 minutes. Stir in water, bay leaves, and 1 tablespoon salt. Nestle thighs into pot, adding any accumulated juices, and bring to simmer. Reduce heat to medium-low, cover, and cook for 30 minutes. Nestle chicken breasts into pot, cover, and cook until breasts register 165 degrees, about 15 minutes.

3 Transfer chicken to cutting board and let cool slightly. Strain broth through fine-mesh strainer into large bowl, pressing on solids to extract as much liquid as possible. Discard solids. Skim excess fat from surface of broth using wide, shallow spoon.

4 Using 2 forks, shred chicken thighs into bite-size pieces; discard bones and reserve meat for another use. Using 2 forks, shred chicken breasts into bite-size pieces and reserve for soup.

5 For the soup Heat oil in now-empty pot over medium heat until shimmering. Add onion, carrot, and celery and cook until softened, 6 to 8 minutes. Stir in thyme and cook until fragrant, about 30 seconds. Stir in broth, bring to simmer, and cook until vegetables are tender, about 15 minutes.

6 Stir in noodles and chicken and cook until noodles are just tender, about 5 minutes. Off heat, stir in parsley and season with salt and pepper to taste. Serve.

CHICKEN AND RAMEN SOUP

SERVES 4 TO 6   TOTAL TIME 1 HOUR

WHY THIS RECIPE WORKS Your Dutch oven doesn't have to be limited to labor-intensive recipes: This quick Asian-style noodle soup is as simple as it is satisfying. We used the Dutch oven to first brown chicken breasts and build a full-flavored base. To keep it easy, we used the noodles from store-bought ramen soup, discarding the seasoning packet, which tasted dusty and was too salty. Store-bought coleslaw mix conveniently provided already shredded cabbage and carrots ready to add to the pot. Ginger, soy sauce, and sesame oil added significant savoriness to our soup. Gently poaching the browned chicken breasts in the broth, and then removing the meat briefly to shred it before returning it to the soup, kept the chicken tender and flavorful. You can find shredded coleslaw mix in the packaged salad aisle at the grocery store.

1 tablespoon vegetable oil

1 pound boneless, skinless chicken breasts, trimmed
Salt and pepper

5 scallions, white and green parts separated and sliced thin

2 tablespoons grated fresh ginger

2 garlic cloves, minced

6 cups chicken broth

2 tablespoons dry sherry

2 tablespoons soy sauce, plus extra for seasoning

2 (3-ounce) packages ramen noodles, seasoning packets discarded

3 cups (8¼ ounces) shredded green coleslaw mix

3 ounces (3 cups) baby spinach

1 tablespoon toasted sesame oil, plus extra for seasoning

1 Heat vegetable oil in Dutch oven over medium-high heat until just smoking. Pat chicken dry with paper towels and season with salt and pepper. Brown chicken lightly on both sides, about 5 minutes; transfer to plate.

2 Add scallion whites, ginger, and garlic to fat left in pot and cook over medium heat until fragrant, about 1 minute. Stir in broth, sherry, and soy sauce, scraping up any browned bits, and bring to simmer.

3 Nestle chicken into pot, adding any accumulated juices. Reduce heat to low, cover, and cook until chicken registers 165 degrees, about 10 minutes. Transfer chicken to cutting board, let cool slightly, then shred into bite-size pieces using 2 forks.

4 Return soup to simmer, stir in noodles and coleslaw mix, and cook until noodles are tender, about 4 minutes. Stir in chicken and spinach and cook until spinach is wilted, about 1 minute. Stir in scallion greens and sesame oil. Season with salt, pepper, extra soy sauce, and extra sesame oil to taste. Serve.

ITALIAN CHICKEN SOUP WITH PARMESAN DUMPLINGS

SERVES 4 TO 6   TOTAL TIME 2 HOURS

WHY THIS RECIPE WORKS This rustic northern Italian specialty features tender dumplings deeply flavored with Parmesan and served in a light chicken broth. We modernized the classic recipe a bit, making it heartier by adding fennel, carrots, and escarole. For the dumplings, we combined fresh toasted bread crumbs with some rendered chicken fat and a generous amount of grated Parmesan for great savory flavor. Egg whites gave the dumplings a lighter texture. To ensure that the dumplings remain intact during cooking, roll them until the surfaces are smooth and no cracks remain.

1½ pounds bone-in chicken thighs, trimmed
   Salt and pepper
1 tablespoon vegetable oil
1 fennel bulb, stalks discarded, bulb halved, cored, and cut into ½-inch pieces
1 onion, chopped fine
2 carrots, peeled and cut into ¾-inch pieces
½ cup dry white wine
8 cups chicken broth
1 Parmesan cheese rind (optional), plus 3 ounces Parmesan, finely grated (1½ cups)
2 slices hearty white sandwich bread, torn into 1-inch pieces
2 large egg whites
¼ teaspoon grated lemon zest
   Pinch ground nutmeg
½ small head escarole (6 ounces), trimmed and cut into ½-inch pieces

1 Pat chicken dry with paper towels and season with salt and pepper. Heat oil in Dutch oven over medium-high heat until just smoking. Add chicken, skin side down, and cook until deep golden brown, about 6 minutes; transfer to large plate and discard skin.

2 Measure out and reserve 1 tablespoon fat from pot for dumplings; pour off all but 1 teaspoon remaining fat. Add fennel, onion, carrots, and ½ teaspoon salt to fat left in pot and cook over medium heat until vegetables are softened and lightly browned, 6 to 8 minutes. Stir in wine, scraping up any browned bits, and cook until almost dry, about 2 minutes.

3 Stir in broth and Parmesan rind, if using. Nestle chicken into pot, adding any accumulated juices, and bring to simmer. Reduce heat to medium-low, cover, and cook until chicken registers 175 degrees, about 30 minutes.

4 Meanwhile, adjust oven rack to middle position and heat oven to 350 degrees. Pulse bread in food processor until finely ground, 10 to 15 pulses. Measure out 1 cup bread crumbs and transfer to parchment paper–lined rimmed baking sheet; discard remaining crumbs. Toast crumbs in oven until light brown, about 5 minutes. Transfer to large bowl, reserving sheet and parchment, and let cool completely.

5 Stir reserved 1 tablespoon fat, grated Parmesan, egg whites, lemon zest, ⅛ teaspoon pepper, and nutmeg into bread crumbs until thoroughly combined. Refrigerate for 15 minutes.

6 Discard Parmesan rind, if using. Transfer chicken to cutting board, let cool slightly, then shred into bite-size pieces using 2 forks; discard bones.

7 Working with 1 teaspoon dough at a time, roll into smooth balls and place on reserved sheet (you should have about 28 dumplings). Return soup to simmer over medium-high heat, then stir in escarole and chicken. Add dumplings and cook until they float to surface and are cooked through, 3 to 5 minutes. Season with salt and pepper to taste. Serve.

QUICK BEEF AND BARLEY SOUP

SERVES 4 TO 6   TOTAL TIME 1 HOUR

WHY THIS RECIPE WORKS This meaty, rich soup lets the star ingredients—beef and barley—shine through. Beef and barley soup usually takes some time to make; to speed things up we turned to sirloin steak tips, which are already tender and full of flavor. Browning the meat in the Dutch oven provided plenty of savory fond. Setting the beef aside while we built a flavorful base with sautéed aromatics, porcini, and tomato paste ensured that the meat stayed tender and didn't overcook. Since beef broth can add a tinny flavor, we mixed it with an equal amount of chicken broth and added some soy sauce to boost savory depth. Letting the barley cook through in our enhanced broth infused the grains with flavor. Sirloin steak tips, also known as flap meat, are sold as whole steaks, strips, and cubes; we prefer to buy whole steaks for this dish.

3 tablespoons extra-virgin olive oil

1½ pounds sirloin steak tips, trimmed and cut into ½-inch pieces

Salt and pepper

3 carrots, peeled and cut into ¼-inch pieces

1 onion, chopped fine

1 tablespoon minced fresh thyme or 1 teaspoon dried

¼ ounce dried porcini mushrooms, rinsed and minced

2 garlic cloves, minced

2 teaspoons tomato paste

3 cups beef broth

3 cups chicken broth

⅔ cup quick-cooking barley

2 teaspoons soy sauce

1 Heat 1 tablespoon oil in Dutch oven over medium-high heat until just smoking. Pat beef dry with paper towels and season with salt and pepper. Brown half of beef on all sides, about 8 minutes; transfer to bowl. Repeat with remaining beef; transfer to bowl.

2 Add carrots, onion, and remaining 2 tablespoons oil to fat left in pot and cook over medium heat until vegetables are softened and lightly browned, 5 to 7 minutes. Stir in thyme, mushrooms, garlic, and tomato paste and cook until fragrant, about 30 seconds. Stir in beef broth, chicken broth, barley, and soy sauce, scraping up any browned bits. Bring to simmer and cook until barley is tender, about 15 minutes.

3 Stir in beef and any accumulated juices and let heat through, about 1 minute. Season with salt and pepper to taste. Serve.

MEXICAN BEEF AND VEGETABLE SOUP

SERVES 6 TO 8   **TOTAL TIME** 1 HOUR 45 MINUTES

WHY THIS RECIPE WORKS Mexico's version of beef and vegetable soup, *caldo de res*, is rich with spices, tender chunks of meat, and vegetables like tomatoes, corn, and squash. Our recipe captures the authentic flavors of this classic soup while eliminating the long cooking time required by most traditional recipes. Our first step in streamlining the recipe was to eliminate bone-in cuts and focus on quicker-cooking boneless cuts. In the end, a beef chuck-eye roast proved to be our cut of choice—it was flavorful, tender, and juicy. We browned the meat and then set it aside while we sautéed our aromatics. We then added the broth (a combination of beef broth and chicken broth gave us the best flavor), returned the beef to the pot, and simmered everything until the meat was tender. Most authentic recipes call for *chayote*, a gourd-like fruit similar to a summer squash; easy-to-find zucchini made a perfect stand-in. Tomatoes and corn are another mainstay in the soup. Canned diced tomatoes provided a more reliable flavor than fresh, but fresh corn on the cob was preferred over frozen kernels. We also included carrots and red potatoes, which contributed pleasant earthiness. To maintain the rustic feel of the soup, we left the corn on the cob and cut the cobs into 1-inch rounds, and we cut the potatoes into large pieces. With a host of complex flavors and contrasting textures, our soup was now much less work than the original, but still just as hearty and delicious. Serve with lime wedges and/or sliced radishes.

1   pound boneless beef chuck-eye roast, trimmed and cut into 1-inch pieces
    Salt and pepper
1   tablespoon vegetable oil
1   onion, chopped
5   garlic cloves, minced
1   tablespoon minced fresh oregano or 1 teaspoon dried
½   teaspoon ground cumin
4   cups beef broth
2   cups chicken broth
1   (14.5-ounce) can diced tomatoes, drained
2   bay leaves
10 ounces red potatoes, unpeeled, cut into 1-inch pieces
2   carrots, peeled and cut into ½-inch pieces
1   zucchini, cut into ½-inch pieces
2   ears corn, husks and silk removed, cut into 1-inch rounds
2   tablespoons minced fresh cilantro

1 Pat beef dry with paper towels and season with salt and pepper. Heat oil in Dutch oven over medium-high heat until just smoking. Brown beef on all sides, 5 to 7 minutes; transfer to bowl.

2 Add onion to fat left in pot and cook over medium heat until softened, about 5 minutes. Stir in garlic, oregano, and cumin and cook until fragrant, about 30 seconds. Stir in beef broth, chicken broth, tomatoes, and bay leaves, scraping up any browned bits, and bring to simmer. Stir in beef and any accumulated juices, reduce heat to low, cover, and cook for 30 minutes.

3 Stir in potatoes and carrots and cook, uncovered, until beef and vegetables are just tender, 20 to 25 minutes. Stir in zucchini and corn and cook until corn is tender, 5 to 10 minutes.

4 Discard bay leaves. Stir in cilantro and season with salt and pepper to taste. Serve.

VIETNAMESE BEEF PHO

SERVES 4 TO 6   TOTAL TIME 2 HOURS

WHY THIS RECIPE WORKS The biggest selling point of this famous soup is its killer broth—a beefy, fragrant, faintly sweet concoction produced by simmering beef bones and water, along with ginger, onions, cinnamon, and star anise, for hours. For a streamlined version, we enhanced store-bought broth with convenient ground beef. Parboiling the beef before making the broth ensured our final soup was free of scum. Onion, fresh ginger, fish sauce, and warm spices gave the broth dimension. To serve, we ladled the hot broth over tender rice noodles and thin slices of strip steak. Look for rice noodles that are about ⅛ inch wide; these are often labeled "small." Do not use Thai Kitchen Stir-Fry Rice Noodles; they are too thick and don't adequately soak up the broth.

 1 pound 85 percent lean ground beef
 2 onions, quartered through root end
12 cups beef broth
 ¼ cup fish sauce, plus extra for serving
 1 (4-inch) piece ginger, peeled and sliced into thin rounds
 1 cinnamon stick
 2 tablespoons sugar, plus extra for seasoning
 6 star anise pods
 6 whole cloves
    Salt
 1 teaspoon black peppercorns
 1 (1-pound) boneless strip steak, trimmed and halved
14–16 ounces (⅛-inch-wide) rice noodles
 ⅓ cup chopped fresh cilantro
 3 scallions, sliced thin (optional)
    Bean sprouts
    Fresh Thai or Italian basil sprigs
    Lime wedges
    Hoisin sauce
    Sriracha sauce

1 Break ground beef into rough 1-inch chunks in Dutch oven. Add water to cover by 1 inch. Bring mixture to boil over high heat and cook for 2 minutes, stirring occasionally. Drain ground beef in colander and rinse well under running water. Return ground beef to now-empty pot.

2 Add 6 onion quarters to pot with ground beef. Slice remaining 2 onion quarters as thin as possible and set aside for garnish. Add broth, 2 cups water, fish sauce, ginger, cinnamon, sugar, star anise, cloves, 2 teaspoons salt, and peppercorns to pot and bring to boil over high heat. Reduce heat to medium-low and simmer, partially covered, for 45 minutes.

3 Pour broth through colander set in large bowl. Discard solids. Strain broth through fine-mesh strainer lined with triple thickness of cheesecloth; add water as needed to equal 11 cups. Return broth to now-empty pot and season with extra sugar and salt (broth should taste overseasoned). Cover and keep warm over low heat.

4 While broth simmers, place steak on large plate and freeze until very firm, 35 to 45 minutes. Once firm, cut against grain into ⅛-inch-thick slices. Return steak to plate and refrigerate until needed.

5 Place noodles in large bowl and cover with hot tap water. Soak until noodles are pliable, 10 to 15 minutes; drain noodles. Meanwhile, bring 4 quarts water to boil in large pot. Add drained noodles and cook until almost tender, 30 to 60 seconds. Drain immediately and divide noodles among individual bowls.

6 Bring broth to rolling boil. Divide steak among individual bowls, shingling slices on top of noodles. Pile reserved onion slices on top of steak slices and sprinkle with cilantro and scallions, if using. Ladle hot broth into each bowl. Serve immediately, passing bean sprouts, basil sprigs, lime wedges, hoisin, Sriracha, and extra fish sauce separately.

SPICY MOROCCAN-STYLE LAMB AND LENTIL SOUP

SERVES 6 TO 8   TOTAL TIME 2 HOURS

WHY THIS RECIPE WORKS *Harira* is an intensely flavored Moroccan soup of lentils, tomatoes, chickpeas, and lamb. We started our soup on the stovetop, where we could brown the lamb and build a flavorful stock, then transferred the Dutch oven to a low oven to make our recipe more hands-off. After cooking, we added some zing by stirring in harissa, a chile-spiced paste that's traditional in the region. You can substitute store-bought harissa, though spiciness can vary by brand. If you can't find lamb shoulder chops, you can substitute an equal amount of lamb shoulder roast trimmed of all visible fat. Do not use French green lentils (*lentilles du Puy*) in this recipe. If you can't find Aleppo pepper, you can substitute ¾ teaspoon paprika and ¾ teaspoon finely chopped red pepper flakes.

Harissa

- 6 tablespoons extra-virgin olive oil
- 6 garlic cloves, minced
- 2 tablespoons paprika
- 1 tablespoon ground coriander
- 1 tablespoon ground dried Aleppo pepper
- 1 teaspoon ground cumin
- ¾ teaspoon caraway seeds
- ½ teaspoon salt

Soup

- 1 pound lamb shoulder chops (blade or round bone), 1 to 1½ inches thick, trimmed and halved
  Salt and pepper
- 1 tablespoon extra-virgin olive oil
- 1 onion, chopped fine
- 1 teaspoon grated fresh ginger
- 1 teaspoon ground cumin
- ½ teaspoon paprika
- ¼ teaspoon ground cinnamon
- ¼ teaspoon cayenne pepper
  Pinch saffron threads, crumbled
- 1 tablespoon all-purpose flour
- 10 cups chicken broth
- ¾ cup green or brown lentils, picked over and rinsed
- 1 (15-ounce) can chickpeas, rinsed
- 4 plum tomatoes, cored and cut into ¾-inch pieces
- ⅓ cup minced fresh cilantro

1 For the harissa Microwave all ingredients in bowl until bubbling, about 1 minute, stirring halfway through microwaving; set aside for serving. (Harissa can be refrigerated for up to 4 days.)

2 For the soup Adjust oven rack to lower-middle position and heat oven to 325 degrees. Pat lamb dry with paper towels and season with salt and pepper. Heat oil in Dutch oven over medium-high heat until just smoking. Brown lamb, about 4 minutes per side; transfer to plate. Pour off all but 2 tablespoons fat from pot.

3 Add onion to fat left in pot and cook over medium heat until softened, about 5 minutes. Stir in ginger, cumin, paprika, cinnamon, cayenne, ¼ teaspoon pepper, and saffron and cook until fragrant, about 30 seconds. Stir in flour and cook for 1 minute. Slowly whisk in broth, scraping up any browned bits and smoothing out any lumps, and bring to simmer.

4 Stir in lamb and any accumulated juices and cook for 10 minutes. Stir in lentils and chickpeas, cover, and transfer pot to oven. Cook until fork slips easily in and out of lamb and lentils are tender, about 1 hour.

5 Transfer lamb to cutting board, let cool slightly, then shred into bite-size pieces using 2 forks; discard fat and bones. Stir lamb into soup and let sit until heated through, about 2 minutes. Stir in tomatoes, cilantro, and ¼ cup harissa, and season with salt and pepper to taste. Serve, passing extra harissa separately.

SPICY THAI-STYLE SHRIMP SOUP

SERVES **4 TO 6**   TOTAL TIME **45 MINUTES**

WHY THIS RECIPE WORKS Based on a Thai soup called tom yum, this quick shrimp soup offers an exotic balance of hot, salty, sweet, and sour elements by way of grocery store ingredients. We substituted easy-to-find jalapeño peppers for traditional Thai chiles, while fish sauce provided the saltiness. The soup's sourness authentically comes from a combination of lemon grass and makrut (sometimes called kaffir) lime leaves, which we replaced with lime juice added to the soup at the last minute. Plain white sugar, a substitute for palm sugar, helped balance the powerful flavors. Cooking the shrimp in the hot broth for just a minute ensured they turned out tender. For a spicier soup, use the larger amount of chiles.

5¼ cups chicken broth
1 (½-inch) piece ginger, cut in half and smashed
2 tablespoons fish sauce
2 large garlic cloves, lightly crushed with skins on
4–6 cilantro stems, including roots, plus ¼ cup coarsely chopped fresh cilantro
1 teaspoon sugar
1–2 jalapeño chiles, stemmed and sliced crosswise into ¼-inch-thick rings
2 tomatoes, cored and chopped coarse
8 ounces cremini, oyster, or white mushrooms, stemmed and quartered if small or cut into sixths if large
8 ounces medium shrimp (41 to 50 per pound), peeled and deveined
3 tablespoons lime juice (2 limes)

1 Bring broth, ginger, fish sauce, garlic, cilantro stems, sugar, half of jalapeños, and one-quarter of tomatoes to simmer in Dutch oven over medium-high heat and cook for 20 minutes. Strain broth through fine-mesh strainer set over large bowl, pressing on solids to extract as much liquid as possible.

2 Return broth to now-empty pot and bring to simmer over medium-high heat. Stir in mushrooms and remaining chiles and cook for 2 minutes. Stir in shrimp and cook for 1 minute. Off heat, stir in lime juice. Divide remaining tomato and chopped cilantro among individual bowls and ladle soup over top. Serve.

PEELING AND DEVEINING SHRIMP

1 Break shell under swimming legs, which will come off as shell is removed. Leave tail intact if desired, or tug tail to remove shell.

2 Use paring knife to make shallow cut along back of shrimp to expose vein. Use tip of knife to lift out vein. Discard vein by wiping blade against paper towel.

NEW ENGLAND CLAM CHOWDER

SERVES 6 TOTAL TIME 1 HOUR 15 MINUTES

WHY THIS RECIPE WORKS There's no better ally for homemade clam chowder than a good Dutch oven: You can use it first to steam open the clams (which is far easier than shucking them, and steaming yields an ultraflavorful clam broth), then to build the soup after simply wiping out the pot. We decided on medium-size cherrystones since they offered good value and great briny taste. We reserved 2 cups of the steaming liquid to add to the chowder; balanced with 3 cups of bottled clam juice, this combination made a chowder that was packed with clam flavor without being too salty. We chose Yukon Gold potatoes, as their moderate levels of starch and moisture blended seamlessly with this creamy chowder. Thickening the chowder with flour helped stabilize it, as it can otherwise easily separate and curdle. Cream turned out to be essential, but our chowder needed only a minimal amount, which provided richness without overpowering the flavor of the clams. Finally, we chose bacon rather than salt pork, a traditional component of chowder, to enrich the flavor with a subtle smokiness. Serve with oyster crackers.

3 cups water
6 pounds medium hard-shell clams, such as cherrystones, scrubbed
2 slices bacon, chopped fine
2 onions, chopped fine
2 celery ribs, chopped fine
1 teaspoon minced fresh thyme or ¼ teaspoon dried
⅓ cup all-purpose flour
3 (8-ounce) bottles clam juice
1½ pounds Yukon Gold potatoes, peeled and cut into ½-inch pieces
1 bay leaf
1 cup heavy cream
2 tablespoons minced fresh parsley
  Salt and pepper

1 Bring water to boil in Dutch oven over medium-high heat. Add clams, cover, and cook for 5 minutes. Stir clams thoroughly and continue to cook, covered, until clams begin to open, 2 to 7 minutes. As clams open, transfer to large bowl and let cool slightly. Discard any unopened clams.

2 Measure out and reserve 2 cups clam steaming liquid, avoiding any gritty sediment that has settled on bottom of pot. Open clams with paring knife, holding clams over bowl to catch any juices. Using knife, sever muscle that attaches clam belly to shell and transfer meat to cutting board. Discard shells. Coarsely chop clams; set aside.

3 Wipe Dutch oven clean with paper towels. Add bacon and cook over medium heat until crisp, 5 to 7 minutes. Stir in onions and celery and cook until softened, 5 to 7 minutes. Stir in thyme and cook until fragrant, about 30 seconds. Stir in flour and cook for 1 minute.

4 Slowly whisk in bottled clam juice and reserved clam steaming liquid, scraping up any browned bits and smoothing out any lumps. Stir in potatoes and bay leaf, bring to simmer, and cook until potatoes are tender, 20 to 25 minutes.

5 Discard bay leaf. Stir in cream and return to brief simmer. Off heat, stir in clams and let sit until heated through, about 1 minute. Stir in parsley and season with salt and pepper to taste. Serve.

FRESH CORN CHOWDER

SERVES 6   TOTAL TIME 1 HOUR

WHY THIS RECIPE WORKS This thick and lush chowder is bursting with fresh corn flavor. To pump up the corn flavor, we first added grated corn and corn milk, which came from scraping the cobs with the back of a butter knife, then we stirred in more whole kernels toward the end. Bacon added richness and a subtle smoky note; we used the rendered fat to sauté onion and garlic. Water diluted the flavor of the chowder, so we used chicken broth instead. With whole milk as our primary dairy component (we rejected using heavy cream by itself because it was too rich), we added a few tablespoons of flour, which thickened our soup nicely. This soup tastes best with sweet corn from the height of the season; do not substitute frozen corn.

10   ears corn, husks and silk removed
 4   slices bacon, chopped fine
 1   onion, chopped fine
 2   garlic cloves, minced
 1   teaspoon minced fresh thyme or ¼ teaspoon dried
 3   tablespoons all-purpose flour
 3   cups chicken broth
 2   cups whole milk
12   ounces red potatoes, unpeeled, cut into
     ¼-inch pieces
 2   bay leaves
 1   cup heavy cream
 2   tablespoons minced fresh parsley
     Salt and pepper

1 Working with 1 ear of corn at a time, stand each of 4 ears on end inside large bowl and cut kernels from cob using paring knife. Grate remaining 6 ears over large holes of box grater into separate bowl. Using back of butter knife, scrape remaining pulp from all cobs into bowl with grated corn.

2 Cook bacon in Dutch oven over medium heat until crisp, 5 to 7 minutes. Stir in onion and cook until softened, about 5 minutes. Stir in garlic and thyme and cook until fragrant, about 30 seconds. Stir in flour and cook for 1 minute. Slowly whisk in broth and milk, scraping up any browned bits and smoothing out any lumps. Stir in potatoes, bay leaves, and grated corn and pulp mixture. Bring to simmer and cook until potatoes are almost tender, about 15 minutes.

3 Stir in remaining corn kernels and cream and cook until corn kernels are tender yet still slightly crunchy, about 5 minutes. Discard bay leaves. Stir in parsley and season with salt and pepper to taste. Serve.

PREPARING FRESH CORN FOR CHOWDER

1 Stand corn upright inside large bowl and cut kernels from cobs using paring knife.

2 Grate remaining ears over large holes of box grater into separate bowl.

3 Using back of butter knife, scrape pulp from all cobs into bowl with grated corn.

CLASSIC TOMATO SOUP

SERVES 6 TO 8   TOTAL TIME 1 HOUR

WHY THIS RECIPE WORKS It's hard to beat a classic tomato soup, whether as a simple lunch on its own or as a dip for a melty grilled cheese. We used canned diced tomatoes so we could make this soup any time of year. To enhance the tomatoes' complexity, we browned most of them in our Dutch oven to concentrate their flavor, and saved some to add toward the end of cooking to keep the soup fresh. But the real key to a satiny, well-balanced soup turned out to be just ½ teaspoon of baking soda, which helped neutralize the metallic taste and acidity of the canned tomatoes. We were tempted to add a variety of classic seasonings, but found they made the soup taste like marinara sauce. Tasters were most satisfied with a single bay leaf, chicken broth, and the richness of heavy cream.

2 (28-ounce) cans diced tomatoes
¾ cup chicken broth, plus extra as needed
3 tablespoons unsalted butter
1 onion, chopped
1 bay leaf
1 teaspoon packed brown sugar
2 tablespoons tomato paste
2 tablespoons all-purpose flour
½ teaspoon baking soda
Salt and pepper
½ cup heavy cream
2 tablespoons minced fresh chives
Extra-virgin olive oil

1 Drain tomatoes in colander set over large bowl, pressing lightly to release juices. Transfer tomato juice to large measuring cup and add broth. You should have about 4 cups tomato juice–broth mixture; add extra broth as needed to equal 4 cups. Set aside.

2 Melt butter in Dutch oven over medium heat. Add onion and cook until softened, about 5 minutes. Add two-thirds of tomatoes, bay leaf, and sugar and cook, stirring occasionally, until tomatoes begin to brown, about 15 minutes.

3 Add tomato paste and flour and cook, stirring frequently, until paste begins to darken, about 1 minute. Slowly whisk in reserved tomato juice–broth mixture, scraping up any browned bits and smoothing out any lumps. Stir in remaining tomatoes, baking soda, and ½ teaspoon salt. Bring to simmer and cook until slightly thickened, about 5 minutes.

4 Discard bay leaf. Working in batches, process soup in blender until smooth, 1 to 2 minutes, then return to clean pot. Stir in cream and bring to brief simmer over medium-low heat. Season with salt and pepper to taste. Drizzle individual portions with oil and sprinkle with chives before serving.

CURRIED BUTTERNUT SQUASH AND APPLE SOUP

SERVES 4 TO 6   TOTAL TIME 1 HOUR 15 MINUTES

WHY THIS RECIPE WORKS Butternut squash soup is a fall staple, but many recipes fail to live up to their potential, ending up too sweet or with too little squash flavor—plus, prepping the squash can be time-consuming and unwieldy. We found the solution to these problems in our Dutch oven. We sautéed a shallot in butter with the reserved squash seeds and fibers before adding water for a flavorful, squash-enhanced liquid that we then used for steaming the squash. The Dutch oven's ample size provided plenty of room for steaming, and we could drop the squash in unpeeled and quartered, which cut out lots of prep time. To complete our soup, we scooped out the cooked squash from its skin and then pureed it with some of the strained steaming liquid for a perfectly smooth texture. Some heavy cream added richness, and a little brown sugar and curry powder balanced the squash's earthy flavor. A tart apple, such as a Granny Smith, adds a nice contrast to the sweet squash, but any type of apple may be used.

6 slices hearty white sandwich bread, crusts removed, cut into ½-inch pieces (3 cups)

3 tablespoons unsalted butter, melted, plus 4 tablespoons unsalted butter
   Salt and pepper

1 large shallot, chopped

2½ pounds butternut squash, quartered and seeded, fibers and seeds reserved

6 cups water

1 large apple, peeled, cored, and quartered

½ cup heavy cream

2 teaspoons curry powder

1 teaspoon packed dark brown sugar

1 Adjust oven rack to middle position and heat oven to 350 degrees. Toss bread with melted butter, season with salt and pepper, and spread onto rimmed baking sheet. Bake until golden brown and crisp, 20 to 25 minutes, stirring halfway through baking. Set aside to cool. (Croutons can be stored at room temperature for up to 3 days.)

2 Melt 2 tablespoons butter in Dutch oven over medium heat. Add shallot and cook until softened, 2 to 3 minutes. Stir in squash seeds and fibers and cook until butter turns orange, about 4 minutes.

3 Stir in water and 1 teaspoon salt and bring to simmer. Place squash, cut side down, and apple in steamer basket and lower basket into pot. Cover and steam until completely tender, 30 to 40 minutes.

4 Using tongs, transfer squash to rimmed baking sheet. Let squash cool slightly, then scrape flesh from skin using soupspoon; discard skin.

5 Strain cooking liquid through fine-mesh strainer into bowl. Working in batches, process squash and 3 cups strained cooking liquid in blender until smooth, 1 to 2 minutes, then return to clean pot. Stir in cream, curry powder, sugar, and remaining 2 tablespoons butter and bring to brief simmer over medium-low heat. Adjust consistency as needed with remaining strained cooking liquid. Season with salt and pepper to taste. Top individual portions with croutons before serving.

WEST AFRICAN SWEET POTATO AND PEANUT SOUP

SERVES 4 TO 6   TOTAL TIME 1 HOUR

WHY THIS RECIPE WORKS This West African soup puts sweet potatoes center stage. Onion and garlic offered aromatic backbone; using butter instead of oil to sauté them brought out the alliums' sweet, nutty notes. Rather than pureeing peanuts into the soup, as many traditional recipes call for, we decided to use creamy peanut butter, which packed a flavor punch and gave the soup a smoother, more luxurious texture. We opted for a combination of chicken broth and water to give the soup a bit of savoriness without overpowering the other flavors. Recipes we found varied widely in the spices they added; in the end, we went with a simple combination of coriander, since its slightly floral flavor and aroma complemented the sweet potato nicely, and cayenne, which brought everything else into focus. A bit of fresh cilantro, stirred in at the end, echoed the coriander with bright freshness. This recipe was developed with standard sweet potatoes (called Beauregards), but Jewel and Red Garnet sweet potatoes also work well. Do stick with the orange-fleshed varieties; white- or purple-fleshed sweet potatoes, in conjunction with the peanut butter, will blend to an unappetizing color. For a spicier soup, use the larger amount of cayenne.

2 tablespoons unsalted butter

1 onion, chopped fine

1 teaspoon packed light brown sugar
   Salt and pepper

3 garlic cloves, minced

½ teaspoon ground coriander

⅛–¼ teaspoon cayenne pepper

2 pounds sweet potatoes, peeled, quartered lengthwise, and sliced thin

3½ cups chicken broth, plus extra as needed

2 cups water

3 tablespoons creamy peanut butter

½ cup unsalted dry-roasted peanuts

¼ cup minced fresh cilantro

1 Melt butter in Dutch oven over medium heat. Add onion, sugar, and 1 teaspoon salt and cook until onion is softened, about 5 minutes. Stir in garlic, coriander, and cayenne and cook until fragrant, about 30 seconds.

2 Add potatoes, broth, water, and peanut butter and bring to simmer. Reduce heat to low, partially cover, and cook until potatoes are tender, 25 to 30 minutes.

3 Working in batches, process soup in blender until smooth, 1 to 2 minutes, then return to clean pot. Adjust consistency as needed with extra hot broth. Season with salt and pepper to taste. Sprinkle individual portions with peanuts and cilantro and. Serve.

ULTIMATE FRENCH ONION SOUP

SERVES 6   TOTAL TIME 4 HOURS 30 MINUTES

WHY THIS RECIPE WORKS Great French onion soup is characterized by a rich broth, sweet-savory caramelized onions, and nutty Gruyère-topped bread—but it can be labor-intensive. By starting the cooking in a 400-degree oven, we needed to stir only periodically before moving the Dutch oven to the stovetop to deeply brown the onions. We deglazed the pot several times with water before adding our broth and additional aromatics. Sweet onions, such as Vidalia or Walla Walla, will make this recipe overly sweet. Use broiler-safe crocks and keep the rims 4 to 5 inches from the broiler element to obtain a proper gratinée of cheese. If using ordinary soup bowls, sprinkle the toasted bread slices with Gruyère and broil them on the baking sheet until the cheese melts, then float them on top of the soup.

4 pounds onions, halved and sliced through root end into ¼-inch-thick pieces
3 tablespoons unsalted butter, cut into 3 pieces
Salt and pepper
2¾–3 cups water
½ cup dry sherry
4 cups chicken broth
2 cups beef broth
6 sprigs fresh thyme, tied with kitchen twine
1 bay leaf
1 (12-inch) baguette, cut into ½-inch slices
8 ounces Gruyère cheese, shredded (2 cups)

1 Adjust oven rack to middle position and heat oven to 400 degrees. Coat inside of Dutch oven with vegetable oil spray. Add onions, butter, and 1 teaspoon salt. Cover, transfer pot to oven, and cook until onions wilt slightly, about 1 hour.

2 Stir onions thoroughly, scraping bottom and sides of pot. Partially cover pot and continue to cook in oven until onions are very soft and golden brown, 1½ to 1¾ hours, stirring onions thoroughly after 1 hour. Do not turn off oven.

3 Remove pot from oven and place over medium-high heat. Continue to cook onions, stirring and scraping pot often, until liquid evaporates, onions brown, and bottom of pot is coated with dark crust, 20 to 25 minutes. (If onions begin to brown too quickly, reduce heat to medium.)

4 Stir in ¼ cup water, scraping up any browned bits. Continue to cook until water evaporates and pot bottom has formed another dark crust, 6 to 8 minutes. Repeat deglazing with ¼ cup water 2 or 3 more times, until onions are very dark brown.

5 Stir in sherry and cook until almost dry, about 5 minutes. Stir in chicken broth, beef broth, 2 cups water, thyme bundle, bay leaf, and ½ teaspoon salt, scraping up any remaining browned bits, and bring to simmer. Reduce heat to medium-low, cover, and cook for 30 minutes. Discard thyme bundle and bay leaf and season with salt and pepper to taste. (Soup can be refrigerated for up to 3 days; return to simmer before proceeding.)

6 Lay baguette slices on rimmed baking sheet and bake until dry, crisp, and lightly golden, about 10 minutes, flipping slices halfway through baking.

7 Position oven rack 8 inches from broiler element and heat broiler. Set individual broiler-safe crocks on separate rimmed baking sheet and fill each with about 1½ cups soup. Top each bowl with 1 or 2 baguette slices (do not overlap slices) and sprinkle evenly with Gruyère. Broil until cheese is melted and bubbly around edges, 3 to 5 minutes. Let cool for 5 minutes before serving.

VEGETABLE SHABU-SHABU WITH SESAME SAUCE

SERVES 6 TO 8   TOTAL TIME 1 HOUR

WHY THIS RECIPE WORKS This Japanese soup features chewy udon noodles, silky tofu, and tender vegetables in a simple, savory broth. Shabu-shabu is traditionally a hot-pot dish in which the ingredients are cooked at the table in boiling broth. We wanted to achieve a similarly satisfying dish at home—without the hot pot—so we turned to our trusty Dutch oven. The typical dashi broth is made from glutamate-rich kombu seaweed and bonito (tuna) flakes. After a good deal of testing, we found that adding a second variety of seaweed (wakame), fish sauce, rice wine, and sugar replicated the fishy depth of the bonito. Shabu-shabu typically includes carrots, napa cabbage or bok choy, enoki or shiitake mushrooms, tofu, and chrysanthemum leaves. Luckily, the hard-to-find chrysanthemum leaves were not missed when omitted. We preferred bok choy to cabbage and the fuller flavor of shiitake mushrooms to enoki; adding the vegetables right to the broth infused them with flavor and resulted in a cohesive soup. A dollop of homemade sesame sauce was the perfect garnish. We prefer the flavor of red miso here, but white miso can be substituted. Toast the sesame seeds in a dry skillet over medium heat until fragrant (about 1 minute) and then remove the pan from the heat so the seeds won't scorch.

Sesame Sauce

- ¼ cup sesame seeds, toasted
- 2 tablespoons mayonnaise
- 1 tablespoon red miso
- 2 teaspoons lemon juice
- 2 teaspoons sugar
- 1 garlic clove, minced
- ½ teaspoon water

Soup

- 8 ounces dried udon noodles
  Salt
- ½ ounce kombu, rinsed
- ½ ounce wakame, rinsed
- ½ cup mirin
- ¼ cup fish sauce
- 1½ teaspoons sugar
- 3 heads baby bok choy (4 ounces each), sliced ⅛ inch thick
- 3 carrots, peeled and sliced ⅛ inch thick
- 14 ounces soft tofu, cut into ½-inch cubes
- 8 ounces shiitake mushrooms, stemmed and sliced thin

1 For the sesame sauce Stir all ingredients together in bowl until smooth.

2 For the soup Bring 8 cups water to boil in Dutch oven. Add noodles and 1½ teaspoons salt and cook, stirring often, until tender. Drain noodles, rinse well under cold water, and set aside.

3 Bring 9 cups water, kombu, and wakame to brief boil in now-empty Dutch oven over high heat. Off heat, discard seaweed.

4 Stir in mirin, fish sauce, and sugar and bring to simmer over medium-high heat. Stir in bok choy and carrots and cook until crisp-tender, 2 to 4 minutes. Stir in tofu, mushrooms, and noodles and let heat through, about 1 minute. Drizzle individual portions with sesame sauce before serving.

EASY BLACK BEAN SOUP

SERVES 4 TO 6   TOTAL TIME 50 MINUTES

WHY THIS RECIPE WORKS We wanted a simple yet flavorful black bean soup that we could make even on busy weeknights, so we started with convenient canned beans. Pureeing a portion of the beans gave our soup body, while a hearty base of aromatics—garlic, oregano, cumin, and chili powder—gave it a lot of flavor. For the liquid, chicken broth proved the best bet because its flavor was not intrusive. Since the soup is cooked so briefly, we looked for a quick-cooking pork product and found that sliced spicy chorizo sausage added meaty richness. A handful of cilantro, stirred in at the end, offered freshness. We prefer to top bowls of this soup with simple, classic garnishes such as sour cream and lime wedges.

4 (15-ounce) cans black beans, rinsed

3 cups chicken broth

1 tablespoon vegetable oil

6 ounces chorizo sausage, halved lengthwise and sliced ¼ inch thick

1 onion, chopped fine

1 red bell pepper, stemmed, seeded, and chopped fine

6 garlic cloves, minced

1 tablespoon minced fresh oregano or 1 teaspoon dried

½ teaspoon ground cumin

½ teaspoon chili powder

½ cup minced fresh cilantro

Salt and pepper

Hot sauce

1 Process 2 cups beans and 1 cup broth in blender until smooth, about 10 seconds.

2 Heat oil in Dutch oven over medium heat until shimmering. Add chorizo, onion, and bell pepper and cook until vegetables are softened and lightly browned, 5 to 7 minutes. Stir in garlic, oregano, cumin, and chili powder and cook until fragrant, about 30 seconds. Stir in remaining 2 cups broth, scraping up any browned bits.

3 Stir in pureed beans and remaining whole beans, bring to simmer, and cook until flavors meld, about 15 minutes. Stir in cilantro and season with salt, pepper, and hot sauce to taste. Serve.

HEARTY MINESTRONE

SERVES 6 TO 8   TOTAL TIME 1 HOUR 45 MINUTES (PLUS SOAKING TIME)

WHY THIS RECIPE WORKS A good minestrone captures the fleeting flavors of summer vegetables in a bowl. We wanted to create the ultimate version: a rich broth that would be packed with flavor and that would feature lots of contrasting textures. Sautéing pancetta and then cooking the vegetables in the rendered fat gave our soup layers of flavor, while a Parmesan rind added richness. Because we were relying on the starch from the beans to give our soup some body, it was necessary to start with dried beans. The last component we considered for our perfect minestrone was the liquid, settling on just the right combination of chicken broth, water, and V8 juice (which added a big wallop of vegetable flavor). If you're pressed for time, you can skip brining and quick-salt-soak the beans: In step 1, combine the salt, water, and beans in a Dutch oven and bring to a boil. Off the heat, cover the pot and let sit for 1 hour. Drain and rinse the beans and proceed with the recipe. In order for the starch from the beans to thicken the soup, it's important to maintain a vigorous simmer in step 3.

Salt and pepper
8 ounces (1¼ cups) dried cannellini or great Northern beans, picked over and rinsed
1 tablespoon extra-virgin olive oil, plus extra for serving
3 ounces pancetta, cut into ¼-inch pieces
2 small onions, cut into ½-inch pieces
2 celery ribs, cut into ½-inch pieces
1 carrot, peeled and cut into ½-inch pieces
1 zucchini, cut into ½-inch pieces
½ small head green cabbage, cored and cut into ½-inch pieces (2 cups)
2 garlic cloves, minced
⅛ teaspoon red pepper flakes
2 cups chicken broth
1 Parmesan cheese rind (optional), plus grated Parmesan for serving
1 bay leaf
1½ cups V8 juice
½ cup chopped fresh basil

1 Dissolve 1½ tablespoons salt in 8 cups cold water in large container. Add beans and soak at room temperature for at least 8 hours or up to 24 hours. Drain and rinse well.

2 Cook oil and pancetta in Dutch oven over medium-high heat, stirring occasionally, until pancetta is lightly browned and fat has rendered, 3 to 5 minutes. Add onions, celery, carrot, and zucchini and cook until vegetables are softened and lightly browned, 7 to 9 minutes. Stir in cabbage, garlic, pepper flakes, and ½ teaspoon salt and cook until cabbage starts to wilt, 1 to 2 minutes. Transfer vegetables to rimmed baking sheet and set aside.

3 Add soaked beans, 8 cups water, broth, Parmesan rind, if using, and bay leaf to now-empty pot. Bring to vigorous simmer over medium-high heat and cook, stirring occasionally, until beans are fully tender and liquid begins to thicken, 45 minutes to 1 hour.

4 Stir reserved vegetables and V8 juice into soup and cook until vegetables are soft, about 15 minutes. Off heat, discard bay leaf and Parmesan rind, if using. Stir in basil and season with salt and pepper to taste. Serve, passing extra oil and grated Parmesan separately.

U.S. SENATE NAVY BEAN SOUP

SERVES 6 TO 8   TOTAL TIME 1 HOUR 30 MINUTES (PLUS SOAKING TIME)

WHY THIS RECIPE WORKS This simple, filling white bean and potato soup is a classic; it's been on the menu in the U.S. Senate dining room for more than a century. The original recipe derives much of its flavor from a ham hock, aromatic vegetables, and butter. We wanted to stay true to the simple ingredient list but ramp up the flavor. We began by choosing dried beans, which tasters preferred over canned for their creamier texture in this bean-focused soup. We also doubled up on ham hocks. Next, we substituted vegetable oil for the butter so the flavor was cleaner. A few whole cloves, removed before serving the soup, added a gentle infusion of spice. And instead of stirring precooked mashed potatoes into the beans, as some recipes suggest, we added cut-up potatoes right to the soup pot and then mashed the cooked spuds to thicken the soup. The finished texture of the soup should be creamy but not too thick. Do not use ground cloves; they will turn the soup an unsightly gray color. If you're pressed for time, you can skip brining and quick-salt-soak the beans: In step 1, combine the salt, water, and beans in a Dutch oven and bring to a boil. Off the heat, cover the pot and let sit for 1 hour. Drain and rinse the beans and proceed with the recipe.

Salt and pepper
1 pound (2½ cups) navy beans, picked over and rinsed
1 tablespoon vegetable oil
1 onion, chopped fine
2 celery ribs, chopped fine
2 garlic cloves, minced
3 whole cloves
2 (12-ounce) smoked ham hocks
8 ounces russet potatoes, peeled and cut into ¼-inch pieces
1 tablespoon cider vinegar

1 Dissolve 3 tablespoons salt in 4 quarts cold water in large container. Add beans and soak at room temperature for at least 8 hours or up to 24 hours. Drain and rinse well.

2 Heat oil in Dutch oven over medium heat until shimmering. Add onion, celery, and 1 teaspoon salt and cook until vegetables are softened, about 5 minutes. Stir in garlic and cook until fragrant, about 30 seconds. Transfer onion mixture to bowl.

3 Insert cloves into skin of 1 ham hock. Add 8 cups water, ham hocks, and beans to now-empty pot and bring to simmer over medium-high heat. Reduce heat to medium-low, partially cover, and cook, stirring occasionally, until beans are tender, 45 minutes to 1 hour.

4 Stir potatoes and onion mixture into soup, bring to simmer, and cook, uncovered, until potatoes are tender, 10 to 15 minutes; remove pot from heat. Transfer ham hocks to cutting board, let cool slightly, then shred into bite-size pieces using 2 forks; discard skin, bones, and cloves.

5 Using potato masher, gently mash beans and potatoes until soup is creamy and lightly thickened, 8 to 10 strokes. Add ½ teaspoon pepper and shredded meat and bring to simmer over medium heat. Stir in vinegar and season with salt and pepper to taste. Serve.

French-Style Pork Stew

HEARTY STEWS AND CHILIS

BEST CHICKEN STEW

SERVES 6 TO 8   TOTAL TIME 2 HOURS 30 MINUTES

WHY THIS RECIPE WORKS Fond—the flavorful browned bits that collect in the pot when searing meat or aromatics—is key for making a stew with deep, robust flavor. An enameled Dutch oven helps build fond thanks to its thick walls, and the light-colored enamel makes it easy to monitor browning. We capitalized on this for a chicken stew that would satisfy like its beef brethren. Searing collagen-rich chicken wings provided lots of chicken flavor and thickening gelatin, while boneless thighs yielded tender stew meat. Lots of sautéed aromatics contributed to a hefty layer of fond, and cooking the stew uncovered in the oven encouraged the creation of even more fond on the pot's sides. Mashed anchovy fillets (rinsed and dried before mashing) can be used instead of anchovy paste. Use small red potatoes measuring 1½ inches in diameter.

2   pounds boneless, skinless chicken thighs, halved crosswise and trimmed
    Salt and pepper
3   slices bacon, chopped
1   pound chicken wings, cut at joint
1   onion, chopped fine
1   celery rib, minced
2   garlic cloves, minced
2   teaspoons anchovy paste
1   teaspoon minced fresh thyme or ¼ teaspoon dried
5   cups chicken broth
1   cup dry white wine, plus extra for seasoning
1   tablespoon soy sauce
3   tablespoons unsalted butter, cut into 3 pieces
⅓   cup all-purpose flour
1   pound small red potatoes, unpeeled, quartered
4   carrots, peeled and cut into ½-inch pieces
2   tablespoons chopped fresh parsley

1 Adjust oven rack to lower-middle position and heat oven to 325 degrees. Arrange chicken thighs on rimmed baking sheet and season with salt and pepper; cover with plastic wrap and set aside.

2 Cook bacon in Dutch oven over medium-low heat, stirring occasionally, until crisp, 5 to 7 minutes. Using slotted spoon, transfer bacon to bowl. Add chicken wings to fat left in pot, increase heat to medium, and cook until well browned on both sides, 10 to 12 minutes; transfer to bowl with bacon.

3 Add onion, celery, garlic, anchovy paste, and thyme to fat left in in pot. Cook, stirring occasionally, until dark fond forms on bottom of pot, 2 to 4 minutes. Increase heat to high. Stir in 1 cup broth, wine, and soy sauce, scraping up any browned bits, and bring to boil. Cook, stirring occasionally, until almost dry and vegetables begin to sizzle again, 12 to 15 minutes.

4 Add butter and stir to melt. Stir in flour and cook for 1 minute. Slowly whisk in remaining 4 cups broth, scraping up any browned bits and smoothing out any lumps. Stir in wings and bacon, potatoes, and carrots and bring to simmer. Transfer pot to oven and cook, uncovered, for 30 minutes, stirring once halfway through cooking.

5 Remove pot from oven. Use wooden spoon to draw gravy up sides of pot and scrape browned bits into stew. Stir in thighs and bring to simmer over high heat. Return pot to oven, uncovered, and cook, stirring occasionally, until chicken and vegetables are tender, about 45 minutes.

6 Remove pot from oven. Discard wings and season stew with up to 2 tablespoons extra wine. Stir in parsley and season with salt and pepper to taste. Serve.

CHICKEN AND SAUSAGE GUMBO

SERVES 6   TOTAL TIME 2 HOURS

WHY THIS RECIPE WORKS This classic New Orleans specialty is built on a roux—a cooked mixture of fat and flour that must be stirred constantly, sometimes for an hour or more, until it is deep brown. To get the same depth of flavor with much less hands-on work, we turned to a dry roux: We toasted the flour alone in the oven until it was the color of cinnamon. Using our Dutch oven prevented hot spots and encouraged even toasting. Whisking half of the broth right into the toasted flour avoided clumps and made it easy to incorporate into the gumbo. Rich and flavorful boneless, skinless chicken thighs and andouille sausage were the proteins favored by tasters. For the sake of efficiency, start toasting the flour in the oven before prepping the remaining ingredients. We strongly recommend using andouille, but in a pinch you can substitute kielbasa, if desired. In step 3, be sure to whisk the broth into the toasted flour in small increments to prevent lumps from forming. Serve over white rice.

1 cup all-purpose flour

1 tablespoon vegetable oil

1 onion, chopped fine

1 green bell pepper, stemmed, seeded, and chopped fine

2 celery ribs, chopped fine

1 tablespoon minced fresh thyme

3 garlic cloves, minced

1 teaspoon paprika

2 bay leaves

½ teaspoon cayenne pepper
  Salt and pepper

4 cups chicken broth, room temperature

2 pounds boneless, skinless chicken thighs, trimmed

8 ounces andouille sausage, halved and sliced ¼ inch thick

6 scallions, sliced thin

1 teaspoon distilled white vinegar
  Hot sauce

1 Adjust oven rack to middle position and heat oven to 425 degrees. Place flour in Dutch oven and bake, stirring occasionally, until color of ground cinnamon, 40 to 55 minutes. (As flour approaches desired color, it will take on very nutty aroma that will smell faintly of burnt popcorn, and it will need to be stirred more frequently.) Remove pot from oven. Transfer flour to medium bowl and let cool. Wipe pot clean with paper towels.

2 Heat oil in now-empty pot over medium heat until shimmering. Add onion, bell pepper, and celery and cook, stirring frequently, until softened, 5 to 7 minutes. Stir in thyme, garlic, paprika, bay leaves, cayenne, ¼ teaspoon salt, and ¼ teaspoon pepper and cook until fragrant, about 1 minute. Stir in 2 cups broth. Nestle chicken into pot in single layer (chicken will not be completely submerged in liquid) and bring to simmer. Reduce heat to medium-low, cover, and cook until chicken is fork-tender, 15 to 17 minutes. Transfer chicken to cutting board, let cool slightly, then shred into bite-size pieces using 2 forks.

3 Meanwhile, slowly whisk remaining 2 cups broth in small increments into toasted flour until thick, smooth, batter-like paste forms. Increase heat to medium and slowly whisk paste into gumbo, making sure each addition is incorporated before adding next. Stir in andouille. Simmer, uncovered, until gumbo thickens slightly, 20 to 25 minutes.

4 Stir chicken and scallions into gumbo. Off heat, stir in vinegar and season with salt to taste. Discard bay leaves. Serve, passing hot sauce separately.

CLASSIC BEEF STEW

SERVES 6 TO 8   TOTAL TIME 3 HOURS 30 MINUTES TO 4 HOURS

WHY THIS RECIPE WORKS We wanted to create a foolproof beef stew that would be rich and satisfying, with fall-apart meat and tender vegetables draped in a rich brown gravy. To begin, we chose chuck-eye roast for its great flavor and plentiful collagen that melted into tender gelatin through cooking. Browning the meat in two batches ensured that it got a thorough sear and didn't steam, boosting the savory flavor of the gravy. Along with traditional stew components like onions, garlic, red wine, and chicken broth, we also added tomato paste, which is rich in glutamates—compounds that give meat its savory taste and contribute considerable flavor. Potatoes, carrots, and peas rounded out our hearty and soul-warming beef stew. Use a good-quality full-bodied wine, such as Cabernet Sauvignon, for this stew. Depending on the size of your Dutch oven, you may need to brown the beef in three batches rather than two.

4 pounds boneless beef chuck-eye roast, pulled apart at seams, trimmed, and cut into 1½-inch pieces
  Salt and pepper
3 tablespoons vegetable oil
2 tablespoons unsalted butter
2 onions, chopped
3 garlic cloves, minced
1 tablespoon minced fresh thyme or 1 teaspoon dried
¼ cup all-purpose flour
1 tablespoon tomato paste
1 cup dry red wine
2½ cups chicken broth, plus extra as needed
1 pound carrots, peeled and sliced 1 inch thick
2 bay leaves
1½ pounds red potatoes, unpeeled, cut into 1-inch pieces
1 cup frozen peas
3 tablespoons minced fresh parsley

1 Adjust oven rack to lower-middle position and heat oven to 325 degrees. Pat beef dry with paper towels and season with salt and pepper. Heat 2 tablespoons oil in Dutch oven over medium-high heat until just smoking. Brown half of beef on all sides, 7 to 10 minutes; transfer to bowl. Repeat with remaining 1 tablespoon oil and remaining beef; transfer to bowl.

2 Melt butter in now-empty pot over medium-low heat. Add onions and 1 teaspoon salt and cook, stirring often, until onions are softened, 5 to 7 minutes. Stir in garlic and thyme and cook until fragrant, about 30 seconds. Stir in flour and tomato paste and cook, stirring constantly, until golden, about 1 minute. Slowly whisk in wine, scraping up any browned bits and smoothing out any lumps. Stir in broth, carrots, bay leaves, and beef, along with any accumulated juices, and bring to simmer.

3 Cover, transfer pot to oven, and cook for 1 hour. Stir in potatoes and continue to cook until meat is just tender, 1½ to 2 hours.

4 Remove pot from oven and discard bay leaves. Stir in peas, cover, and let sit for 10 minutes. Adjust consistency with extra hot broth as needed. Stir in parsley and season with salt and pepper to taste. Serve.

HUNGARIAN GOULASH

SERVES 6   TOTAL TIME   3 HOURS TO 3 HOURS 30 MINUTES

WHY THIS RECIPE WORKS Traditional Hungarian goulash is the simplest of stews, calling for little more than beef, onions, and paprika. This stew is traditionally cooked for hours over a low fire, making the even heat of the Dutch oven a perfect fit. To recover this recipe from overly busy American versions, we stuck with a simple ingredient list. Tasters preferred traditional sweet paprika to hot or smoked, but when we used enough to pack the flavor punch we wanted, the spice contributed a gritty, dusty texture. Consulting a few Hungarian restaurants, we discovered they used "paprika cream," so we created our own by pureeing a drained jar of roasted red peppers with a little tomato paste, vinegar, and the paprika; this gave the stew the bold flavor and smooth texture we were after. We also found that searing the meat competed with the paprika's flavor, so we simply softened the onions first, then stirred in the paprika cream mixture and the meat and left everything to cook. Paprika is vital to this recipe, so it's best to use a fresh container; do not substitute hot or smoked paprika for the sweet paprika. Serve with sour cream and buttered egg noodles.

4   pounds boneless beef chuck-eye roast, pulled apart at seams, trimmed, and cut into 1½-inch pieces
     Salt and pepper
1½   cups jarred roasted red peppers, rinsed
⅓   cup paprika
2   tablespoons tomato paste
1   tablespoon distilled white vinegar
3   pounds onions, chopped fine
2   tablespoons vegetable oil
4   carrots, peeled and sliced 1 inch thick
1   bay leaf
1   cup beef broth, warm, plus extra as needed

1 Adjust oven rack to lower-middle position and heat oven to 325 degrees. Season beef with salt and pepper. Process red peppers, paprika, tomato paste, and 2 teaspoons vinegar in food processor until smooth, 1 to 2 minutes, scraping down sides of bowl as needed.

2 Combine onions, oil, and 1 teaspoon salt in Dutch oven, cover, and cook over medium heat, stirring occasionally, until onions soften but have not yet begun to brown, 8 to 10 minutes. (If onions begin to brown, reduce heat to medium-low and stir in 1 tablespoon water.)

3 Stir in pepper mixture and cook, uncovered, until onions begin to stick to bottom of pot, about 2 minutes. Stir in beef, carrots, and bay leaf and use rubber spatula to scrape down sides of pot. Cover, transfer pot to oven, and cook until meat is almost tender and surface of liquid is ½ inch below top of meat, 2 to 2½ hours, stirring every 30 minutes.

4 Stir in warm broth until surface of liquid measures ¼ inch from top of meat (beef should not be fully submerged). Cover and continue to cook in oven until meat is tender, about 30 minutes.

5 Remove pot from oven. Discard bay leaf. Skim excess fat from surface of stew using wide, shallow spoon. Adjust consistency with extra hot broth as needed. Stir in remaining 1 teaspoon vinegar and season with salt and pepper to taste. Serve.

PORTUGUESE BEEF STEW

SERVES 6   TOTAL TIME 4 HOURS 15 MINUTES

WHY THIS RECIPE WORKS *Alcatra*, a classic and simple Portuguese beef stew, features tender chunks of beef braised with onions, garlic, warm spices, and wine. Unlike beef stews that require either searing the beef to build savory flavor or adding flavor boosters like tomato paste and anchovies, this recipe favors a simpler approach that highlights the warm and bright flavors of the spices and wine as much as it does the meatiness of the beef. We use beef shank because it is lean (which means the cooking liquid doesn't need to be skimmed) and full of collagen, which breaks down into gelatin and gives the sauce body. Submerging the sliced onions in the liquid causes them to form a meaty-tasting compound, called MMP, that enhances the savory flavor of the broth. Beef shank is sold both long-cut and crosscut (and with and without bones). We prefer the long-cut shank since it has more collagen. You can substitute 4 pounds of bone-in crosscut shank if that's all you can find. Remove the bones before cooking and save them for another use. Crosscut shank cooks more quickly, so check the stew for doneness in step 2 after 3 hours. A 4-pound boneless beef chuck-eye roast, pulled apart at the seams, trimmed, and cut into 2½-inch pieces, can be substituted for the shank. Serve with crusty bread or boiled potatoes.

3 pounds boneless long-cut beef shank, trimmed of all visible fat and cut crosswise into 2½-inch pieces
Salt and pepper

5 garlic cloves, peeled and smashed

5 allspice berries

4 bay leaves

1½ teaspoons black peppercorns

2 large onions, halved and sliced

2¼ cups dry white wine

¼ teaspoon ground cinnamon

8 ounces Spanish-style chorizo sausage, sliced ¼ inch thick

1 Adjust oven rack to lower-middle position and heat oven to 325 degrees. Season beef with 1 teaspoon salt.

2 Cut 8-inch square of triple-thickness cheesecloth. Place garlic, allspice berries, bay leaves, and peppercorns in center of cheesecloth and tie into bundle with kitchen twine. Arrange onions and spice bundle in Dutch oven in even layer. Add wine and cinnamon. Arrange beef in single layer on top of onions. Cover, transfer pot to oven, and cook until beef is tender, about 3½ hours.

3 Remove pot from oven and add chorizo. Using tongs, flip each piece of beef over, making sure that chorizo is submerged. Cover and let sit until chorizo is heated through, about 20 minutes. Discard spice bundle. Season with salt and pepper to taste. Serve.

FRENCH-STYLE PORK STEW

SERVES 8   TOTAL TIME 2 HOURS 30 MINUTES

WHY THIS RECIPE WORKS In the realm of stews, pork is often either overlooked in favor of other proteins or overpowered by more-assertive ingredients. We wanted a robust and satisfying (but not heavy) stew that put pork at the forefront. We took inspiration from a classic French dish, *potée*, a stew that uses multiple parts of the pig, at least one of which is always smoked, to yield a deep, meaty flavor. For our version, we chose a mix of pork butt for a base of tasty, succulent meat; collagen-rich smoked ham hocks, which would impart a silky consistency and smokiness; and kielbasa for a firm bite and additional smoky flavor. For our vegetables, the traditional potatoes, carrots, and cabbage were perfect. We started to build a flavorful backbone in our Dutch oven by cooking onion, garlic, and herbes de Provence. We then added our liquid (mostly water, to keep the stew from becoming heavy, plus chicken broth, to prevent the flavors from becoming washed out) and the pork and ham hocks. Because the pork would take 2 hours to become perfectly tender, we added our other ingredients in stages to prevent them from becoming mushy. About halfway through, we removed the ham hocks to shred the meat, which we added back to the stew. A final sprinkle of fresh parsley rounded out our flavors and added freshness. Pork butt roast is often labeled Boston butt in the supermarket. Serve with crusty bread.

2 tablespoons vegetable oil

1 onion, chopped

  Salt and pepper

3 garlic cloves, minced

2 teaspoons herbes de Provence

3 pounds boneless pork butt roast, trimmed and cut into 1½-inch pieces

1¼ pounds smoked ham hocks, rinsed

5 cups water

4 cups chicken broth, plus extra as needed

1 pound Yukon Gold potatoes, unpeeled, cut into ¾-inch pieces

4 carrots, peeled and cut into ½-inch pieces

12 ounces kielbasa sausage, halved lengthwise and sliced ½ inch thick

½ head savoy cabbage, cored and sliced thin (8 cups)

¼ cup minced fresh parsley

1 Adjust oven rack to lower-middle position and heat oven to 325 degrees. Heat oil in Dutch oven over medium heat until shimmering. Add onion, ½ teaspoon salt, and ¼ teaspoon pepper and cook until onion is softened and lightly browned, 5 to 7 minutes. Stir in garlic and herbes de Provence and cook until fragrant, about 30 seconds. Add pork, ham hocks, water, and broth and bring to simmer. Cover, transfer pot to oven, and cook until pork is tender, 1¼ to 1½ hours.

2 Remove pot from oven. Transfer ham hocks to cutting board, let cool slightly, then shred into bite-size pieces using 2 forks; discard skin and bones and set aside. Stir potatoes and carrots into stew, return pot to oven, and cook, covered, until vegetables are almost tender, 20 to 25 minutes.

3 Stir in ham hocks, kielbasa, and cabbage, cover, and continue to cook in oven until kielbasa is heated through and cabbage is wilted and tender, 15 to 20 minutes.

4 Remove pot from oven. Adjust consistency of stew with extra hot broth as needed. Stir in parsley and season with salt and pepper to taste. Serve.

NEW MEXICAN PORK STEW

SERVES 6 TO 8   TOTAL TIME 2 HOURS 45 MINUTES

WHY THIS RECIPE WORKS New Mexican *posole* is a warming, chile-spiced stew made with pork and hominy, a type of corn that has been treated to remove its hull and germ. Traditional versions can require a laundry list of ingredients, while "simplified" recipes often rely on flavorless convenience products. We wanted our posole to be streamlined but still maintain the complex flavor that makes this stew so appealing. Toasting dried ancho chiles deepened their flavor, and steeping them in hot broth provided an extra boost. We browned boneless pork ribs in our Dutch oven to create savory fond. Canned hominy was easy to find; browning the kernels in the ribs' rendered fat turned them sweet and toasty, and reserving the cooked hominy until the end preserved these qualities. Braising the stew in the oven uncovered allowed the flavors to concentrate and meld. Do not use store-bought chili powder here. When shopping for dried chiles, look for those that are pliable and smell slightly fruity. Depending on the size of your Dutch oven, you may need to brown the pork in two batches rather than one. Serve posole with sliced radishes, sliced green cabbage, chopped avocado, hot sauce, and lime wedges.

¾ ounce (about 3) dried ancho chiles
8 cups chicken broth, plus extra as needed
2 pounds boneless country-style pork ribs, trimmed
   Salt and pepper
3 tablespoons vegetable oil
3 (15-ounce) cans white hominy, rinsed
2 onions, chopped
5 garlic cloves, minced
1 tablespoon minced fresh oregano
1 tablespoon lime juice

1 Adjust oven rack to middle position and heat oven to 325 degrees. Place anchos on baking sheet and bake until puffed and fragrant, about 6 minutes. When cool enough to handle, remove stems and seeds. Combine anchos and 1 cup broth in bowl. Cover and microwave until bubbling, about 2 minutes. Let sit until softened, 10 to 15 minutes.

2 Pat pork dry with paper towels and season with salt and pepper. Heat 2 tablespoons oil in Dutch oven over medium-high heat until just smoking. Add pork and brown on all sides, about 10 minutes; transfer to plate. Add hominy to fat left in pot and cook, stirring frequently, until fragrant and hominy begins to darken, 2 to 3 minutes. Transfer hominy to bowl.

3 Add remaining 1 tablespoon oil to fat left in pot and heat over medium heat until shimmering. Add onions and cook until softened, about 5 minutes. Stir in garlic and cook until fragrant, about 30 seconds. Transfer onion mixture to blender and add softened ancho mixture. Process until smooth, about 1 minute. Add remaining 7 cups broth to now-empty pot, scraping up any browned bits. Stir in onion-ancho mixture, pork and any accumulated juices, oregano, ½ teaspoon salt, and ½ teaspoon pepper and bring to simmer. Transfer pot to oven and cook, uncovered, until meat is tender, 1¼ to 1½ hours.

4 Remove pot from oven. Transfer pork to cutting board, let cool slightly, then shred into bite-size pieces using 2 forks; discard fat. Stir hominy into stew, bring to simmer over medium heat, and cook, covered, until tender, about 30 minutes.

5 Skim excess fat from surface of stew using wide, shallow spoon. Stir in pork and let sit until heated through, about 1 minute. Adjust consistency with extra hot broth as needed. Stir in lime juice and season with salt and pepper to taste. Serve.

IRISH LAMB STEW

SERVES 6 TOTAL TIME 3 HOURS

WHY THIS RECIPE WORKS At its most traditional, Irish stew is made with just lamb, onions, potatoes, and water. There's no browning or precooking to develop flavor, which often results in a bland stew that lacks complexity. We set out to change that and create a lamb stew that would be sustaining, satisfying, and memorable. While most recipes call for boneless cuts of lamb, tasters liked the rich taste and velvety texture of broth fortified with marrow-rich bones. To make sure that our recipe remained a stew and not a braise, we cut the meat off the bones (we chose lamb shoulder chops for their superior flavor) and cut it into small pieces. As a bonus, the pieces had more surface area to build flavorful browning. Simply adding the bones to the Dutch oven as the stew simmered gave the stew plenty of body, and the bones were easily removed before serving. To further thicken the stew, we stirred in ¼ cup of flour, and added medium-starch Yukon Gold potatoes halfway through cooking. The potatoes released some starch while also holding their shape nicely. Though we prefer 1½-inch-thick chops here, 1-inch-thick chops will suffice. If possible, try to buy the chops from a butcher, since most supermarket chops are too thin. Depending on the size of your Dutch oven, you may need to brown the lamb chops in three batches rather than two.

4½ pounds lamb shoulder chops (blade or round bone), 1 to 1½ inches thick, trimmed, meat removed from bones and cut into 1½-inch pieces, bones reserved
Salt and pepper

3 tablespoons vegetable oil

2½ pounds onions, chopped coarse

¼ cup all-purpose flour

1 tablespoon minced fresh thyme or 1 teaspoon dried

3 cups water, plus extra as needed

2 pounds Yukon Gold potatoes, peeled and cut into 1-inch pieces

¼ cup minced fresh parsley

1 Adjust oven rack to lower-middle position and heat oven to 325 degrees. Pat lamb dry with paper towels and season with salt and pepper. Heat 1 tablespoon oil in Dutch oven over medium-high heat until just smoking. Brown half of lamb on all sides, about 8 minutes; transfer to bowl. Repeat with 1 tablespoon oil and remaining lamb; transfer to bowl.

2 Add remaining 1 tablespoon oil, onions, and 1¼ teaspoons salt to fat left in pot and cook over medium heat, stirring frequently and scraping up any browned bits, until onions are browned, about 8 minutes. Stir in flour and thyme and cook for 1 minute. Slowly whisk in water, scraping up any remaining browned bits and smoothing out any lumps, and bring to simmer. Add reserved bones, then lamb and any accumulated juices. Cover, transfer pot to oven, and cook for 1 hour.

3 Place potatoes on top of lamb and bones, cover, and continue to cook in oven until lamb is tender, about 1 hour.

4 Remove pot from oven and discard bones. Stir potatoes into stew and let sit for 5 minutes. Skim excess fat from surface of stew using wide, shallow spoon. Adjust consistency with extra hot water as needed. Stir in parsley and season with salt and pepper to taste. Serve.

SPANISH SHELLFISH STEW

SERVES 4 TO 6 TOTAL TIME 1 HOUR

WHY THIS RECIPE WORKS *Zarzuela*, Spain's answer to French bouillabaisse, is a saffron-scented, tomato-based shellfish stew that's thickened with a *picada*, a mixture of ground almonds, bread crumbs, and olive oil. Unlike many seafood stews, this one contains no fish stock or clam juice, instead relying on the shellfish to release their rich liquors into the pot as they cook. With this in mind, we enriched the broth by steeping the flavor-packed shrimp shells in wine while we prepared the other ingredients. A traditional Spanish *sofrito* of onion, red bell pepper, and garlic gave the stew a rich foundation. Staggering the addition of the clams, mussels, scallops, and shrimp ensured that each element was perfectly cooked. Stirring in the picada at the end provided richness and also thickened the stew. Fresh parsley and a squeeze of lemon offered a bright, fresh finish. Be sure to buy shrimp with their shells on and reserve the shells.

¼ cup extra-virgin olive oil

8 ounces medium-large shrimp (31 to 40 per pound), peeled and deveined, shells reserved

1½ cups dry white wine or dry vermouth

1 onion, chopped fine

1 red bell pepper, stemmed, seeded, and chopped fine

3 garlic cloves, minced

1 teaspoon paprika

¼ teaspoon saffron threads, crumbled

⅛ teaspoon red pepper flakes

2 tablespoons brandy

1 (28-ounce) can whole peeled tomatoes, drained with juice reserved, chopped

2 bay leaves

1½ pounds littleneck clams, scrubbed

8 ounces mussels, scrubbed and debearded

12 ounces large sea scallops, tendons removed

1 recipe Picada (recipe follows)

1 tablespoon minced fresh parsley

Salt and pepper

Lemon wedges

1 Heat 1 tablespoon oil in Dutch oven over medium heat until shimmering. Add shrimp shells and cook, stirring frequently, until they begin to turn spotty brown and pot starts to brown, 2 to 4 minutes. Off heat, stir in wine, transfer to bowl, and cover and let steep until ready to use. Wipe out Dutch oven with paper towels.

2 Heat remaining 3 tablespoons oil in Dutch oven over medium-high heat until shimmering. Add onion and bell pepper and cook until softened and lightly browned, 5 to 7 minutes. Stir in garlic, paprika, saffron, and pepper flakes and cook until fragrant, about 30 seconds. Stir in brandy, scraping up any browned bits. Stir in tomatoes and their juice and bay leaves and cook until slightly thickened, 5 to 7 minutes.

3 Strain wine mixture through fine-mesh strainer into Dutch oven, pressing on solids to extract as much liquid as possible; discard solids. Bring to simmer and cook until flavors meld, 3 to 5 minutes.

4 Nestle clams into pot, cover, and cook for 4 minutes. Nestle mussels and scallops into pot, cover, and continue to cook until most clams have opened, about 3 minutes. Arrange shrimp evenly over stew, cover, and continue to cook until shrimp are opaque throughout, scallops are firm and opaque in center, and clams and mussels have opened, 1 to 2 minutes.

5 Off heat, discard bay leaves and any clams and mussels that refuse to open. Stir in picada and parsley and season with salt and pepper to taste. Serve in wide, shallow bowls with lemon wedges.

PICADA

MAKES ABOUT 1 CUP

Chopped or whole unsalted almonds can be substituted for the slivered almonds; however, they may require longer processing times.

¼ cup slivered almonds

2 slices hearty white sandwich bread, torn into quarters

2 tablespoons extra-virgin olive oil

⅛ teaspoon salt

Pinch pepper

Adjust oven rack to middle position and heat oven to 375 degrees. Pulse almonds in food processor to fine crumbs, about 20 pulses. Add bread, oil, salt, and pepper and pulse bread to coarse crumbs, about 10 pulses. Spread mixture evenly on rimmed baking sheet and bake, stirring often, until golden brown, about 10 minutes. Set aside to cool. (Picada can be stored for up to 2 days.)

SICILIAN FISH STEW

SERVES 4 TO 6 TOTAL TIME 1 HOUR

WHY THIS RECIPE WORKS In Sicily, fish is combined with tomatoes and favorite local ingredients to create a simple stew. Although easy to prepare, this stew requires a balancing act of sweet, sour, and salty flavors. Many Sicilian dishes exhibit the strong influence of Arabic cooking through the use of dried fruits and nuts. Although these flavors are delicious, they must be used judiciously to keep them from upstaging each other and the fish. This stew is typically made with firm white-fleshed fillets, such as snapper. However, tasters felt that the snapper's mild flavor was lost amid the bold flavors of the stew and preferred the stronger flavor and meaty texture of swordfish. To prevent the fish from overcooking and drying out, we found it best to add it when the stew was nearly done, simmering it until partially cooked and letting it finish cooking via the residual heat in our covered Dutch oven. For the base of the stew, we created a quick stock using aromatic onions, celery, and garlic simmered with white wine, whole peeled tomatoes, and clam juice, and mixed in golden raisins and capers for sweet and briny pops of flavor. To finish our stew, we put together a twist on gremolata, a classic Italian herb condiment usually made with lemon zest and parsley. Here, we swapped out those elements for orange zest and mint to underline the sweet and fragrant flavors in the dish, and we stirred in toasted pine nuts for added crunch. Tuna and halibut are good substitutes for the swordfish. Serve with crusty bread.

¼ cup pine nuts, toasted
¼ cup chopped fresh mint
4 garlic cloves, minced
1 teaspoon grated orange zest
2 tablespoons extra-virgin olive oil
2 onions, chopped fine
1 celery rib, minced
   Salt and pepper
1 teaspoon minced fresh thyme or ¼ teaspoon dried
   Pinch red pepper flakes
½ cup dry white wine
1 (28-ounce) can whole peeled tomatoes, drained with juice reserved, chopped coarse
2 (8-ounce) bottles clam juice
¼ cup golden raisins
2 tablespoons capers, rinsed
1½ pounds skinless swordfish steaks, 1 to 1½ inches thick, cut into 1-inch pieces

1 Combine pine nuts, mint, one-quarter of garlic, and orange zest in bowl; set aside for serving. Heat oil in Dutch oven over medium heat until shimmering. Add onions, celery, ½ teaspoon salt, and ¼ teaspoon pepper and cook until vegetables are softened, about 5 minutes. Stir in thyme, pepper flakes, and remaining garlic and cook until fragrant, about 30 seconds.

2 Stir in wine and reserved tomato juice, bring to simmer, and cook until reduced by half, about 4 minutes. Stir in tomatoes, clam juice, raisins, and capers, return to simmer, and cook until flavors meld, about 15 minutes.

3 Season swordfish with salt and pepper. Add swordfish to pot and spoon some cooking liquid over top. Bring to simmer and cook for 4 minutes. Off heat, cover and let sit until swordfish flakes apart when gently prodded with paring knife, about 3 minutes. Season with salt and pepper to taste. Serve, sprinkling individual bowls with pine nut mixture.

HEARTY TUSCAN WHITE BEAN STEW

SERVES 8   TOTAL TIME 2 HOURS 15 MINUTES (PLUS SOAKING TIME)

WHY THIS RECIPE WORKS Cannellini (white kidney beans) are famous in Tuscany, and cooks there go to great lengths to ensure that these beans are worthy of star status, even putting the beans in an empty wine bottle to slow-cook overnight in a fire's dying embers. So when we set out to make a heartier stew version of the region's classic white bean soup, we focused on perfecting the beans. Brining guaranteed the creamiest and most tender texture. To imitate the traditional low, slow cooking environment (no dying fire or wine bottle required), we turned to a very low oven and cooked the stew in a covered Dutch oven to further insulate it. Pancetta, carrots, onion, celery, and garlic made an aromatic base for our stew, and we added tomatoes toward the end of cooking, since their acid would otherwise prevent the beans from softening. Finally, we briefly steeped a sprig of rosemary in the stew to provide herbal notes without overpowering the other flavors. If pancetta is unavailable, substitute four slices of bacon. If you're pressed for time, you can skip brining and quick-salt-soak the beans: In step 1, combine the salt, water, and beans in a Dutch oven and bring to a boil. Off the heat, cover the pot and let sit for 1 hour. Drain and rinse the beans and proceed with the recipe. Serve with crusty bread.

Salt and pepper
1 pound (2½ cups) dried cannellini beans, picked over and rinsed
1 tablespoon extra-virgin olive oil, plus extra for serving
6 ounces pancetta, cut into ¼-inch pieces
1 large onion, chopped
2 carrots, peeled and cut into ½-inch pieces
2 celery ribs, cut into ½-inch pieces
8 garlic cloves, peeled and smashed
4 cups chicken broth
2 bay leaves
1 pound kale or collard greens, stemmed and chopped
1 (14.5-ounce) can diced tomatoes, drained
1 sprig fresh rosemary

1 Dissolve 3 tablespoons salt in 4 quarts cold water in large container. Add beans and soak at room temperature for at least 8 hours or up to 24 hours. Drain and rinse well.

2 Adjust oven rack to lower-middle position and heat oven to 250 degrees. Cook oil and pancetta in Dutch oven over medium heat, stirring occasionally, until pancetta is lightly browned and fat has rendered, 6 to 10 minutes.

3 Add onion, carrots, and celery and cook, stirring occasionally, until softened and lightly browned, 10 to 16 minutes. Stir in garlic and cook until fragrant, about 1 minute. Stir in broth, 3 cups water, bay leaves, and beans and bring to boil. Cover, transfer pot to oven, and cook until beans are almost tender (very center of beans will still be firm), 45 minutes to 1 hour.

4 Stir in kale and tomatoes, cover, and continue to cook in oven until beans and greens are fully tender, 30 to 40 minutes.

5 Remove pot from oven and submerge rosemary sprig in stew. Cover and let sit for 15 minutes. Discard bay leaves and rosemary sprig and season stew with salt and pepper to taste. If desired, use back of spoon to press some beans against side of pot to thicken stew. Drizzle individual portions with extra oil before serving.

CARIBBEAN-STYLE SWISS CHARD AND BUTTERNUT SQUASH STEW

SERVES 4 TO 6   TOTAL TIME 1 HOUR

WHY THIS RECIPE WORKS *Callaloo* is a lively, pesto-green stew that's both creamy and spicy, with a rich, coconutty broth studded with leafy greens and other vegetables. The name comes from the main ingredient, callaloo leaves, which are leafy green plants grown throughout the Caribbean. Traditionally the earthy, citrusy greens are enriched with salt pork, chiles, aromatics, and coconut milk. Variations on the stew abound, but we opted to create a vegetarian version to keep the focus right where we wanted it: on the vegetables. First and foremost, we needed to find an appropriate substitute for the callaloo leaves, which can be difficult to find stateside. Swiss chard proved the best option, offering hearty, earthy flavor, a hint of citrus, and a delicate texture. A single habanero chile provided subtle but persistent heat, while some garlic and thyme lent aromatic backbone. Some callaloo recipes call for pumpkin, but we opted to use easy-to-find butternut squash instead. A handful of recipes called for a few dashes of angostura bitters, an aromatic alcohol infused with herbs and citrus. While not a must, the bitters gave the stew a uniquely authentic flavor. We pureed a small portion of the stew to give it a thick consistency and bright green color, while leaving most of the greens and squash in large bites. You can substitute delicata or carnival squash for the butternut squash if you prefer. For more spice, do not remove the ribs and seeds from the chile.

2   tablespoons vegetable oil
2   onions, chopped fine
4   scallions, minced
     Salt
4   garlic cloves, minced
1   habanero or Scotch bonnet chile, stemmed, seeded, and minced
1   teaspoon minced fresh thyme or ¼ teaspoon dried
     Pinch cayenne pepper
3½   cups vegetable broth
2   pounds butternut squash, peeled, seeded, and cut into ½-inch pieces (6 cups)
1   pound Swiss chard, stemmed and cut into 1-inch pieces
1   cup canned coconut milk
     Angostura bitters (optional)

1 Heat oil in Dutch oven over medium heat until shimmering. Add onions, scallions, and ½ teaspoon salt and cook until vegetables are softened, 5 to 7 minutes. Stir in garlic, habanero, thyme, and cayenne and cook until fragrant, about 30 seconds.

2 Stir in broth and squash, scraping up any browned bits. Bring to simmer and cook for 15 minutes. Stir in chard and cook until squash and chard are tender, 10 to 15 minutes. Stir in coconut milk and return to brief simmer.

3 Process 2 cups stew in blender until smooth, about 45 seconds; return to pot. Season with salt and bitters, if using, to taste. Serve.

QUICK BEEF AND BEAN CHILI

SERVES 4 TO 6   TOTAL TIME 45 MINUTES

WHY THIS RECIPE WORKS A quick and easy chili is something all cooks should have in their arsenal—with this recipe, a satisfying and family-friendly meal is less than an hour away. We found that browning the ground meat gave it a pebbly texture with the quick cooking time, so we sautéed it in our Dutch oven just until it was no longer pink. Store-bought chili powder packed a flavor punch; we added a generous amount, along with some cumin and garlic, and bloomed their flavors. We processed half of the beans with half of the tomatoes to create a thick and flavorful base for our chili in record time. Serve with your favorite chili toppings.

2 (15-ounce) cans red kidney beans, rinsed
2 (14.5-ounce) cans diced tomatoes
1½ pounds 85 percent lean ground beef
1 onion, chopped fine
4 garlic cloves, minced
3 tablespoons chili powder
2 teaspoons ground cumin
2 teaspoons sugar
¼ cup chopped fresh cilantro
   Salt and pepper

1 Process half of beans and half of tomatoes and their juice in food processor to coarse paste, about 30 seconds.

2 Combine ground beef and onion in Dutch oven and cook over medium heat, breaking up meat with wooden spoon, until meat is no longer pink, about 5 minutes. Stir in garlic, chili powder, cumin, and sugar and cook until fragrant, about 1 minute. Stir in bean-tomato mixture and remaining beans and tomatoes and their juice, and bring to simmer. Reduce heat to low, cover, and cook, stirring occasionally, until thickened, about 15 minutes. Off heat, stir in cilantro and season with salt and pepper to taste. Serve.

HEARTY BEEF AND VEGETABLE CHILI

SERVES 6 TO 8   TOTAL TIME 3 HOURS

WHY THIS RECIPE WORKS Our ultimate beef and vegetable chili takes time, but that patience is rewarded with a deeply flavorful and satisfying chili that's worth the wait. We started with well-marbled, inexpensive beef chuck-eye for its ability to become meltingly tender. We browned it in our Dutch oven for rich flavor and then stewed it in the oven long enough to make it fork-tender. An aromatic base of garlic, cumin, chipotle, and chili powder gave our stew real depth of flavor and some heat. The heat balanced out the sweetness of our sweet potatoes and red bell pepper, and mild beer added further complexity. We added a quarter of the potatoes in the beginning, knowing that they would break down to thicken our stew, and we waited to stir in the beans with the tomatoes so that they cooked enough to absorb flavor but not so much that they fell apart. Once our meat was tender, we added the rest of the potatoes and bell pepper, cooking them just long enough to have toothsome chunks in our stew. Light-bodied American lagers, such as Budweiser, work best in this recipe. Depending on the size of your Dutch oven, you may need to brown the beef in three batches rather than two. Serve with your favorite chili toppings.

3½ pounds boneless beef chuck-eye roast, pulled apart at seams, trimmed, and cut into 1-inch pieces
    Salt and pepper
3 tablespoons vegetable oil
1 onion, chopped
1½ pounds sweet potatoes, peeled and cut into ½-inch pieces
3 garlic cloves, minced
1 tablespoon ground cumin
1 tablespoon minced canned chipotle chile in adobo sauce
2 teaspoons chili powder
1 (28-ounce) can diced tomatoes
1½ cups beer
2 (15-ounce) cans black beans, rinsed
1 red bell pepper, stemmed, seeded, and cut into ½-inch pieces
4 scallions, sliced thin

1 Adjust oven rack to lower-middle position and heat oven to 300 degrees. Pat beef dry with paper towels and season with salt and pepper. Heat 1 tablespoon oil in Dutch oven over medium-high heat until just smoking. Brown half of beef on all sides, 6 to 8 minutes; transfer to bowl. Repeat with 1 tablespoon oil and remaining beef; transfer to bowl.

2 Add remaining 1 tablespoon oil, onion, and ¾ cup sweet potatoes to fat left in pot and cook over medium heat until just beginning to brown, 5 to 7 minutes. Stir in garlic, cumin, chipotle, chili powder, and 1 teaspoon salt and cook until fragrant, about 30 seconds. Stir in tomatoes and their juice and beer, scraping up any browned bits. Stir in beans and beef, along with any accumulated juices, and bring to simmer.

3 Cover, transfer pot to oven, and cook, stirring occasionally, until sweet potatoes are broken down and beef is just tender, about 1¾ hours.

4 Stir in remaining sweet potatoes and bell pepper and continue to cook in oven, covered, until meat and sweet potatoes are tender, about 20 minutes.

5 Remove pot from oven, uncover, and let chili sit until thickened slightly, about 15 minutes. Adjust consistency with hot water as needed. Season with salt and pepper to taste. Sprinkle individual portions with scallions before serving.

CARNE ADOVADA

SERVES 6 TOTAL TIME 3 HOURS 30 MINUTES TO 4 HOURS

WHY THIS RECIPE WORKS This rich and robust New Mexican stew is as much about the chiles as it is about the pork. For a version that would showcase these key ingredients while staying true to the dish's traditional simplicity, we started with a generous 4 ounces of mild dried New Mexican chiles. To preserve the chiles' fruity flavor, we skipped toasting them, only steeping them in hot water to make them pliable. We then made a flavorful puree by blending the chiles with honey and vinegar (both traditional additions), along with garlic, spices, and just enough of the flavorful chile soaking liquid to make a smooth and luxurious puree. Boneless pork butt's generous marbling held up well to braising, and salting the meat for an hour while preparing the chile sauce seasoned it throughout and helped it stay juicy. Moving the Dutch oven to the oven made for more hands-off cooking; we didn't even need to brown the meat since the pieces that were not submerged in sauce during cooking could brown in the Dutch oven's ambient heat. Pork butt roast is often labeled Boston butt in the supermarket. When shopping for dried chiles, look for those that are pliable and smell slightly fruity. We prefer using Mexican oregano here, but Mediterranean can be substituted. Serve with rice and beans, crispy potatoes, or flour tortillas with shredded lettuce and chopped tomato.

4 pounds boneless pork butt roast, trimmed and cut into 1½-inch pieces
Salt
4 ounces (8 to 12) dried New Mexican chiles, stemmed, seeded, and torn into 1-inch pieces
2 tablespoons honey
2 tablespoons distilled white vinegar
5 garlic cloves, peeled
2 teaspoons dried Mexican oregano
2 teaspoons ground cumin
½ teaspoon cayenne pepper
⅛ teaspoon ground cloves
Lime wedges

1 Toss pork with 1½ teaspoons salt in bowl and refrigerate for 1 hour.

2 Bring 4 cups water to boil. Place New Mexican chile pieces in medium bowl. Pour boiling water over chiles, making sure they are completely submerged, and let sit until chiles are softened, about 30 minutes. Adjust oven rack to lower-middle position and heat oven to 325 degrees.

3 Drain chiles in fine-mesh strainer set over bowl and reserve 2 cups of soaking liquid (discard any remaining soaking liquid). Process chiles, honey, vinegar, garlic, oregano, cumin, cayenne, cloves, and ½ teaspoon salt in blender until chiles are finely ground and thick paste forms, about 30 seconds. With blender running, add 1 cup soaking liquid and blend until puree is smooth, 1½ to 2 minutes, adding up to additional ¼ cup liquid to maintain vortex. Add remaining soaking liquid and continue to blend sauce at high speed, 1 minute longer.

4 Combine pork and chile sauce in Dutch oven and bring to simmer, stirring to coat pork evenly, over medium-high heat. Cover, transfer pot to oven, and cook until pork is tender, 2 to 2½ hours.

5 Remove pot from oven. Using wooden spoon, scrape any browned bits from sides of pot and stir until pork and sauce are recombined and sauce is smooth and homogeneous. Let sit, uncovered, for 10 minutes. Adjust consistency with extra hot water as needed. Season with salt to taste. Serve with lime wedges.

ROASTED POBLANO AND WHITE BEAN CHILI

SERVES 4 TO 6   TOTAL TIME 1 HOUR 45 MINUTES

WHY THIS RECIPE WORKS White bean chili is a fresher, lighter cousin of the thick red chili most Americans know and love. Because there are no tomatoes to mask the other flavors, the fresh chiles take center stage. A trio of poblanos, Anaheims, and jalapeños provided the complexity and modest heat we were looking for. We broiled the poblanos and Anaheims to develop depth and smokiness. To keep the flavor of the jalapeños bright, we chopped them, put them in the food processor with onions, and then sautéed the mixture. To offset the vegetal flavor of the chiles, we broiled fresh sweet corn, and then added it to the chili just before serving. In addition, simmering the cobs with the beans and chiles created sweet undertones that permeated the chili. To thicken the chili, we processed some of the roasted peppers with a portion of the beans and broth. For more spice, do not remove the ribs and seeds from the chiles. If you can't find Anaheim chiles, add two additional poblanos and one additional jalapeño to the chili. Serve with sour cream, tortilla chips, and lime wedges.

5   poblano chiles, stemmed, halved, and seeded
3   Anaheim chiles, stemmed, halved, and seeded
3   tablespoons vegetable oil
3   ears corn, kernels cut from cobs and cobs reserved
2   onions, cut into large pieces
2   jalapeño chiles, stemmed, seeded, and chopped
2   (15-ounce) cans cannellini beans, rinsed
4   cups vegetable broth
6   garlic cloves, minced
1   tablespoon tomato paste
1   tablespoon ground cumin
1½ teaspoons ground coriander
    Salt and pepper
1   (15-ounce) can pinto beans, rinsed
4   scallions, green parts only, sliced thin
¼   cup minced fresh cilantro
1   tablespoon lime juice

1 Adjust oven rack 6 inches from broiler element and heat broiler. Toss poblanos and Anaheims with 1 tablespoon oil in large bowl and arrange, skin side up, on aluminum foil–lined rimmed baking sheet. Broil until chiles begin to blacken and soften, about 10 minutes, rotating sheet halfway through broiling. Transfer chiles to bowl, cover with plastic wrap, and let steam until skins peel off easily, 10 to 15 minutes. Peel poblanos and Anaheims, then cut into ½-inch pieces, reserving any accumulated juices.

2 Meanwhile, toss corn kernels with 1 tablespoon oil in medium bowl, spread evenly over now-empty sheet, and broil, stirring occasionally, until beginning to brown, 5 to 10 minutes; let cool on sheet.

3 Pulse onions and jalapeños in food processor to consistency of chunky salsa, 6 to 8 pulses; transfer to separate bowl. Process 1 cup cannellini beans, 1 cup broth, and ½ cup poblano-Anaheim mixture and any accumulated juices in now-empty processor until smooth, about 45 seconds.

4 Heat remaining 1 tablespoon oil in Dutch oven over medium heat until shimmering. Add onion-jalapeño mixture and cook until softened, 5 to 7 minutes. Stir in garlic, tomato paste, cumin, coriander, and ½ teaspoon salt and cook until tomato paste begins to darken, about 2 minutes. Stir in remaining 3 cups broth, scraping up any browned bits. Stir in bean-chile mixture, remaining roasted chiles, remaining cannellini beans, pinto beans, and corn cobs. Bring to gentle simmer and cook until thickened and flavors meld, about 40 minutes.

5 Discard corn cobs. Stir in corn kernels and let sit until heated through, about 1 minute. Off heat, stir in scallions, cilantro, and lime juice, and season with salt and pepper to taste. Serve.

PUMPKIN TURKEY CHILI

SERVES 8   TOTAL TIME 2 HOURS 45 MINUTES

WHY THIS RECIPE WORKS Turkey is a great healthy alternative to beef for chili, but turkey chilis often lack depth and richness. We wanted a chili with flavor bold enough that we wouldn't miss the beef. To safeguard against rubbery turkey, we treated the meat with salt and baking soda, which helped it hold on to moisture. To give our dish a smoky, aromatic backbone, we made our own chili powder by grinding toasted ancho chiles, cumin, coriander, paprika, and oregano. We loaded the chili with red bell peppers and black beans for great textural contrast. Still, our chili needed more richness. We found the answer in a unique ingredient—pumpkin puree. Folding this into the chili gave it a rich, silky texture and subtle squash-y flavor without being overly sweet. Be sure to use ground turkey, not ground turkey breast (also labeled 99 percent fat-free), in this recipe. When shopping for dried chiles, look for those that are pliable and smell slightly fruity. Serve with your favorite chili toppings.

1   pound ground turkey

2   cups plus 1 tablespoon water
    Salt and pepper

¼   teaspoon baking soda

1   ounce (about 4) dried ancho chiles, stemmed, seeded, and torn into 1-inch pieces

1½   tablespoons ground cumin

1½   teaspoons ground coriander

1½   teaspoons dried oregano

1½   teaspoons paprika

1   (28-ounce) can whole peeled tomatoes

2   tablespoons extra-virgin olive oil

2   onions, chopped fine

2   red bell peppers, stemmed, seeded, and cut into ½-inch pieces

6   garlic cloves, minced

1   cup canned unsweetened pumpkin puree

2   (15-ounce) cans black beans, rinsed

1 Toss turkey, 1 tablespoon water, ¼ teaspoon salt, and baking soda in bowl until thoroughly combined. Set aside for 20 minutes.

2 Toast anchos in Dutch oven over medium-high heat, stirring frequently, until fragrant, 4 to 6 minutes, reducing heat if anchos begin to smoke. Transfer to food processor and let cool for about 5 minutes.

3 Add cumin, coriander, oregano, paprika, and 1 teaspoon pepper to food processor with anchos and process until finely ground, about 2 minutes; transfer mixture to bowl. Process tomatoes and their juice in now-empty processor until smooth, about 30 seconds.

4 Heat oil in now-empty pot over medium heat until shimmering. Add onions, bell peppers, and ½ teaspoon salt and cook until vegetables are softened, 8 to 10 minutes. Increase heat to medium-high, add turkey, and cook, breaking up meat with wooden spoon, until no longer pink, 4 to 6 minutes. Stir in spice mixture and garlic and cook until fragrant, about 30 seconds. Stir in tomatoes, pumpkin, and remaining 2 cups water and bring to simmer. Reduce heat to low, cover, and cook, stirring occasionally, for 1 hour.

5 Stir in beans, cover, and cook until slightly thickened, about 45 minutes. (If chili begins to stick to bottom of pot or looks too thick, stir in extra water as needed.) Season with salt to taste. Serve.

ROASTS AND BRAISES

Braised Short Ribs with Wild Mushroom Farrotto

BRAISED CHICKEN WITH MUSHROOMS AND TOMATOES

SERVES 4   TOTAL TIME 1 HOUR 30 MINUTES

WHY THIS RECIPE WORKS Chicken *cacciatore*, Italian for "hunter-style," is a rustic meal of chicken braised in a tomato-mushroom sauce. Bone-in chicken thighs offered the richest flavor, but the skin became soggy after cooking. To avoid this, we browned the skin-on thighs to create some flavorful fond on the bottom of the Dutch oven, then removed the skin before simmering the meat. A combination of red wine, chicken broth, diced tomatoes, and fresh thyme yielded a balanced, complex sauce. Cooking the thighs to 195 degrees (past the technical doneness of 175) allowed their collagen to melt into gelatin, turning them supertender and enriching the sauce. Portobello mushrooms contributed a meaty flavor, and fresh sage, added at the end, highlighted the braise's woodsy notes. The Parmesan rind is optional, but we highly recommend it for the rich, savory flavor it adds. Depending on the size of your Dutch oven, you may need to brown the chicken thighs in two batches rather than one. Serve over egg noodles or polenta.

8 (5- to 7-ounce) bone-in chicken thighs, trimmed
Salt and pepper
1 tablespoon extra-virgin olive oil
1 onion, chopped
6 ounces portobello mushroom caps, cut into ¾-inch pieces
4 garlic cloves, minced
2 teaspoons minced fresh thyme
1½ tablespoons all-purpose flour
1½ cups dry red wine
½ cup chicken broth
1 (14.5-ounce) can diced tomatoes, drained
1 Parmesan cheese rind (optional)
2 teaspoons minced fresh sage

1 Adjust oven rack to middle position and heat oven to 300 degrees. Pat chicken dry with paper towels and season with salt and pepper. Heat oil in Dutch oven over medium-high heat until just smoking. Brown thighs, 5 to 6 minutes per side. Transfer thighs to plate and discard skin.

2 Pour off all but 1 tablespoon fat from pot. Add onion, mushrooms, and ½ teaspoon salt and cook, stirring occasionally, until vegetables are softened and beginning to brown, 6 to 8 minutes. Stir in garlic and thyme and cook until fragrant, about 30 seconds. Stir in flour and cook for 1 minute. Slowly whisk in wine, scraping up any browned bits and smoothing out any lumps.

3 Stir in broth, tomatoes, and Parmesan rind, if using, and bring to simmer. Nestle thighs into pot, adding any accumulated juices, cover, and transfer to oven. Cook until chicken registers 195 degrees, 35 to 40 minutes.

4 Remove pot from oven and transfer chicken to serving platter. Discard cheese rind, if using. Stir sage into sauce and season with salt and pepper to taste. Spoon sauce over chicken and serve.

BRAISED CHICKEN THIGHS WITH CHICKPEAS AND FENNEL

SERVES 4   TOTAL TIME 1 HOUR 45 MINUTES

WHY THIS RECIPE WORKS Braising usually involves a large—and often tough—cut of meat. The slow cooking technique breaks down fat and connective tissue, turning the meat tender and allowing deep flavors to develop. But it's also a great method for quicker-cooking proteins, such as rich, meaty chicken thighs. Since the chicken spends less time in the pot, we needed bold ingredients to replace the deep flavors that would otherwise come from slow cooking. We looked to the Mediterranean for inspiration: Vibrant lemon and briny olives added complexity, while fennel, with its lively licorice-like flavor, brought a soft but sturdy balance to the dish. To keep the cooking to a single pot, we browned the chicken in our Dutch oven and then set the meat aside while parcooking the fennel and aromatics. Chickpeas turned the dish into a complete meal; mashing a portion of them thickened the stew-y base. When braising chicken, we often remove the skin since it typically turns soggy. Here, however, we strategically placed the thighs on top of the chickpeas and fennel, elevating the skin just above the sauce so it could crisp in the oven. Keeping the pot uncovered also allowed the sauce to reduce slightly, deepening its flavors. Be sure to leave the core in the fennel so the wedges don't fall apart. Depending on the size of your Dutch oven, you may need to brown the chicken thighs in two batches rather than one.

2 (15-ounce) cans chickpeas, rinsed
8 (5- to 7-ounce) bone-in chicken thighs, trimmed
Salt and pepper
1 tablespoon extra-virgin olive oil
1 large fennel bulb, stalks discarded, bulb halved and cut into 8 wedges through core
4 garlic cloves, minced
2 teaspoons grated lemon zest plus 1½ tablespoons juice
1 teaspoon ground coriander
½ teaspoon red pepper flakes
½ cup dry white wine
1 cup pitted large brine-cured green olives, halved
¾ cup chicken broth
1 tablespoon honey
2 tablespoons chopped fresh parsley

1 Adjust oven rack to middle position and heat oven to 300 degrees. Place ½ cup chickpeas in bowl and mash to coarse puree with potato masher; set aside.

2 Pat chicken dry with paper towels and season with salt and pepper. Heat oil in Dutch oven over medium-high heat until just smoking. Place thighs, skin side down, in pot and cook until skin is crisped and well browned, 8 to 10 minutes. Transfer thighs, skin side up, to plate.

3 Pour off all but 2 tablespoons fat from pot. Arrange fennel cut side down in pot and sprinkle with ¼ teaspoon salt. Cover and cook over medium heat until lightly browned, 3 to 5 minutes per side. Add garlic, lemon zest, coriander, and pepper flakes and cook until fragrant, about 30 seconds. Stir in wine, scraping up any browned bits, and cook until almost evaporated, about 2 minutes.

4 Stir in olives, broth, honey, mashed chickpeas, lemon juice, and remaining whole chickpeas and bring to simmer. Nestle thighs into pot, adding any accumulated juices and keeping skin above surface of sauce. Transfer pot to oven and cook, uncovered, until fennel is tender and chicken registers 195 degrees, about 1 hour. Sprinkle with parsley and serve.

SICHUAN BRAISED CHICKEN LEG QUARTERS WITH SHIITAKE MUSHROOMS

SERVES 4   TOTAL TIME 1 HOUR 45 MINUTES

WHY THIS RECIPE WORKS Sichuan cuisine is known for its unapologetically bold flavors, which we thought would translate well to a simple braise. We opted to use meaty chicken leg quarters, which could stand up to the powerful flavors in the sauce, along with shiitake mushrooms for textural contrast. Scallions, garlic, ginger, and red pepper flakes made for a fragrant base, while oyster sauce added savoriness without making the dish overly salty. Braising the chicken skin side up in an uncovered Dutch oven on a high oven rack allowed the heat to reflect off the oven's top, helping crisp the skin on the chicken. For authentic flair, we stirred in a generous 2 teaspoons of Sichuan peppercorns: The spice's floral, almost lemony flavor and the unique tingling sensation it produced on the tongue offset the richness of the dish. Toasted sesame oil and a pinch of sugar rounded out the flavors. You can substitute 8 (5- to 7-ounce) bone-in chicken thighs for the leg quarters, if desired. Depending on the size of your Dutch oven, you may need to brown the chicken in two batches. Serve over rice.

4 (10-ounce) chicken leg quarters, trimmed

1 tablespoon vegetable oil

8 ounces shiitake mushrooms, stemmed and sliced thin

6 scallions, white parts minced, green parts sliced thin

6 garlic cloves, minced

2 tablespoons grated fresh ginger

¼ teaspoon red pepper flakes

1 cup water, plus extra as needed

¼ cup oyster sauce

1 tablespoon toasted sesame oil

2 teaspoons Sichuan peppercorns, toasted and ground

½ teaspoon sugar

1 Adjust oven rack to upper-middle position and heat oven to 300 degrees. Pat chicken dry with paper towels. Heat vegetable oil in Dutch oven over medium-high heat until just smoking. Place chicken, skin side down, in pot and cook until skin is crisped and well browned, 8 to 10 minutes. Transfer chicken, skin side up, to plate.

2 Pour off all but 1 tablespoon fat from pot. Add mushrooms and cook over medium heat until softened and lightly browned, about 5 minutes. Stir in scallion whites, garlic, ginger, and pepper flakes and cook until fragrant, about 30 seconds. Stir in water and oyster sauce, scraping up any browned bits, and bring to simmer.

3 Nestle chicken into pot, adding any accumulated juices and keeping skin above surface of sauce. Transfer pot to oven and cook, uncovered, until chicken registers 195 degrees, about 1 hour.

4 Remove pot from oven and transfer chicken to serving platter. Stir sesame oil, peppercorns, and sugar into sauce. Adjust consistency with extra hot water as needed. Spoon sauce over chicken and sprinkle with scallion greens. Serve.

CHICKEN IN A POT WITH RED POTATOES, CARROTS, AND SHALLOTS

SERVES 4   TOTAL TIME 2 HOURS

WHY THIS RECIPE WORKS Classic French *poulet en cocotte* relies on the moist environment of a covered Dutch oven to yield unbelievably tender meat (albeit with soft skin) and a concentrated jus made of the chicken's own juices. To make this dish into a complete meal, we added root vegetables to the pot but found that they were underdone even after an hour of baking. Adding liquid (a combination of chicken broth and wine) tenderized the vegetables, but the jus lost its appealing intensity. To counter this, we browned the chicken and vegetables to build fond. Browning our bird also crisped the skin slightly, and we wondered if we could preserve and enhance its crispness by cooking the chicken uncovered. To our satisfaction, we found that the uncovered roasting intensified the sauce without excessive evaporation, and the vegetables emerged tender and bathed in flavor. Our chicken in a pot now had the best of all worlds: succulent meat, crisped skin, superflavorful vegetables, and a killer sauce.

1 (3½- to 4-pound) whole chicken, giblets discarded
  Salt and pepper
1 tablespoon vegetable oil
1½ pounds red potatoes, unpeeled, cut into 1-inch pieces
1 pound carrots, peeled and cut into 1-inch pieces
4 shallots, peeled and halved
3 garlic cloves, minced
1 teaspoon minced fresh thyme or ¼ teaspoon dried
½ cup dry white wine
½ cup chicken broth, plus extra as needed
1 bay leaf
2 tablespoons unsalted butter
1 tablespoon lemon juice
1 tablespoon minced fresh parsley

1 Adjust oven rack to lower-middle position and heat oven to 350 degrees. Pat chicken dry with paper towels, tuck wingtips behind back, and season with salt and pepper. Heat oil in Dutch oven over medium-high heat until just smoking. Place chicken, breast side down, in pot and cook until lightly browned, about 5 minutes. Carefully flip chicken breast side up and continue to cook until well browned on second side, 6 to 8 minutes; transfer to large plate.

2 Pour off all but 1 tablespoon fat from pot. Add potatoes, carrots, shallots, and ½ teaspoon salt and cook over medium heat until vegetables are just beginning to brown, 5 to 7 minutes. Stir in garlic and thyme and cook until fragrant, about 30 seconds. Add wine, broth, and bay leaf, scraping up any browned bits.

3 Place chicken, breast side up, on top of vegetables, adding any accumulated juices. Transfer pot to oven and roast, uncovered, until breast registers 160 degrees and thighs register 175 degrees, 55 to 65 minutes, rotating pot halfway through roasting.

4 Remove pot from oven. Transfer chicken to carving board and let rest for 15 minutes. Using slotted spoon, transfer vegetables to serving platter and tent with aluminum foil to keep warm.

5 Discard bay leaf. Pour liquid left in pot into fat separator and let settle for 5 minutes. (You should have ¾ cup defatted liquid; add extra broth as needed to equal ¾ cup.) Return defatted liquid to now-empty pot, bring to simmer over medium-high heat, and cook until it measures ½ cup, 5 to 7 minutes. Off heat, whisk in butter and lemon juice, and season with salt and pepper to taste. Sprinkle vegetables with parsley, carve chicken, and serve with sauce.

ROAST CHICKEN WITH CRANBERRY-WALNUT STUFFING

SERVES 4   TOTAL TIME 2 HOURS

WHY THIS RECIPE WORKS An herb butter–rubbed chicken boasting a cranberry-walnut stuffing sounds like a meal fit for a holiday table, but our version takes the stuffing out of the chicken and moves the cooking to a Dutch oven for a fuss-free, anytime dish. The Dutch oven's tall sides easily contained the chicken and a hefty portion of stuffing. We sautéed some classic aromatics and herbs such as celery, onion, sage, and thyme to give the dish a solid flavor base, then nestled the butter-rubbed chicken into the pot and surrounded it with cubes of sturdy Italian bread. Placing the bread cubes around the chicken rather than underneath it allowed them to toast in the oven as well as soak up the chicken's flavorful juices. While the chicken rested, we completed the stuffing, moistening it with a small amount of chicken broth and stirring in sweet-tart dried cranberries, buttery toasted walnuts, and fresh parsley.

4 tablespoons unsalted butter, melted,
   plus 1 tablespoon unsalted butter
4 teaspoons minced fresh sage
4 teaspoons minced fresh thyme
   Salt and pepper
1 (3½- to 4-pound) whole chicken, giblets discarded
1 onion, chopped coarse
2 celery ribs, chopped coarse
5 ounces Italian bread, cut into ½-inch pieces (4 cups)
⅓ cup chicken broth
⅓ cup dried cranberries
¼ cup walnuts, toasted and chopped coarse
2 tablespoons minced fresh parsley

1 Adjust oven rack to middle position and heat oven to 425 degrees. Combine melted butter, 2 teaspoons sage, 2 teaspoons thyme, 1 teaspoon salt, and ½ teaspoon pepper in bowl. Pat chicken dry with paper towels, tuck wingtips behind back, and rub all over with butter mixture.

2 Melt remaining 1 tablespoon butter in Dutch oven over medium heat. Add onion, celery, ¼ teaspoon salt, and ¼ teaspoon pepper and cook until vegetables are softened, about 5 minutes. Stir in remaining 2 teaspoons sage and remaining 2 teaspoons thyme and cook until fragrant, about 30 seconds.

3 Off heat, place chicken, breast side up, in pot, then tuck bread evenly around sides of chicken. Transfer pot to oven and roast, uncovered, until breast registers 160 degrees and thighs register 175 degrees, about 1 hour, rotating pot halfway through roasting.

4 Remove pot from oven. Transfer chicken to carving board, brushing any bread pieces back into pot, and let rest for 15 minutes.

5 Meanwhile, stir broth, cranberries, and walnuts into bread mixture and cover to keep warm. Stir parsley and any accumulated chicken juices into stuffing. Carve chicken and serve with stuffing.

ROAST TURKEY BREAST WITH SHALLOT-PORCINI GRAVY

SERVES 6 TO 8 TOTAL TIME 3 HOURS 15 MINUTES TO 3 HOURS 45 MINUTES

WHY THIS RECIPE WORKS Unlike a whole roast turkey, roast bone-in turkey breast is unfussy and a great option for a Sunday dinner, especially when served with a rich gravy. Unfortunately, turkey breast has a reputation for turning out dry, which can dissuade cooks from preparing it. We've used several tricks to prevent dry meat, but no method delivers a juicier turkey breast than roasting it in a covered Dutch oven at very low heat. With all the moisture trapped in the pot, the turkey essentially braises in its own flavorful juices, and the gentle heat decreases the risk of overcooking the delicate white meat. A good gravy can be as fussy as the turkey itself, involving drippings, stock, and a roux. For a simpler but ultraflavorful gravy, we surrounded the turkey breast with shallots, celery, dried porcini mushrooms for earthy depth, tomato paste for an umami boost, and thyme and a bay leaf for backbone. As they cooked in the turkey's rendered juices, the seasonings became so flavorful that, while the meat rested, we simply transferred the contents of the pot to a blender (minus the herbs), added broth and lemon juice, and pureed them until luxuriously smooth. *Voilà*—perfectly juicy turkey and an ultrasimple gravy. If using a self-basting turkey breast (such as a frozen Butterball) or kosher turkey, do not season with salt in step 2.

1 (5- to 6-pound) bone-in whole turkey breast
  Salt and pepper
2 tablespoons extra-virgin olive oil
8 shallots, chopped
2 celery ribs, chopped
½ ounce dried porcini mushrooms, rinsed and minced
2 teaspoons tomato paste
4 sprigs fresh thyme
1 bay leaf
¼ cup chicken broth
1 tablespoon lemon juice

1 Adjust oven rack to lowest position and heat oven to 250 degrees. Place turkey breast on counter, skin side down. Using kitchen shears, cut through ribs, following vertical line of fat where breast meets back, from tapered end of breast to wing joint. Using your hands, bend back away from breast to pop shoulder joints out of sockets. Using paring knife, cut through joints between bones to separate back from breast; discard back. Trim excess fat from breast.

2 Pat breast dry with paper towels and season with salt and pepper. Heat oil in Dutch oven over medium-high heat until just smoking. Brown breast on all sides, about 12 minutes; transfer to plate.

3 Pour off all but 2 tablespoons fat from pot. Add shallots and celery and cook over medium heat until softened and lightly browned, 5 to 7 minutes. Stir in mushrooms, tomato paste, thyme sprigs, and bay leaf and cook until fragrant, about 1 minute. Off heat, return breast, skin side up, to pot, adding any accumulated juices. Cover, transfer pot to oven, and cook until turkey registers 160 degrees, 2 to 2½ hours.

4 Remove pot from oven. Transfer turkey to carving board and let rest for 20 minutes. Meanwhile, discard thyme sprigs and bay leaf. Transfer vegetables and any cooking liquid from pot to blender. Add broth and lemon juice and process until smooth, about 30 seconds. Return gravy to now-empty pot and set over low heat to keep warm. Season with salt and pepper to taste. Carve turkey, discarding skin, if desired. Serve, passing gravy separately.

HARISSA-RUBBED TURKEY BREAST WITH MASHED SWEET POTATOES

SERVES 6 TO 8   TOTAL TIME 3 HOURS 30 MINUTES TO 4 HOURS

WHY THIS RECIPE WORKS Turkey and gravy is classic, but this versatile protein also takes well to stronger flavors. And with our Dutch oven we could achieve not only a perfect roast turkey breast, but also a distinctive side dish to accompany it. We found inspiration for this complete meal in North Africa, where the chile paste known as harissa is a common condiment. We created our own harissa by blooming garlic, paprika, coriander, Aleppo pepper, cumin, and caraway seeds in oil. We then rubbed the mixture under the turkey's skin and let the bird rest for an hour in the fridge so the flavor could penetrate. For the side dish, we opted for earthy sweet potatoes, a common ingredient in many North African cuisines, and cut them into small pieces so they would cook at the same rate as the turkey. Putting the potatoes in the bottom of the Dutch oven and resting the turkey on top allowed them to soak up the turkey's flavorful juices and meant we didn't need to add any additional cooking liquid to the pot, which helped intensify the flavors. We roasted the turkey and potatoes uncovered at 325 degrees for an hour so the turkey could develop some browning, then we cranked the heat to 500 degrees at the end to deeply bronze the skin. While the breast rested, we mashed our potatoes to a smooth consistency, stirring in some half-and-half and cilantro before serving for a creamy, rich texture and a bit of fresh flavor. If you can't find Aleppo pepper, you can substitute ¾ teaspoon paprika and ¾ teaspoon finely chopped red pepper flakes. If using a self-basting turkey breast (such as a frozen Butterball) or kosher turkey, omit the salt in step 1.

½ cup extra-virgin olive oil

6 garlic cloves, minced

2 tablespoons paprika

1 tablespoon ground coriander

1 tablespoon ground dried Aleppo pepper

1 teaspoon ground cumin

¾ teaspoon caraway seeds
   Salt and pepper

1 (5- to 6-pound) bone-in turkey breast

4 pounds sweet potatoes, peeled and cut into
   ¾-inch pieces

⅓ cup half-and-half, warmed

2 tablespoons chopped fresh cilantro

1 Microwave 6 tablespoons oil, garlic, paprika, coriander, Aleppo pepper, cumin, caraway seeds, and 1½ teaspoons salt in bowl until bubbling and very fragrant, about 1 minute, stirring halfway through microwaving. Let cool to room temperature. Measure out and reserve ¼ cup harissa for serving.

2 Place turkey breast on counter, skin side down. Using kitchen shears, cut through ribs, following vertical line of fat where breast meets back, from tapered end of breast to wing joint. Using your hands, bend back away from breast to pop shoulder joints out of sockets. Using paring knife, cut through joints between bones to separate back from breast; discard back. Trim excess fat from breast.

3 Place breast, skin side up, on counter. Using your fingers, carefully loosen and separate turkey skin from each side of breast. Peel back skin, leaving it attached at top and center of breast. Rub 1 tablespoon remaining harissa onto each side of breast, then place skin back over meat. Rub 1 tablespoon remaining harissa onto underside of breast cavity. Place turkey on large plate and refrigerate, uncovered, for 1 hour.

4 Adjust oven rack to middle position and heat oven to 325 degrees. Toss potatoes with remaining 2 tablespoons oil and ½ teaspoon salt, then arrange in even

layer in Dutch oven. Pat turkey dry with paper towels and brush with remaining 1 tablespoon harissa. Place turkey, skin side up, on top of potatoes. Transfer pot to oven and roast, uncovered, until turkey registers 130 degrees, 1 to 1¼ hours.

5 Remove pot from oven and increase oven temperature to 500 degrees. When oven reaches 500 degrees, return pot to oven and roast, uncovered, until turkey skin is deeply browned and breast registers 160 degrees, 15 to 30 minutes.

6 Remove pot from oven. Transfer turkey to carving board and let rest for 30 minutes. Meanwhile, using potato masher, mash potatoes until smooth; cover to keep warm.

7 Stir warm half-and-half and cilantro into potatoes, and season with salt and pepper to taste. Carve turkey and serve with potatoes, passing reserved harissa separately.

BRAISED SHORT RIBS WITH WILD MUSHROOM FARROTTO

SERVES **4 TO 6**   TOTAL TIME **4 HOURS 45 MINUTES**

WHY THIS RECIPE WORKS Bone-in short ribs are perfect for braising: When cooked slowly, they boast a rich, beefy flavor and a tender, velvety texture. But the marbling that makes them taste so good can also be a serious liability, resulting in a greasy final dish. To avoid this, we first roasted them for about an hour without anything else in the pot; this enabled us to render and discard a significant amount of fat. We then built a deeply flavorful braising liquid using a combination of cremini and dried porcini mushrooms, aromatics, beef broth, and the porcini's soaking liquid. When the ribs were close to done, we again defatted the cooking liquid and decided to use it to make farrotto, which is similar to risotto but uses hearty farro. To get a creamy, risotto-like consistency, we cracked about half of the farro in a blender to allow the grains to release more of their starch. We removed the short ribs from the pot, stirred the farro into the liquid, then put the short ribs back in and covered the pot to ensure that the grains would cook evenly. Stirring in some Parmesan, butter, and sherry vinegar at the end made for a rich yet bright side for our ribs. To give the dish a fresh finish, we topped it with a simple gremolata—a mixture of parsley, chives, lemon zest, and garlic. English-style short ribs contain a single rib bone. We prefer the flavor and texture of whole farro. Do not use quick-cooking or pearled farro.

4 pounds bone-in English-style short ribs, bone 4 to 5 inches long, 1 to 1½ inches of meat on top of bone, trimmed
 Salt and pepper
¾ ounce dried porcini mushrooms, rinsed
4 cups water
1½ cups whole farro
4 tablespoons unsalted butter
12 ounces cremini mushrooms, trimmed and sliced thin
1 onion, chopped fine
2 teaspoons minced fresh thyme
3 garlic cloves, minced
2 cups beef broth, plus extra as needed
1½ ounces Parmesan cheese, grated (¾ cup)
2 teaspoons sherry vinegar
¼ cup chopped fresh parsley
2 tablespoons minced fresh chives
2 teaspoons grated lemon zest

1 Adjust oven rack to lower-middle position and heat oven to 450 degrees. Pat short ribs dry with paper towels and season with salt and pepper. Arrange ribs in single layer in Dutch oven. Transfer pot to oven and roast, uncovered, until short ribs are browned, about 1 hour, flipping short ribs halfway through roasting.

2 Microwave porcini mushrooms and 1 cup water in covered bowl until steaming, about 1 minute. Let sit until softened, about 5 minutes. Drain mushrooms in fine-mesh strainer lined with coffee filter. Reserve liquid and finely chop porcini mushrooms. Pulse farro in blender until about half of grains are broken into smaller pieces, about 6 pulses; set aside.

3 Remove pot from oven and reduce oven temperature to 300 degrees. Transfer ribs to plate and discard any fat and juices left in pot. Melt 2 tablespoons butter in now-empty pot over medium heat. Add cremini mushrooms and onion and cook, stirring occasionally, until softened and dry, 8 to 10 minutes. Stir in porcini mushrooms, thyme, and two-thirds of garlic and cook until fragrant, about 30 seconds.

4 Stir in reserved porcini soaking liquid, broth, and remaining 3 cups water, scraping up any browned bits, and bring to simmer. Nestle ribs, bone side up, into pot, adding any accumulated juices. Cover, return pot to oven, and cook for 2 hours.

5 Remove pot from oven and transfer ribs to plate. Using wide, shallow spoon, skim excess fat from surface of braising liquid. Stir in farro, then return ribs to pot, adding any accumulated juices. Cover, return pot to oven, and cook until ribs are tender and fork slips easily in and out of meat, 30 to 40 minutes.

6 Remove pot from oven. Transfer ribs to serving platter, brushing any farro back into pot; discard any loose bones. Add Parmesan, vinegar, and remaining 2 tablespoons butter to farro and stir vigorously until mixture becomes creamy, about 2 minutes. Adjust consistency with extra hot broth as needed. Season with salt and pepper to taste.

7 To make gremolata, combine parsley, chives, lemon zest, and remaining garlic in small bowl. Sprinkle individual portions of ribs and farrotto with gremolata before serving.

SIMPLE POT ROAST

SERVES 6 TO 8   TOTAL TIME 4 HOURS 30 MINUTES TO 5 HOURS

WHY THIS RECIPE WORKS When it comes to pot roast, keeping it simple is sometimes best. We started with a chuck-eye roast, a well-marbled cut that is great for braising. Splitting the roast in two allowed us to trim excess fat and cut down on cooking time. A stovetop sear created a nicely caramelized exterior; transferring the covered Dutch oven to the oven promoted even cooking and prevented scorching over the long cooking time. Adding carrots, potatoes, and parsnips to the pot partway through braising ensured that the vegetables didn't overcook and become mushy. We added wine to the sauce after braising so that its flavor stayed bright; reducing it briefly on the stovetop ensured that our sauce didn't taste boozy. Use a good-quality medium-bodied wine, such as a Côtes du Rhône or a Pinot Noir, for this dish. Depending on the size of your Dutch oven, you may need to brown the roasts in two batches rather than one.

1 (3½- to 4-pound) boneless beef chuck-eye roast, pulled into 2 pieces at natural seam and trimmed of large pieces of fat
    Salt and pepper
3 tablespoons vegetable oil
1 onion, chopped
1 celery rib, chopped
4 garlic cloves, minced
2 teaspoons sugar
1 teaspoon minced fresh thyme or ¼ teaspoon dried
1 cup chicken broth
1 cup beef broth
1 cup water
1½ pounds carrots, peeled and cut into 3-inch pieces
1½ pounds red potatoes, unpeeled, cut into 1½-inch pieces
1½ pounds parsnips, peeled and cut into 3-inch pieces
⅓ cup dry red wine

1 Adjust oven rack to lower-middle position and heat oven to 300 degrees. Tie roasts crosswise with kitchen twine at 1-inch intervals. Pat dry with paper towels and season with salt and pepper. Heat 2 tablespoons oil in Dutch oven over medium-high heat until just smoking. Brown roasts on all sides, 8 to 10 minutes; transfer to plate.

2 Add remaining 1 tablespoon oil, onion, and celery to fat left in pot and cook over medium heat until vegetables are softened, about 5 minutes. Stir in garlic, sugar, and thyme and cook until fragrant, about 30 seconds. Stir in chicken broth, beef broth, and water, scraping up any browned bits, and bring to simmer. Return roasts to pot along with any accumulated juices. Cover, transfer pot to oven, and cook for 2 hours, flipping roasts halfway through cooking.

3 Remove pot from oven. Nestle carrots into pot around roasts and sprinkle potatoes and parsnips over top. Return covered pot to oven and cook until vegetables and beef are tender and fork slips easily in and out of meat, 1 to 1½ hours.

4 Remove pot from oven. Transfer roasts to carving board, tent with aluminum foil, and let rest while finishing sauce. Transfer vegetables to large bowl, season with salt and pepper to taste, and cover to keep warm.

5 Using wide, shallow spoon, skim excess fat from surface of braising liquid. Stir in wine, bring to simmer over medium-high heat, and cook until sauce measures 2 cups, about 15 minutes. Season with salt and pepper to taste.

6 Discard twine, slice roasts against grain into ½-inch-thick slices, and arrange on serving platter. Spoon some of sauce over meat and serve with vegetables, passing remaining sauce separately.

BEEF BRAISED IN BAROLO

SERVES 6 TO 8   TOTAL TIME 4 HOURS 30 MINUTES

WHY THIS RECIPE WORKS The Italian version of pot roast is an inexpensive cut of beef braised in wine. But what a difference that wine makes. Full-bodied Barolo has been called the "wine of kings" and can be somewhat expensive, so this pot roast has to be special. We wanted moist, tender meat enveloped in a silky sauce that would do justice to the regal wine. We chose chuck-eye roast, which wouldn't dry out after a long braise. As with our Simple Pot Roast (page 159), we separated the meat into two pieces and removed the central layer of fat; this also allowed the dish to cook more quickly. We tied the roasts to hold their shape and then browned them in the fat rendered from pancetta, which added rich flavor. Next, we browned aromatics and poured a whole bottle of wine into the pot. Barolo has such a bold flavor that we needed something to temper it, and that proved to be a can of diced tomatoes. When the meat was done, we removed it from the pot, reduced the sauce, and strained out the vegetables. Dark, full-flavored, and lustrous, this sauce bestowed nobility on our humble cut of meat. Purchase pancetta that is cut to order, about ¼ inch thick. If pancetta is not available, substitute an equal amount of salt pork (find the meatiest piece possible); cut it into ¼-inch pieces and boil it in 3 cups of water for about 2 minutes to remove excess salt. After draining, use it as you would pancetta. Depending on the size of your Dutch oven, you may need to brown the roasts in two batches rather than one.

1 (3½- to 4-pound) boneless beef chuck-eye roast, pulled into 2 pieces at natural seam and trimmed of large pieces of fat
  Salt and pepper
4 ounces pancetta, cut into ¼-inch pieces
2 onions, chopped
2 carrots, chopped
2 celery ribs, chopped
1 tablespoon tomato paste
3 garlic cloves, minced
1 tablespoon all-purpose flour
½ teaspoon sugar
1 (750-ml) bottle Barolo wine
1 (14.5-ounce) can diced tomatoes, drained
1 sprig fresh thyme, plus 1 teaspoon minced
1 sprig fresh rosemary
10 sprigs fresh parsley

1 Adjust oven rack to middle position and heat oven to 300 degrees. Tie roasts crosswise with kitchen twine at 1-inch intervals. Pat dry with paper towels and season with salt and pepper. Cook pancetta in Dutch oven over medium heat, stirring occasionally, until browned and crisp, about 8 minutes. Using slotted spoon, transfer pancetta to paper towel–lined plate; set aside.

2 Pour off all but 2 tablespoons fat from pot, then heat fat left in pot over medium-high heat until just smoking. Brown roasts on all sides, 8 to 10 minutes; transfer to plate.

3 Add onions, carrots, celery, and tomato paste to fat left in pot and cook over medium heat until vegetables are softened and lightly browned, 5 to 7 minutes. Stir in garlic, flour, sugar, and reserved pancetta and cook until fragrant, about 30 seconds. Stir in wine and tomatoes, scraping up any browned bits. Add thyme sprig, rosemary sprig, and parsley sprigs and bring to simmer.

4 Nestle roasts into pot, adding any accumulated juices. Cover, transfer pot to oven, and cook until beef is tender and fork slips easily in and out of meat, about 3 hours, flipping roasts every hour.

5 Transfer roasts to carving board, tent with aluminum foil, and let rest while finishing sauce. Using wide, shallow spoon, skim excess fat from surface of braising liquid. Stir in minced thyme, bring to boil over high heat, and cook, whisking vigorously, until vegetables have broken down and thickened sauce measures about 3½ cups, about 18 minutes.

6 Strain sauce through fine-mesh strainer into bowl, pressing on solids to extract as much liquid as possible; discard solids. (You should have 1½ cups strained sauce; if necessary, return sauce to Dutch oven and reduce to 1½ cups.) Season with salt and pepper to taste.

7 Discard twine, slice roasts against grain into ½-inch-thick slices, and arrange on serving platter. Spoon some of sauce over meat and serve, passing remaining sauce separately.

SLOW-ROASTED CHUCK ROAST WITH HORSERADISH–SOUR CREAM SAUCE

SERVES 8 TO 10   TOTAL TIME 3 HOURS 15 MINUTES TO 3 HOURS 45 MINUTES

WHY THIS RECIPE WORKS Inexpensive beef chuck-eye isn't just a great cut for braising; it also makes a first-rate roast if you treat it correctly. In this simple recipe, we transform it into a tender, juicy roast by salting the meat and then cooking it in the oven at a low temperature. This allowed the meat's enzymes to act as natural tenderizers, breaking down its tough connective tissue. We split the meat in half to remove the central layer of fat, then tied the pieces into a single cylindrical roast, which enabled the meat to cook evenly. Roasting the meat in a Dutch oven made it easy to brown the meat first on the stovetop, then transfer it to a 300-degree oven to gently cook. While it roasted, we created a flavorful rub, which would burn if applied at the onset of cooking. A brush of egg white helped the rub stick to the meat. A final quick stint in a hot oven bloomed the spices and imparted additional browning. For a simple accompaniment, we created a creamy horseradish sauce. Buy refrigerated prepared horseradish, not the shelf-stable kind, which contains preservatives and additives. Prepared horseradish can vary drastically in spiciness; start with the smaller amount and add more to taste.

1 (4- to 5-pound) boneless beef chuck-eye roast, pulled into 2 pieces at natural seams and trimmed of large pieces of fat
  Salt and pepper
2 tablespoons vegetable oil
2 tablespoons mustard seeds
4 teaspoons black peppercorns
3 tablespoons chopped fresh rosemary
⅔ cup sour cream
¼–½ cup prepared horseradish, drained
1 large egg white

1 Sprinkle beef with 2 teaspoons salt. Tie meat pieces together at 1-inch intervals using kitchen twine to create 1 evenly shaped roast. Transfer to plate, cover with plastic wrap, and refrigerate for at least 1 hour or up to 24 hours.

2 Adjust oven rack to middle position and heat oven to 300 degrees. Heat oil in Dutch oven over medium-high heat until just smoking. Pat roast dry with paper towels and season with pepper. Brown roast on all sides, 8 to 10 minutes. Transfer pot to oven and roast, uncovered, until meat registers 150 degrees, 1 to 1½ hours, flipping roast halfway through roasting.

3 Meanwhile, process mustard seeds and black peppercorns in spice grinder until coarsely ground. Transfer to small bowl and stir in rosemary. Whisk sour cream, horseradish, ¾ teaspoon salt, and ⅛ teaspoon pepper together in separate bowl; cover and refrigerate until ready to serve.

4 Remove pot from oven and increase oven temperature to 450 degrees. Transfer roast to rimmed baking sheet. Pour off any fat left in pot. Whisk egg white in medium bowl until frothy. Brush roast with egg white on all sides and sprinkle with mustard seed mixture, rolling roast and pressing on mixture to adhere. Return roast to now-empty pot, transfer pot to oven, and cook, uncovered, until roast is browned and fragrant, about 10 minutes, flipping roast halfway through roasting.

5 Remove pot from oven. Transfer roast to carving board and let rest for 15 minutes. Discard twine and slice roast against grain into ½-inch-thick slices. Serve with horseradish sauce.

CUBAN BRAISED SHREDDED BEEF

SERVES 6 TO 8 TOTAL TIME 3 HOURS 15 MINUTES

WHY THIS RECIPE WORKS Cuban *ropa vieja* is a hearty, rustic dish of braised and shredded beef, sliced peppers and onions, chopped green olives, and a brothy sauce. Traditionally, the dish requires simmering beef in one pot, and then using the meat and some of its broth in a separate sauté of onions, peppers, and spices. To simplify, we combined the two steps into the ease of a Dutch oven braise, which also meant that all the beef's flavorful juices ended up in the final dish. We eschewed typical flank steak, which can turn out dry, in favor of brisket, which has great beefy flavor and enough collagen to guarantee tender, juicy shreds. Cutting the brisket into 2-inch-wide strips sped up cooking and made shredding a breeze. Searing the meat before braising and adding glutamate-rich anchovies gave the dish serious savory flavor. We caramelized the onions and peppers and then set them aside while cooking the beef so they would retain some texture. Reserving the briny green olives for the end kept their flavor sharp. Depending on the size of your Dutch oven, you may need to brown the beef in two batches rather than one. Serve with rice.

1 (2-pound) beef brisket, 1½ to 2½ inches thick, fat trimmed to ¼ inch
  Salt and pepper
5 tablespoons vegetable oil
2 onions, halved and sliced thin
2 red bell peppers, stemmed, seeded, and sliced into ¼-inch-wide strips
2 anchovy fillets, rinsed, patted dry, and minced
4 garlic cloves, minced
2 teaspoons ground cumin
1½ teaspoons dried oregano
½ cup dry white wine
2 cups chicken broth
1 (8-ounce) can tomato sauce
2 bay leaves
¾ cup pitted brine-cured green olives, chopped coarse
¾ teaspoon white wine vinegar, plus extra for seasoning
  Lime wedges

1 Adjust oven rack to middle position and heat oven to 300 degrees. Cut brisket against grain into 2-inch-wide strips. Cut any strips longer than 5 inches in half crosswise. Season beef with salt and pepper.

2 Heat 4 tablespoons oil in Dutch oven over medium-high heat until just smoking. Brown beef on all sides, 8 to 10 minutes; transfer to plate. Add onions and bell peppers to fat left in pot and cook until softened and pan develops some fond, 10 to 15 minutes; transfer to bowl.

3 Heat remaining 1 tablespoon oil in now-empty pot over medium heat until shimmering. Add anchovies, garlic, cumin, and oregano and cook until fragrant, about 30 seconds. Stir in wine, scraping up any browned bits, and cook until mostly evaporated, about 1 minute. Stir in broth, tomato sauce, and bay leaves and bring to simmer. Nestle beef into pot, adding any accumulated juices. Cover, transfer pot to oven, and cook until beef is just tender, 2 to 2¼ hours, flipping meat halfway through cooking.

4 Remove pot from oven. Transfer beef to cutting board, let cool slightly, then shred into ¼-inch-thick pieces using 2 forks.

5 Meanwhile, add olives and reserved vegetables to pot and bring to simmer over medium-high heat. Cook until sauce is thickened and measures 4 cups, 5 to 7 minutes. Discard bay leaves. Stir in beef and cook until heated through, about 2 minutes. Off heat, stir in vinegar and season with salt, pepper, and extra vinegar to taste. Serve with lime wedges.

SMOTHERED PORK CHOPS WITH BROCCOLI

SERVES 4 TOTAL TIME 2 HOUR 15 MINUTES

WHY THIS RECIPE WORKS A roomy Dutch oven is a true multitasker—especially when it comes to creative one-pot cooking. While developing our take on Southern-style smothered pork chops in a rich, oniony gravy, we wondered whether we could make a side dish in the same pot—without saturating our whole meal with the heavy gravy. We discovered that we could braise the pork chops until they were nearly tender, then use a steamer basket to elevate broccoli florets above the chops, utilizing the moisture already in the pot to steam the vegetable to crisp-tender perfection. Cutting slits in the pork chops prevented them from curling and made fitting the steamer basket in the pot easy. You will need a collapsible steamer basket for this recipe.

3 slices bacon, chopped fine

4 (8- to 10-ounce) bone-in blade-cut pork chops, ¾ inch thick, trimmed

Salt and pepper

¼ cup extra-virgin olive oil

1 onion, halved and sliced thin

4 garlic cloves, minced

1 teaspoon minced fresh thyme or ¼ teaspoon dried

½ teaspoon red pepper flakes

2 tablespoons water

2 tablespoons all-purpose flour

1¾ cups chicken broth

2 bay leaves

1 pound broccoli florets, cut into 1-inch pieces

2 tablespoons minced fresh parsley

1 Adjust oven rack to lower-middle position and heat oven to 300 degrees. Cook bacon in Dutch oven over medium heat until crisp, 5 to 7 minutes. Using slotted spoon, transfer bacon to paper towel–lined plate. Pour off all but 2 tablespoons fat from pot.

2 Cut 2 slits, about 2 inches apart, through fat on edges of each pork chop. Pat chops dry with paper towels and season with salt and pepper. Heat fat left in pot over medium-high heat until just smoking. Add chops (they will overlap slightly) and brown on both sides, 7 to 10 minutes; transfer to separate plate.

3 Add 2 tablespoons oil, onion, and ¼ teaspoon salt to fat left in pot and cook over medium heat until onion is softened and lightly browned, 5 to 7 minutes. Stir in garlic, thyme, and pepper flakes and cook until fragrant, about 30 seconds. Stir in water, scraping up any browned bits. Reduce heat to medium-low, add flour, and cook, stirring often, until well browned, about 5 minutes.

4 Slowly whisk in broth, scraping up any browned bits and smoothing out any lumps. Add bay leaves and bring to simmer. Nestle chops into pot, adding any accumulated juices. Cover, transfer pot to oven, and cook until chops are almost fork-tender, about 1 hour.

5 Remove pot from oven. Place steamer basket on top of chops and add broccoli to basket. Cover, return pot to oven, and cook until broccoli is tender, about 20 minutes.

6 Remove pot from oven and remove basket of broccoli from pot. Toss broccoli in bowl with remaining 2 tablespoons oil, and season with salt and pepper to taste. Transfer chops to serving platter, tent with aluminum foil, and let rest while finishing sauce.

7 Using wide, shallow spoon, skim any fat from surface of sauce. Bring to simmer over medium-high heat and cook until thickened, about 5 minutes. Discard bay leaves and season with salt and pepper to taste. Spoon sauce over chops, sprinkle with bacon and parsley, and serve with broccoli.

MILK-BRAISED PORK LOIN

SERVES 4 TO 6   TOTAL TIME 3 HOURS 30 MINUTES

WHY THIS RECIPE WORKS *Maiale al latte*, or pork cooked in milk, is not only one of the most delicious roasts in the Italian canon but also one of the simplest. Traditionally, a boneless pork roast is browned in a little fat and then braised in milk, often with a few garlic cloves and some fresh sage. The meat turns out supple and juicy, and the milk cooks down to form a lush, deeply savory sauce. But the sauce is typically unattractive, drab in color and lumpy from the curdled dairy, plus the dish can have a one-note richness. We set out to make the sauce look more appealing and add some complexity. We chose a boneless loin roast since this lean cut wouldn't make the dish overly rich. Brining the pork seasoned it throughout and kept it moist during cooking. Adding a touch of fat from rendered salt pork offered two major benefits: It boosted the meaty flavor of the dish, and the fat coated the milk proteins, preventing them from bonding, which minimized curdling. We also added a pinch of baking soda to the braising liquid, which encouraged deeper browning—good for both flavor and appearance. Whisking some white wine, punchy Dijon mustard, and fresh parsley into the sauce at the end of cooking brightened its flavor and made the sauce look even more appealing. The milk will bubble up when added to the pot. If necessary, remove the pot from the heat and stir to break up the foam before returning it to the heat. We prefer natural pork, but if your pork is enhanced (injected with a salt solution), do not brine. Instead, skip to step 2.

Salt and pepper
¼ cup sugar
1 (2- to 2½-pound) boneless pork loin roast, fat trimmed to ¼ inch
2 ounces salt pork, chopped coarse
3 cups whole milk
5 garlic cloves, peeled
1 teaspoon minced fresh sage
¼ teaspoon baking soda
½ cup dry white wine
3 tablespoons chopped fresh parsley
1 teaspoon Dijon mustard

1 Dissolve ¼ cup salt and sugar in 2 quarts cold water in large container. Submerge roast in brine, cover, and refrigerate for 1½ to 2 hours.

2 Adjust oven rack to middle position and heat oven to 250 degrees. Remove roast from brine, pat dry with paper towels, and tie at 1-inch intervals with kitchen twine. Bring salt pork and ½ cup water to simmer in Dutch oven over medium heat. Simmer until water evaporates and salt pork begins to sizzle, 5 to 6 minutes. Continue to cook, stirring frequently, until salt pork is lightly browned and fat has rendered, 2 to 3 minutes. Using slotted spoon, discard salt pork, leaving fat in pot.

3 Increase heat to medium-high and heat fat in pot until just smoking. Brown roast on all sides, 8 to 10 minutes; transfer to plate. Add milk, garlic, sage, and baking soda to fat left in pot and bring to simmer, scraping up any browned bits. Cook, stirring frequently, until milk is lightly browned and has consistency of heavy cream, 14 to 16 minutes. Reduce heat to medium-low and continue to cook, stirring and scraping bottom of pot constantly, until milk thickens to consistency of thin batter, 1 to 3 minutes. Remove pot from heat.

4 Return roast and any accumulated juices to pot, cover, and transfer to oven. Cook until pork registers 140 degrees, 30 to 50 minutes, flipping roast halfway through cooking.

5 Remove pot from oven. Transfer roast to carving board, tent with aluminum foil, and let rest for 20 to 25 minutes.

6 Add wine and any accumulated meat juices to pot and bring to simmer over medium-high heat, whisking vigorously to smooth out sauce. Cook until sauce has consistency of thin gravy, 2 to 3 minutes. Off heat, stir in 2 tablespoons parsley and mustard, and season with salt and pepper to taste. Discard twine and slice roast into ¼-inch-thick slices; arrange on serving platter. Spoon sauce over slices and sprinkle with remaining 1 tablespoon parsley. Serve.

PORK LOIN WITH FENNEL AND HERB COUSCOUS

SERVES 6   TOTAL TIME 3 HOURS 30 MINUTES

WHY THIS RECIPE WORKS Inspired by the lively flavors of North African cuisine, we set out to create a satisfying one-pot meal featuring easy-to-prepare boneless pork loin. To keep the lean meat juicy through cooking, we brined it and braised it at a low temperature in a covered Dutch oven to hold in moisture. Searing the roast before braising created flavorful browning, and to further enhance the mild pork's flavor we infused our braising liquid with potent aromatics including fennel stalks, onion, garlic, and orange zest. Once the pork had braised to perfection, we let it rest while we whipped up an equally flavor-packed side dish using the braising liquid: First, we sautéed fennel bulbs, then stirred in quick-cooking couscous and the defatted braising liquid and let everything sit until the couscous was fluffy and tender. Dried apricots offered a touch of sweetness, while fennel fronds enhanced the anise-y flavor. A quick serving sauce, made with cilantro, garlic, orange juice, and a few North African spices, came together easily in a food processor. We prefer natural pork, but if your pork is enhanced (injected with a salt solution), do not brine. Instead, skip to step 2.

Salt and pepper
1 (2½- to 3-pound) boneless pork loin roast,
   fat trimmed to ¼ inch
2 cups fresh cilantro leaves
9 garlic cloves, minced
¾ teaspoon ground cumin
¾ teaspoon paprika
¼ teaspoon cayenne pepper
2 teaspoons grated orange zest plus 1¼ cups juice
   (3 oranges)
½ cup plus 3 tablespoons extra-virgin olive oil
1 onion, chopped fine
2 fennel bulbs, fronds minced to get ⅓ cup,
   stalks chopped to get 1 cup, bulbs halved,
   cored, and cut into ½-inch pieces
1½ cups chicken broth
1½ cups couscous
½ cup dried apricots, chopped

1 Dissolve ¼ cup salt in 2 quarts cold water in large container. Submerge roast in brine, cover, and refrigerate for 1½ to 2 hours.

2 Pulse cilantro, half of garlic, cumin, paprika, cayenne, and ½ teaspoon salt in food processor until coarsely chopped, about 10 pulses, scraping down sides of bowl as needed. Add ¼ cup orange juice and pulse briefly to combine. Transfer mixture to bowl and stir in ½ cup oil. Cover and let sit at room temperature until ready to serve.

3 Adjust oven rack to middle position and heat oven to 250 degrees. Remove roast from brine, pat dry with paper towels, and tie at 1-inch intervals with kitchen twine. Heat 2 tablespoons oil in Dutch oven over medium-high heat until just smoking. Brown roast on all sides, 8 to 10 minutes; transfer to plate.

4 Add onion and fennel stalks to fat left in pot and cook until softened, about 5 minutes. Stir in orange zest and remaining garlic and cook until fragrant, about 30 seconds. Stir in broth and remaining 1 cup orange juice, scraping up any browned bits, and bring to simmer.

5 Return roast and any accumulated juices to pot, cover, and transfer to oven. Cook until pork registers 140 degrees, 30 to 50 minutes, flipping pork halfway through cooking. Remove pot from oven. Transfer roast to carving board, tent with aluminum foil, and let rest while finishing couscous.

6 Strain cooking liquid through fine-mesh strainer into fat separator and let settle for 5 minutes; discard solids. Wipe pot clean with paper towels. Heat remaining 1 tablespoon oil in now-empty pot over medium heat until shimmering. Add fennel bulb pieces and ½ teaspoon salt and cook until fennel is softened and lightly browned, 6 to 8 minutes. Off heat, stir in couscous, apricots, and 1½ cups defatted cooking liquid. Cover and let sit until liquid is fully absorbed and grains are tender, about 7 minutes. Add fennel fronds and fluff couscous with fork to combine. Season with salt and pepper to taste.

7 Discard twine and slice pork into ¼-inch-thick slices. Serve with couscous, passing herb sauce separately.

ROASTED PORK LOIN WITH BARLEY, BUTTERNUT SQUASH, AND SWISS CHARD

SERVES 6   TOTAL TIME 3 HOURS 30 MINUTES

WHY THIS RECIPE WORKS We used the French method of cooking *en cocotte* (covered in a heavy pot in a very low oven) to produce juicy, perfectly cooked pork loin along with creamy barley in this one-pot recipe. The low-heat, trapped-moisture method kept the pork from overcooking. Once it was done, we finished cooking the barley on the stovetop, adding cubed butternut squash and Swiss chard stems toward the end of cooking so they could just become tender. In the final minutes, we stirred in the quick-cooking chard leaves, adding some Parmesan cheese for a bit of richness. We prefer natural pork, but if your pork is enhanced (injected with a salt solution), do not brine. Instead, skip to step 2. Arrowhead Mills and Quaker pearled barley yield the most consistent results in this recipe. If you use a different brand, you may need to extend the cooking time in step 5, adding water as necessary.

Salt and pepper
1 (2½- to 3-pound) boneless pork loin roast, fat trimmed to ¼ inch
2 tablespoons minced fresh thyme
3 tablespoons vegetable oil
1 onion, chopped
1 cup pearled barley, rinsed
3 garlic cloves, minced
¼ cup dry white wine
4 cups chicken broth
½ small butternut squash, peeled, seeded, and cut into ½-inch pieces (2½ cups)
8 ounces Swiss chard, stems chopped, leaves cut into 1-inch pieces
1 ounce Parmesan cheese, grated (½ cup)
2 teaspoons cider vinegar

1 Dissolve ¼ cup salt in 2 quarts cold water in large container. Submerge roast in brine, cover, and refrigerate for 1½ to 2 hours.

2 Adjust oven rack to middle position and heat oven to 250 degrees. Remove roast from brine, pat dry with paper towels, and tie at 1-inch intervals with kitchen twine. Season roast with pepper and sprinkle with 1 tablespoon thyme. Heat 2 tablespoons oil in Dutch oven over medium-high heat until just smoking. Brown roast on all sides, 8 to 10 minutes; transfer to plate.

3 Add remaining 1 tablespoon oil, onion, barley, and ¼ teaspoon salt to fat left in pot. Cook over medium heat until onion is softened, about 5 minutes. Stir in garlic and remaining 1 tablespoon thyme and cook until fragrant, about 30 seconds. Stir in wine, scraping up any browned bits, and cook until evaporated, about 30 seconds. Stir in broth and bring to simmer.

4 Return roast and any accumulated juices to pot, cover, and transfer to oven. Cook until pork registers 140 degrees, 30 to 50 minutes. Remove pot from oven. Transfer roast to carving board, tent with aluminum foil, and let rest while barley and vegetables finish cooking.

5 Bring barley to simmer over medium-high heat and cook, covered, until barley is just cooked through but still somewhat firm in center, 10 to 15 minutes. Stir in squash and chard stems and cook, covered, until vegetables are tender, 10 to 15 minutes. Stir in chard leaves, decrease heat to medium, and cook, uncovered, until leaves are tender and mixture is thickened to risotto-like consistency, 2 to 5 minutes. Off heat, stir in Parmesan and vinegar. Season with salt and pepper to taste.

6 Discard twine and slice roast into ½-inch-thick slices. Serve with barley and vegetables.

CHINESE-STYLE BARBECUED SPARERIBS

SERVES 6 TO 8 AS AN APPETIZER OR 4 TO 6 AS A MAIN COURSE   TOTAL TIME 3 HOURS

WHY THIS RECIPE WORKS Chinese-style barbecued ribs are usually marinated for several hours and then slow-roasted and basted repeatedly to build up a thick crust. We skipped both of those time-consuming steps and instead braised the ribs, cut into individual pieces to speed cooking and create more surface area, in a highly seasoned liquid, which helped the flavor penetrate thoroughly and quickly. Then we strained, defatted, and reduced the braising liquid to make a full-bodied glaze in which we tossed the ribs before roasting them on a rack in a hot oven to color and crisp their exteriors. It's not necessary to remove the membrane on the bone side of the ribs. These ribs are chewier than American-style ribs; if you prefer them more tender, cook them for an additional 15 minutes in step 1. Adding water to the baking sheet during roasting helps prevent smoking. You can serve the first batch immediately or tent them with aluminum foil to keep them warm.

1 (6-inch) piece ginger, peeled and sliced thin
8 garlic cloves, peeled
1 cup honey
¾ cup hoisin sauce
¾ cup soy sauce
½ cup Chinese rice wine or dry sherry
2 teaspoons five-spice powder
1 teaspoon red food coloring (optional)
1 teaspoon ground white pepper
2 (2- to 2½-pound) racks St. Louis–style spareribs, trimmed and cut into individual ribs
2 tablespoons toasted sesame oil

1 Pulse ginger and garlic in food processor until finely chopped, 10 to 12 pulses, scraping down sides of bowl as needed. Transfer ginger-garlic mixture to Dutch oven. Add honey, hoisin, soy sauce, ½ cup water, rice wine, five-spice powder, food coloring, if using, and pepper and whisk until combined. Add ribs and toss to coat (ribs will not be fully submerged). Bring to simmer over medium-high heat, then reduce heat to low, cover, and cook for 1¼ hours, stirring occasionally.

2 Adjust oven rack to middle position and heat oven to 425 degrees. Using tongs, transfer ribs to large bowl. Strain braising liquid through fine-mesh strainer set over large container, pressing on solids to extract as

much liquid as possible; discard solids. Let cooking liquid settle for 10 minutes. Using wide, shallow spoon, skim excess fat from surface of liquid.

3 Return braising liquid to now-empty pot and add oil. Bring to boil over high heat and cook until syrupy and reduced to 2½ cups, 16 to 20 minutes.

4 Set wire rack in aluminum foil–lined rimmed baking sheet and pour ½ cup water into sheet. Transfer half of ribs to pot with braising liquid and toss to coat. Arrange ribs, bone side up, on prepared rack, letting excess glaze drip off. Roast until edges of ribs start to caramelize, 5 to 7 minutes. Flip ribs and continue to roast until second side starts to caramelize, 5 to 7 minutes longer. Transfer ribs to serving platter. Repeat with remaining ribs. Serve.

CUTTING SPARERIBS

Using sharp knife, slice between ribs to cut racks into individual pieces.

CITRUS-BRAISED PORK TACOS

SERVES 6   TOTAL TIME 3 HOURS

WHY THIS RECIPE WORKS In Mexico, the dish known as *cochinita pibil* is made by rubbing a whole suckling pig with warm spices and juice from bitter oranges, then wrapping it in banana leaves and slowly pit-roasting it until it is succulent and richly flavored. To achieve a similar dish at home, we turned to well-marbled pork butt roast and traded the banana leaves and pit of coals for a Dutch oven, which, when placed in a moderate oven, allowed the pork to braise gently to tenderness. To give the pork its distinctive flavor, usually achieved with hard-to-find ingredients like bitter oranges and annatto, we used frozen orange juice concentrate, tomato paste for color and depth, and bay leaves for herbal flavor. A quick habanero sauce, made with a traditional cooked-carrot base, and pickled red onions balanced out the rich meat. Pork butt roast is often labeled Boston butt. If you want a spicier sauce, you can add the remaining habanero; if you are spice-averse, substitute a less-spicy jalapeño for the habanero.

Pork

- 2 tablespoons vegetable oil
- 1 onion, chopped fine
- 3 garlic cloves, minced
- 1 teaspoon ground cumin
- 1 teaspoon dried oregano
- ½ teaspoon ground allspice
- ½ teaspoon ground cinnamon
- ⅓ cup tomato paste
- 1½ cups water
- ¼ cup frozen orange juice concentrate, thawed
- 3 tablespoons distilled white vinegar
- 1½ tablespoons Worcestershire sauce
- 5 bay leaves
  Salt and pepper
- 1 (2½- to 3-pound) boneless pork butt roast, trimmed and cut into 1-inch chunks

Pickled Red Onions

- 1 red onion, halved and sliced thin
- 1 cup distilled white vinegar
- ⅓ cup sugar
- ¼ teaspoon salt

Habanero Sauce

- 1 cup water
- 1 carrot, peeled and chopped
- 1 vine-ripened tomato, cored and chopped
- ¼ cup chopped onion
- ½ habanero chile, stemmed
- 1 garlic clove, smashed and peeled
  Salt and pepper
- 1 tablespoon distilled white vinegar
- 1½ teaspoons lime juice, plus lime wedges for serving

18 (6-inch) corn tortillas, warmed

1 For the pork Adjust oven rack to lower-middle position and heat oven to 300 degrees. Heat oil in Dutch oven over medium heat until shimmering. Add onion and cook until lightly browned, 4 to 6 minutes. Stir in garlic, cumin, oregano, allspice, and cinnamon and cook until fragrant, about 30 seconds. Add tomato paste and cook, stirring constantly, until paste begins to darken, about 45 seconds. Stir in water, orange juice concentrate, 2 tablespoons vinegar, Worcestershire, bay leaves, 2 teaspoons salt, and 1 teaspoon pepper, scraping up any browned bits.

2 Add pork and bring to boil. Transfer pot to oven and cook, uncovered, until pork is tender, about 2 hours, stirring once halfway through cooking.

3 For the pickled red onions Meanwhile, place onion in medium bowl. Bring vinegar, sugar, and salt to simmer in small saucepan over medium-high heat, stirring occasionally, until sugar dissolves. Pour over onions and cover loosely. Let onions cool completely, about 30 minutes. (Onions can be refrigerated for up to 1 week.)

4 For the habanero sauce Combine water, carrot, tomato, onion, habanero, garlic, and ½ teaspoon salt in now-empty saucepan. Bring to boil over medium heat and cook until carrot is tender, about 10 minutes. Off heat, let carrot mixture cool slightly, about 5 minutes.

Transfer carrot mixture to blender, add vinegar and lime juice, and process until smooth, 1 to 2 minutes. Season sauce with salt and pepper to taste; set aside. (Sauce can be refrigerated for up to 1 week.)

5 Remove pot from oven; discard bay leaves. Using potato masher, mash pork until finely shredded. Bring to simmer over medium-high heat and cook until most of liquid has evaporated, 3 to 5 minutes. Off heat, stir in remaining 1 tablespoon vinegar and season with salt and pepper to taste. Serve pork on tortillas with pickled red onions, habanero sauce, and lime wedges.

INDOOR PULLED PORK WITH SWEET AND TANGY BARBECUE SAUCE

SERVES 8 TO 10   TOTAL TIME 5 HOURS 30 MINUTES

WHY THIS RECIPE WORKS Barbecued pulled pork is hard to beat: Tender shreds of smoky, juicy meat are enrobed in a tangy-sweet sauce and piled high on a soft bun. But when outdoor cooking is out of the question, is this dish off the table? We wanted an indoor recipe for pulled pork that would boast the same smoky, tender meat as our favorite grilled versions. We discovered that starting the roast in a covered Dutch oven was key—the trapped steam and moisture allowed the large roast to cook through without drying out. Tasters approved of the meltingly tender meat but noted that it lacked the crisp crust of true barbecued pork. To fix this, we uncovered the pot for the last 30 minutes of cooking to create the coveted crust. Splitting the pork butt in half created more surface area, which translated into even more crust and a shorter overall cooking time. To infuse the pork with smoky flavor, we added a bit of liquid smoke to the brine and incorporated more into a wet rub. We also sprinkled the pork with a mixture of smoked paprika, cayenne, salt, pepper, and sugar. Pork butt roast is often labeled Boston butt in the supermarket. Lexington Vinegar Barbecue Sauce or South Carolina Mustard Barbecue Sauce (recipes follow) can be substituted for the Sweet and Tangy Barbecue Sauce. Serve the pork on hamburger buns with pickle chips.

Pork

Salt and pepper
½ cup plus 2 tablespoons sugar
3 tablespoons plus 2 teaspoons liquid smoke
1 (5-pound) boneless pork butt roast, trimmed and cut in half
¼ cup yellow mustard
2 tablespoons smoked paprika
1 teaspoon cayenne pepper

Sweet and Tangy Barbecue Sauce

1½ cups ketchup
¼ cup molasses
2 tablespoons Worcestershire sauce
1 tablespoon hot sauce

1 For the pork Dissolve 1 cup salt, ½ cup sugar, and 3 tablespoons liquid smoke in 4 quarts cold water in large container. Submerge pork in brine, cover, and refrigerate for 1½ to 2 hours.

2 Adjust oven rack to lower-middle position and heat oven to 325 degrees. Combine mustard and remaining 2 teaspoons liquid smoke in bowl. Combine paprika, cayenne, 2 teaspoons salt, 2 tablespoons pepper, and remaining 2 tablespoons sugar in second bowl. Remove pork from brine and pat dry with paper towels. Rub with mustard mixture, then sprinkle with paprika mixture. Place pork in Dutch oven. Cover, transfer pot to oven, and cook for 2½ hours.

3 Remove pot from oven and transfer pork to bowl. Pour liquid in pot into fat separator and set aside. Return pork to now-empty pot, return to oven, and cook, uncovered, until pork is well browned, tender, and registers 200 degrees, about 30 minutes.

4 Remove pot from oven. Transfer pork to carving board, tent loosely with aluminum foil, and let rest for 20 minutes. Using 2 forks, shred pork into bite-size pieces; discard fat.

5 For the sweet and tangy barbecue sauce Pour ½ cup defatted cooking liquid into medium bowl. Whisk in all of sauce ingredients until combined. Transfer pork to large bowl and toss with 1 cup sauce. Season with salt and pepper to taste. Serve, passing remaining sauce separately.

LEXINGTON VINEGAR BARBECUE SAUCE
MAKES ABOUT 2½ CUPS

- 1 cup cider vinegar
- ½ cup ketchup
- ½ cup water
- 1 tablespoon sugar
- ¾ teaspoon red pepper flakes
  Salt and pepper

Place all ingredients in medium bowl, add ½ cup defatted cooking liquid reserved from step 3, and whisk to combine; season with salt and pepper to taste.

SOUTH CAROLINA MUSTARD BARBECUE SAUCE
MAKES ABOUT 2½ CUPS

- 1 cup yellow mustard
- ½ cup distilled white vinegar
- ¼ cup packed light brown sugar
- ¼ cup Worcestershire sauce
- 2 tablespoons hot sauce
  Salt and pepper

Place all ingredients in medium bowl, add ½ cup defatted cooking liquid reserved from step 3, and whisk to combine; season with salt and pepper to taste.

BRAISED LAMB SHOULDER CHOPS WITH TOMATOES AND WARM SPICES

SERVES 4   TOTAL TIME 2 HOURS 15 MINUTES TO 2 HOURS 45 MINUTES

WHY THIS RECIPE WORKS When buying lamb chops, many people turn to the tried-and-true—and expensive—rib or loin chop. But for braising we love shoulder chops: This inexpensive cut is less exacting to cook, and its assertive flavor and somewhat chewy texture take beautifully to the moist cooking method. To ensure tender meat and a rich, flavorful sauce, we started by searing the chops to create fond and then built our sauce right in the pot. To stand up to the robustly flavored chops, we used plenty of assertive ingredients such as onion; garlic; warm spices like coriander, cumin, and cinnamon; and canned tomatoes for balanced acidity. Cooking the chops in the oven, covered, turned them tender and supple. Adding parsley at the last minute offered a hit of freshness to offset the richly flavored sauce.

4   (8- to 12-ounce) lamb shoulder chops (blade or round bone), about ¾ inch thick, trimmed
    Salt and pepper
1   tablespoon extra-virgin olive oil
1   onion, chopped fine
2   garlic cloves, minced
1   teaspoon ground coriander
½   teaspoon ground cumin
½   teaspoon ground cinnamon
⅛   teaspoon cayenne pepper
¾   cup chicken broth
1   (28-ounce) can whole peeled tomatoes, drained with juice reserved, chopped
2   tablespoons minced fresh parsley

1 Adjust oven rack to middle position and heat oven to 300 degrees. Pat chops dry with paper towels and season with salt and pepper. Heat oil in Dutch oven over medium-high heat until just smoking. Brown half of chops, about 3 minutes per side; transfer to plate. Repeat with remaining chops; transfer to plate.

2 Add onion to fat left in pot and cook over medium heat until softened, about 5 minutes. Stir in garlic, coriander, cumin, cinnamon, and cayenne and cook until fragrant, about 30 seconds. Stir in broth and tomatoes and their juice, scraping up any browned bits, and bring to simmer.

3 Nestle chops into pot, adding any accumulated juices. Cover, transfer pot to oven, and cook until lamb is tender and fork slips easily in and out of meat, 1½ to 2 hours, flipping chops halfway through cooking.

4 Remove pot from oven and transfer chops to serving platter. Stir parsley into braising liquid and season with salt and pepper to taste. Spoon sauce over chops and serve.

LEG OF LAMB WITH GARLIC AND ROSEMARY JUS

SERVES 8 TO 10   TOTAL TIME 2 HOURS 45 MINUTES

WHY THIS RECIPE WORKS Like chicken, leg of lamb is commonly cooked *en cocotte* in France, in a covered pot at low heat, yielding its own flavorful jus, with no braising liquid necessary. We were drawn to the promise of succulent, tender meat with minimal hands-on work. Although a bone-in leg of lamb makes for a dramatic presentation, we had no chance of fitting one in our Dutch oven, so we turned to boneless and tied it into an even cylinder. Browning the roast boosted savory flavor and rendered some of the lamb's fat, which kept our finished dish from becoming greasy or gamy. Some sliced garlic and rosemary—classic flavorings with lamb—provided aromatic depth. A stint in a low oven produced perfectly tender meat and a flavorful jus. We prefer the subtler flavor and larger size of lamb labeled "domestic" or "American" for this recipe.

1 (4- to 5-pound) boneless half leg of lamb, trimmed
   Salt and pepper
2 tablespoons extra-virgin olive oil
8 garlic cloves, peeled and sliced thin
2 sprigs fresh rosemary

1 Place roast with rough interior side (which was against bone) facing up on cutting board and season with salt and pepper. Starting from short side, roll roast tightly and tie with kitchen twine at 1-inch intervals. Pat dry with paper towels and season exterior with salt and pepper. Transfer to plate, cover, and refrigerate for at least 1 hour or up to 24 hours.

2 Adjust oven rack to lowest position and heat oven to 250 degrees. Heat oil in Dutch oven over medium-high heat until just smoking. Brown roast on all sides, 8 to 10 minutes; transfer to plate.

3 Pour off fat from pot. Return roast to now-empty pot along with any accumulated juices. Add garlic and rosemary sprigs, cover, and transfer to oven. Cook until lamb registers 120 to 125 degrees (for medium-rare) or 130 to 135 degrees (for medium), 45 to 60 minutes, flipping roast halfway through cooking.

4 Remove pot from oven. Transfer roast to carving board, tent with aluminum foil, and let rest for 20 minutes. Discard rosemary sprigs and cover pot to keep jus warm.

5 Discard twine, slice roast into ½-inch-thick slices, and transfer to serving platter. Spoon jus over lamb and serve.

TYING A BONELESS LAMB ROAST

1 Starting from short side, roll roast tightly.

2 Tie with kitchen twine at 1-inch intervals.

SPICED LAMB POT ROAST WITH FIGS

SERVES 8 TO 10   TOTAL TIME 4 HOURS 45 MINUTES TO 5 HOURS 15 MINUTES

WHY THIS RECIPE WORKS Less common (and less expensive) than leg of lamb, a lamb shoulder roast is an intensely flavorful cut. It's ideal for slow braising, which breaks down the collagen and fats that add flavor and body to the cooking liquid, and produces fall-apart tender meat. We found that braising it in the oven—and turning it once halfway through cooking—provided more even heat than cooking on the stovetop, and browning the shoulder first added complex flavors. What really elevated this dish, however, was to simmer the lamb in ruby port along with rosemary and aromatics. After the long braise, the liquid turned rich and deeply flavored. While the lamb rested, we defatted the liquid, reduced it, and then stirred in figs, creating a auce that had a great balance of salty, sweet, and tart notes. For even more flavor, and to help the lamb stay juicy throughout cooking, we seasoned the roast inside and out with a mixture of ground coriander, ground fennel seed, and salt. A sprinkling of parsley added pleasant freshness. We prefer the subtler flavor and larger size of lamb labeled "domestic" or "American" for this recipe. For more information on tying a boneless lamb roast, see page 182.

1 tablespoon ground coriander
2 teaspoons ground fennel
Salt and pepper
1 (4- to 5-pound) boneless lamb shoulder, trimmed
2 tablespoons extra-virgin olive oil
1 onion, chopped fine
5 garlic cloves, minced
2 cups ruby port
2 sprigs fresh rosemary
12 ounces fresh figs, stemmed and quartered
¼ cup chopped fresh parsley

1 Combine coriander, fennel, 1½ teaspoons salt, and 1½ teaspoons pepper in bowl. Place roast with rough interior side (which was against bone) facing up on cutting board and sprinkle with 4 teaspoons spice mixture. Starting from short side, roll roast tightly and tie with kitchen twine at 1-inch intervals. Sprinkle exterior with remaining spice mixture. Transfer to plate, cover, and refrigerate for at least 1 hour or up to 24 hours.

2 Adjust oven rack to lower-middle position and heat oven to 300 degrees. Pat roast dry with paper towels. Heat oil in Dutch oven over medium-high heat until just smoking. Brown roast on all sides, 8 to 10 minutes; transfer to plate.

3 Pour off all but 1 tablespoon fat from pot. Add onion and cook over medium heat until softened, about 5 minutes. Stir in garlic and cook until fragrant, about 30 seconds. Stir in port, scraping up any browned bits, and bring to simmer. Return roast to pot, adding any accumulated juices. Add rosemary sprigs, cover, and transfer pot to oven. Cook until lamb is tender and fork slips easily in and out of meat, 2¼ to 2¾ hours, flipping roast halfway through cooking.

4 Remove pot from oven. Transfer roast to carving board, tent with aluminum foil, and let rest while finishing sauce. Discard rosemary sprigs and strain braising liquid through fine-mesh strainer into fat separator; reserve solids. Allow braising liquid to settle for 5 minutes. Add defatted braising liquid and reserved solids to now-empty pot and bring to simmer over medium-high heat. Cook until slightly thickened and reduced to 1½ cups, about 10 minutes. Stir in figs and cook until heated through, about 2 minutes. Season with salt and pepper to taste.

5 Discard twine, slice roast into ½-inch-thick slices, and transfer to serving platter. Spoon sauce over lamb and sprinkle with parsley. Serve.

BRAISED COD PEPERONATA

SERVES 4   TOTAL TIME 1 HOUR

WHY THIS RECIPE WORKS A brief stovetop braise is the perfect way to cook delicate white fish like cod, since it keeps the fish moist and silky while creating a sauce at the same time. To give the mild fillets a boost of flavor, we paired them with a Spanish-style peperonata, a combination of cooked bell peppers and onions, to which we added tomatoes, wine, paprika, and fresh thyme for depth of flavor. We then simply nestled the cod right into the pepper mixture and covered the Dutch oven. The sauce infused the fish fillets as they braised and protected them from the heat so they stayed tender. Haddock and hake are good substitutes for the cod.

2 tablespoons extra-virgin olive oil, plus extra
   for serving
1 onion, halved and sliced thin
2 red bell peppers, stemmed, seeded, and sliced thin
   Salt and pepper
4 garlic cloves, minced
2 teaspoons paprika
1 (14.5-ounce) can diced tomatoes, drained
½ cup dry white wine
1 teaspoon minced fresh thyme or ¼ teaspoon dried
4 (6- to 8-ounce) skinless cod fillets, 1 to
   1½ inches thick
2 tablespoons chopped fresh basil
   Sherry or balsamic vinegar

1 Heat oil in Dutch oven over medium heat until shimmering. Add onion, bell peppers, and ½ teaspoon salt and cook until vegetables are softened, about 5 minutes. Stir in garlic and paprika and cook until fragrant, about 30 seconds. Stir in tomatoes, wine, and thyme and bring to simmer.

2 Season cod with salt and pepper. Nestle cod, skinned side down, into pot and spoon some of sauce over fish. Cover, reduce heat to medium-low, and cook until fish flakes apart when gently prodded with paring knife and registers 140 degrees, about 10 minutes.

3 Season sauce with salt and pepper to taste. Sprinkle with basil and vinegar, and drizzle with extra oil before serving.

HAKE IN SAFFRON BROTH WITH CHORIZO AND POTATOES

SERVES 4   TOTAL TIME 1 HOUR

WHY THIS RECIPE WORKS This elegant and easy dish relies on bold Spanish flavors like fragrant saffron and spicy chorizo to bring mild hake to life. The hake's delicate texture and light flavor made it perfect for a moist cooking method, so we created a flavorful saffron broth with aromatics, white wine, and clam juice, which pulled double duty as both a braising liquid and a broth to serve with the fish. Spanish-style chorizo and onions, browned to bring out savory notes, lent subtle heat and depth to the broth. Tasters thought the dish was delicious, but they wanted a starchy element in the mix to round out the meal. Waxy red potatoes, sliced into coins to mirror the slices of chorizo, brought in just the right creaminess and soaked up some of the flavorful broth. A hit of lemon added brightness to the broth at the end of cooking, and a sprinkle of parsley and a drizzle of olive oil on the flaky fish, immersed in the fragrant saffron liquid, brought it all together. Haddock and cod are good substitutes for the hake. Use small red potatoes measuring 1 to 2 inches in diameter. Serve with crusty bread to dip into the broth.

1 tablespoon extra-virgin olive oil, plus extra for serving

1 onion, chopped fine

3 ounces Spanish-style chorizo sausage, sliced ¼ inch thick

4 garlic cloves, minced

¼ teaspoon saffron threads, crumbled

1 (8-ounce) bottle clam juice

¾ cup water

½ cup dry white wine

4 ounces small red potatoes, unpeeled, sliced ¼ inch thick

1 bay leaf

4 (6- to 8-ounce) skinless hake fillets, 1 to 1½ inches thick
Salt and pepper

1 teaspoon lemon juice

2 tablespoons minced fresh parsley

1 Heat oil in Dutch oven over medium heat until shimmering. Add onion and chorizo and cook until onion is softened and lightly browned, 5 to 7 minutes. Stir in garlic and saffron and cook until fragrant, about 30 seconds. Stir in clam juice, water, wine, potatoes, and bay leaf and bring to simmer. Reduce heat to medium-low, cover, and cook until potatoes are almost tender, about 10 minutes.

2 Pat hake dry with paper towels and season with salt and pepper. Nestle hake, skinned side down, into pot and spoon some broth over top. Bring to simmer, cover, and cook until potatoes are fully tender and hake flakes apart when gently prodded with paring knife and registers 140 degrees, 10 to 12 minutes.

3 Carefully transfer hake to individual shallow bowls. Using slotted spoon, divide potatoes and chorizo evenly among bowls. Discard bay leaf. Stir lemon juice into broth and season with salt and pepper to taste. Spoon broth over hake, sprinkle with parsley, and drizzle with extra oil. Serve.

BRAISED WHITE BEANS WITH LINGUIÇA AND CLAMS

SERVES 6 TO 8   TOTAL TIME 2 HOURS 30 MINUTES (PLUS SOAKING TIME)

WHY THIS RECIPE WORKS While white beans are usually matched with rich meats in a braise (think cassoulet), we paired them with briny clams and smoky linguiça sausage for a Portuguese-inspired meal that was satisfying without being too heavy. We browned the sausage in our Dutch oven, added a hefty amount of aromatics, spices, and tomato paste for a deeply flavorful backbone, stirred in white wine and water, then slowly braised the beans in the oven until tender. We chose dried beans so they could absorb the flavorful braising liquid and in turn thicken the sauce by releasing their starch. We tucked clams into the beans partway through cooking, which prevented them from turning rubbery. A quick topping made from toasted panko and lemon zest added brightness and crunch to the dish. If linguiça is unavailable, substitute chorizo. If you're pressed for time, you can quick-salt-soak your beans: In step 1, combine the salt, water, and beans in a Dutch oven and bring them to a boil over high heat. Remove the pot from the heat, cover, and let stand for 1 hour. Drain and rinse the beans, wipe the pot clean, and proceed with the recipe.

Salt and pepper
1 pound (2½ cups) dried cannellini beans, picked over and rinsed
1 tablespoon extra-virgin olive oil
½ cup panko bread crumbs
1 teaspoon grated lemon zest, plus lemon wedges for serving
1 pound linguiça sausage, cut into ½-inch pieces
1 onion, chopped fine
1 red bell pepper, stemmed, seeded, and chopped fine
4 garlic cloves, minced
1 tablespoon tomato paste
1 tablespoon smoked paprika
½ teaspoon cayenne pepper
½ cup dry white wine
2 pounds littleneck clams, scrubbed
¼ cup minced fresh parsley

1 Dissolve 3 tablespoons salt in 4 quarts cold water in large container. Add beans and soak at room temperature for at least 8 hours or up to 24 hours. Drain and rinse well.

2 Adjust oven rack to lower-middle position and heat oven to 250 degrees. Heat oil in Dutch oven over medium heat. Add panko and cook, stirring constantly, until golden brown, 5 to 7 minutes. Transfer panko to bowl and stir in lemon zest and ¼ teaspoon pepper; set aside. Wipe pot clean with paper towels.

3 Add sausage to pot and cook over medium heat until rendered and browned, 5 to 7 minutes. Stir in onion and bell pepper and cook until softened, about 5 minutes. Stir in garlic, tomato paste, paprika, cayenne, and ⅛ teaspoon pepper and cook until fragrant, about 30 seconds. Stir in wine, scraping up any browned bits. Stir in 4 cups water and beans and bring to boil. Cover, transfer pot to oven, and cook until beans are almost tender (very center of beans will still be firm), 1 to 1¼ hours.

4 Remove pot from oven and increase oven temperature to 350 degrees. Using wide, shallow spoon, skim excess fat from surface of beans. Nestle clams, hinge side down, into beans. Cover, return pot to oven, and cook until clams have opened, 35 to 45 minutes.

5 Remove pot from oven and let sit, covered, for 5 minutes. Discard any clams that refuse to open. Stir parsley into panko mixture. Sprinkle individual portions with panko mixture and serve with lemon wedges.

FOOLPROOF FRYING

Coconut Shrimp with Mango Dipping Sauce

EXTRA-CRUNCHY FRIED CHICKEN

SERVES 4 TOTAL TIME 1 HOUR (PLUS BRINING TIME)

WHY THIS RECIPE WORKS Making fried chicken at home can be a messy, labor-intensive ordeal that rarely yields the satisfyingly crunchy crust that makes fried chicken great. Our Dutch oven helped us sidestep many of these common pitfalls. The high sides of the Dutch oven helped contain the mess, as did keeping the pot covered during the first half of the frying time. A covered pot had a couple more advantages as well: It captured escaping steam and made the chicken even more moist, and it helped the oil recover heat quickly once the chicken was added. This more-constant oil temperature was essential for getting fried chicken that was neither too brown nor too greasy. As for the chicken itself, we brined it in salted buttermilk to make sure it was well seasoned and juicy. For the crunchy coating, we found that flour alone didn't provide much crunch; instead, we combined the flour with a little baking powder, then added just enough buttermilk to make a thick mixture that clung tightly to the meat. Depending on the size of your Dutch oven, you may need to fry the chicken in two batches; keep the first batch warm on a clean wire rack in a 200-degree oven and return the oil to 375 degrees before frying the second batch. If desired, you can remove the skin from the chicken before soaking it in the buttermilk, but the chicken will be slightly less crunchy.

2 tablespoons salt

2 cups plus 6 tablespoons buttermilk

1 (3½- to 4-pound) whole chicken, cut into 8 pieces (4 breast pieces, 2 drumsticks, 2 thighs), wings and giblets discarded

3 cups all-purpose flour

2 teaspoons baking powder

¾ teaspoon dried thyme

½ teaspoon pepper

¼ teaspoon garlic powder

1 quart peanut or vegetable oil

1 Dissolve salt in 2 cups buttermilk in large container. Submerge chicken in brine, cover, and refrigerate for 1 hour.

2 Whisk flour, baking powder, thyme, pepper, and garlic powder together in large bowl. Add remaining 6 tablespoons buttermilk; with your fingers, rub flour mixture and buttermilk together until buttermilk is evenly incorporated and mixture resembles coarse, wet sand.

3 Set wire rack inside rimmed baking sheet. Working with 1 piece at a time, remove chicken from brine, letting excess drip back into container, and dredge in flour mixture, pressing to adhere. Gently shake excess flour mixture from each piece of chicken and transfer to prepared wire rack.

4 Line platter with triple layer of paper towels. Add oil to Dutch oven until it measures about ¾ inch deep and heat over medium-high heat to 375 degrees. Place chicken pieces, skin side down, in hot oil, cover, and fry until deep golden brown, 8 to 10 minutes. Remove lid after 4 minutes and lift chicken pieces to check for even browning; rearrange if some pieces are browning faster than others. Adjust burner, if necessary, to maintain oil temperature between 300 and 315 degrees.

5 Turn chicken pieces over and continue to fry, uncovered, until chicken pieces are deep golden brown on second side and breasts register 160 degrees and thighs and drumsticks register 175 degrees, 6 to 8 minutes. Using tongs, transfer chicken to prepared platter; let sit for 5 minutes. Serve.

RANCH FRIED CHICKEN

SERVES 4 TO 6   **TOTAL TIME** 1 HOUR 15 MINUTES

WHY THIS RECIPE WORKS We wanted to get the fresh, tangy flavor of ranch dressing into a coating for fried chicken. But the herbs that give ranch its hallmark flavor quickly lost their taste in hot oil. We got around this problem by swapping in thinner boneless chicken thighs for the usual bone-in chicken pieces; the thighs needed much less time to cook through, so the herbs didn't spend as much time in the oil. We incorporated the herbs—chives, cilantro, and dill—in three places: in the buttermilk mixture and the flour coating for the chicken, as well as in a creamy dipping sauce for serving.

Buttermilk Mixture

- 1 cup buttermilk
- 2 tablespoons minced fresh chives
- 2 tablespoons minced fresh cilantro
- 2 teaspoons minced fresh dill
- 2 teaspoons distilled white vinegar
- 1 garlic clove, minced
- ½ teaspoon salt
- Pinch cayenne pepper

Chicken and Coating

- 8 (5- to 7-ounce) boneless, skinless chicken thighs, trimmed
- Salt and pepper
- 1¼ cups all-purpose flour
- ½ cup cornstarch
- 3 tablespoons minced fresh chives
- 3 tablespoons minced fresh cilantro
- 1 tablespoon minced fresh dill
- 1½ teaspoons garlic powder
- 2 quarts peanut or vegetable oil

Ranch Sauce

- ½ cup mayonnaise
- Salt and pepper

1 For the buttermilk mixture Whisk all ingredients together in large bowl. Set aside ¼ cup buttermilk mixture in small bowl for ranch sauce.

2 For the chicken and coating Pat chicken dry with paper towels and season with salt and pepper. Whisk flour, cornstarch, chives, cilantro, dill, garlic powder, 1½ teaspoons salt, and ¾ teaspoon pepper together in large bowl.

3 Set wire rack in rimmed baking sheet. Working with 1 piece at a time, dip chicken in remaining buttermilk mixture to coat, letting excess drip back into bowl, then dredge in coating, pressing to adhere. Transfer chicken to prepared wire rack. (Chicken can be refrigerated, uncovered, for up to 2 hours.)

4 Add oil to Dutch oven until it measures about 1½ inches deep and heat over medium-high heat to 350 degrees. Set second wire rack in second rimmed baking sheet and line half of rack with triple layer of paper towels. Add half of chicken to hot oil and fry until golden brown and registers 175 degrees, 7 to 9 minutes. Adjust burner, if necessary, to maintain oil temperature between 325 and 350 degrees.

5 Transfer chicken to paper towel–lined side of second wire rack to drain on each side for 30 seconds, then move to unlined side of rack. Return oil to 350 degrees and repeat with remaining chicken.

6 For the ranch sauce Whisk mayonnaise into reserved buttermilk mixture. Season with salt and pepper to taste. Serve chicken, passing sauce separately.

KOREAN FRIED CHICKEN WINGS

SERVES 4 TO 6   TOTAL TIME 1 HOUR 15 MINUTES

WHY THIS RECIPE WORKS Korean fried chicken is exceptionally crispy, with a paper-thin coating achieved by double frying. Each piece is then painted with an addictively tangy, sweet-spicy sauce. To keep the coating crisp even under the sauce, we followed tradition and double-fried the wings. Our sauce mixed spicy, sweet, and savory for the perfect balance of flavors. We tried different types of coatings for our chicken—a simple dusting of cornstarch, a light batter of cornstarch and water, and a heavy batter of eggs, cornstarch, and water. We preferred the middle ground—the cornstarch and water batter—which yielded a light, crisp crust, especially if we let the excess batter drip off before frying. A rasp-style grater makes quick work of turning the garlic into a paste. *Gochujang*, Korean hot red chili paste, can be found in Asian markets and some supermarkets; tailor the heat level of your wings by adjusting the amount you use. If you can't find gochujang, substitute an equal amount of Sriracha sauce and add only 2 tablespoons of water to the sauce. Depending on the size of your Dutch oven, you may need to fry the wings in two batches rather than one in step 4; keep the first batch warm on a second wire rack set in a second rimmed baking sheet in a 200-degree oven, and return the oil to 375 degrees before frying the second batch.

1 tablespoon toasted sesame oil
1 teaspoon garlic, minced to paste
1 teaspoon grated fresh ginger
1¾ cups water
3 tablespoons sugar
2–3 tablespoons gochujang
1 tablespoon soy sauce
2 quarts peanut or vegetable oil
1 cup all-purpose flour
3 tablespoons cornstarch
3 pounds chicken wings, cut at joints, wingtips discarded

1 Combine sesame oil, garlic, and ginger in large bowl and microwave until mixture is bubbly and garlic and ginger are fragrant but not browned, 40 to 60 seconds. Whisk in ¼ cup water, sugar, gochujang, and soy sauce until smooth; set aside.

2 Add peanut oil to Dutch oven until it measures about 1½ inches deep and heat over medium-high heat to 350 degrees. Set wire rack in rimmed baking sheet. Whisk flour, cornstarch, and remaining 1½ cups water in second large bowl until smooth.

3 Place half of wings in batter and stir to coat. Using tongs, remove wings from batter 1 at a time, allowing excess batter to drip back into bowl, and add to hot oil. Increase heat to high and fry, stirring occasionally to prevent wings from sticking, until coating is light golden and beginning to crisp, about 7 minutes. (Oil temperature will drop sharply after adding wings.) Using wire skimmer or slotted spoon, transfer wings to prepared wire rack. Return oil to 350 degrees and repeat with remaining wings; transfer to wire rack and let wings rest for 5 minutes.

4 Reduce heat to medium and heat oil to 375 degrees. Carefully return all wings to oil and fry, stirring occasionally, until deep golden brown and very crispy, about 7 minutes. Return wings to rack and let sit for 2 minutes. Transfer wings to reserved sauce and toss until coated. Return wings to rack and let sit for 2 minutes to allow coating to set. Transfer to serving platter and serve.

TEXAS CHICKEN-FRIED STEAKS

SERVES 4   TOTAL TIME 1 HOUR 30 MINUTES

WHY THIS RECIPE WORKS Chicken-fried steak is typically an inexpensive cut of meat that is pounded to tenderness, breaded, fried, and served with a peppery gravy. We chose steak tips for the best flavor and texture, and scored them to improve tenderness. We then pounded seasoned flour right into the meat to ensure the coating stuck fast. Once the steaks were dredged, we let them rest in the fridge for 15 minutes to set the crust, then recoated them just before frying. Using our Dutch oven to shallow-fry rather than deep-fry the steaks contained the splatter. Avoid using low-fat or skim milk in the gravy. Sirloin steak tips are often sold as flap meat. We prefer to buy a whole 1-pound steak and cut our own steak tips.

Gravy

- 3 tablespoons unsalted butter
- 3 tablespoons all-purpose flour
- ½ teaspoon garlic powder
- 1½ cups chicken broth
- 1½ cups whole milk
- ¾ teaspoon salt
- ½ teaspoon pepper

Steaks

- 3½ cups all-purpose flour
- ½ cup cornstarch
- 1 tablespoon garlic powder
- 1 tablespoon onion powder
- 2 teaspoons baking powder
  Salt and pepper
- ½ teaspoon cayenne pepper
- 4 large eggs
- ¼ cup whole milk
- 4 (4-ounce) sirloin steak tips
- 1 quart peanut or vegetable oil

1 For the gravy Melt butter in 12-inch skillet over medium heat. Stir in flour and garlic powder and cook until golden, about 2 minutes. Slowly whisk in broth, milk, salt, and pepper and simmer until thickened, about 5 minutes. Cover and set aside.

2 For the steaks Whisk flour, cornstarch, garlic powder, onion powder, baking powder, 2 teaspoons pepper, 1 teaspoon salt, and cayenne together in bowl. Transfer 1 cup seasoned flour mixture to shallow dish.

Beat eggs in second shallow dish. Stir milk into remaining flour mixture, rub with your fingers until mixture resembles coarse meal, and transfer to third shallow dish.

3 Set wire rack in rimmed baking sheet. Pat steaks dry with paper towels and season with salt and pepper. Lightly score both sides of steaks in ¼-inch crosshatch pattern. Working with 1 piece at a time, coat steaks lightly with seasoned flour, place between 2 sheets of plastic wrap, and pound to ⅛- to ¼-inch thickness with meat pounder. Coat steaks again with seasoned flour, dip in egg, and dredge in milk-flour mixture, pressing firmly to adhere. Transfer steaks to prepared wire rack and refrigerate for 15 minutes; do not discard milk-flour mixture.

4 Adjust oven rack to middle position and heat oven to 200 degrees. Set second wire rack in second rimmed baking sheet. Add oil to Dutch oven until it measures about ¾ inch deep and heat over medium-high heat to 350 degrees. Working with 2 steaks at a time, return steaks to milk-flour mixture and turn to coat. Fry steaks until deep golden brown and crispy, 4 to 6 minutes, flipping as needed to ensure even browning. Adjust burner, if necessary, to maintain oil temperature between 325 and 350 degrees. Transfer to second prepared wire rack and keep warm in oven. Repeat with remaining 2 steaks.

5 Meanwhile, warm gravy over medium-low heat, stirring occasionally. Serve steaks, passing gravy separately.

FRIED PORK SANDWICHES

SERVES 4   TOTAL TIME 45 MINUTES

WHY THIS RECIPE WORKS This simple sandwich, known in the Midwest as an Iowa skinny, is composed of a pan-fried pork tenderloin cutlet, lettuce, tomato, and mayonnaise served on a bun. The flavor of the pork is the star of the show, and the textural interplay of crispy crust, juicy meat, cool veggies, and creamy mayo means that each bite is interesting and fresh. We began our recipe with the most important element: the pork. The cutlet is typically prepared from one of two cuts of pork: boneless loin chops or tenderloin. Our tasters unanimously favored the cutlets made from the tenderloin, which yielded more tender, less-fatty cutlets with mild yet distinct flavor. Some versions of this sandwich use cutlets that extend well beyond the bun's edges, but we needed to make sure our cutlets could fit comfortably in our Dutch oven, so we opted for 4-ounce portions and shallow-fried the cutlets two at a time. Adding saltines to our bread-crumb coating boosted the coating's flavor. With some fresh tomato, crisp iceberg, and a swipe of creamy mayo on a soft bun, our Iowa skinnies were complete. Pickles also make a good topping for these sandwiches.

1 (1-pound) pork tenderloin, trimmed
   Salt and pepper
3 slices hearty white sandwich bread, torn into quarters
16 square or 18 round saltines
½ cup all-purpose flour
2 large eggs
¼ cup mayonnaise, plus extra for serving
1 quart peanut or vegetable oil
4 hamburger buns
1 tomato, cored and sliced thin
   Shredded iceberg lettuce

1 Cut tenderloin in half, then cut each half in half again, cutting tapered tail pieces slightly thicker than middle medallions. Working with 1 piece at a time, place pork, cut side up, between 2 sheets of plastic wrap and pound to ¼-inch thickness with meat pounder. Pat cutlets dry with paper towels and season with salt and pepper.

2 Pulse bread and saltines in food processor to fine crumbs, about 20 pulses; transfer to shallow dish. Spread flour in second shallow dish. Whisk eggs and mayonnaise together in third shallow dish.

3 Set wire rack in rimmed baking sheet. Working with 1 cutlet at a time, dredge in flour, dip in egg mixture, then coat with bread-crumb mixture, pressing gently to adhere. Transfer cutlets to prepared wire rack and let rest for 5 minutes. (Cutlets can be refrigerated for up to 1 hour.)

4 Adjust oven rack to middle position and heat oven to 200 degrees. Line platter with triple layer of paper towels. Add oil to Dutch oven until it measures about ¾ inch deep and heat over medium-high heat to 350 degrees. Fry 2 cutlets until deep golden brown and crispy, 4 to 6 minutes, flipping as needed to ensure even browning. Adjust burner, if necessary, to maintain oil temperature between 325 and 350 degrees. Transfer cutlets to prepared platter and keep warm in oven. Repeat with remaining cutlets. Serve on hamburger buns with tomato, lettuce, and extra mayonnaise.

FISH AND CHIPS

SERVES 4   TOTAL TIME 1 HOUR 30 MINUTES

WHY THIS RECIPE WORKS For authentic pub-style fish and chips, we began with the fries (or "chips"). Our tried-and-true test kitchen method—starting sliced Yukon Gold potatoes in room-temperature oil, then bringing the oil up to temperature to cook the fries—worked well. To get everything on the table at the same time, we parcooked the fries, set them aside while we cooked the fish, then put the potatoes back in the hot oil at the end to finish cooking. As for the fish, a simple beer batter worked perfectly to create an airy-yet-crisp exterior. Try to find large Yukon Gold potatoes, 10 to 12 ounces each, that are similar in size. If you prefer, you can substitute seltzer for the beer. Haddock and halibut can be substituted for the cod. Serve with Tartar Sauce or Rémoulade.

  1 cup all-purpose flour
  1 cup cornstarch
     Salt and pepper
  1 teaspoon baking powder
1½ cups mild lager, such as Budweiser
  1 (2-pound) skinless cod fillet, about 1 inch thick
2½ pounds large Yukon Gold potatoes, unpeeled
  2 quarts peanut or vegetable oil
     Lemon wedges

1 Whisk flour, cornstarch, 1½ teaspoons salt, and baking powder together in large bowl. Whisk in beer until smooth. Cover with plastic wrap and refrigerate for at least 20 minutes or up to 1 hour.

2 Cut cod crosswise into 8 equal fillets (about 4 ounces each). Pat cod dry with paper towels and season with salt and pepper; refrigerate until ready to use.

3 Square off each potato by cutting ¼-inch-thick slice from each of its 4 long sides. Cut potatoes lengthwise into ¼-inch-thick planks. Stack 3 to 4 planks and cut into ¼-inch-thick fries. Repeat with remaining planks. (Do not place potatoes in water.)

4 Line rimmed baking sheet with triple layer of paper towels. Combine potatoes and oil in Dutch oven and bring to rolling boil over high heat, about 7 minutes. Continue to fry, without stirring, until potatoes are

limp but exteriors are beginning to firm, about 15 minutes longer. Using tongs, stir potatoes, gently scraping up any that stick, and continue to fry, stirring occasionally, until just lightly golden brown, about 4 minutes (fries will not be fully cooked at this point). Using wire skimmer or slotted spoon, transfer fries to prepared sheet. Skim off any browned bits left in pot.

5 Set wire rack in second rimmed baking sheet. Transfer fish to batter and toss to evenly coat. Heat oil over medium-high heat to 375 degrees. Using fork, remove 4 pieces of fish from batter, allowing excess batter to drip back into bowl, and add to hot oil, briefly dragging fish along surface of oil to prevent sticking.

6 Fry fish, stirring gently to prevent pieces from sticking together, until deep golden brown and crispy, about 4 minutes per side. Adjust burner, if necessary, to maintain oil temperature between 350 and 375 degrees. Using wire skimmer or slotted spoon, transfer fish to prepared wire rack and skim off any browned bits left in pot. Return oil to 375 degrees and repeat with remaining 4 pieces of fish.

7 Return oil to 375 degrees. Add fries to oil and fry until deep golden brown and crispy, about 1 minute. Return fries to prepared sheet and season with salt. Transfer fish and chips to serving platter. Serve with lemon wedges.

TARTAR SAUCE
MAKES ABOUT 1 CUP

- ¾ cup mayonnaise
- ¼ cup dill pickle relish
- 1½ teaspoons distilled white vinegar
- ½ teaspoon Worcestershire sauce
- ½ teaspoon pepper
- ⅛ teaspoon salt

Combine all ingredients in small bowl. Cover and refrigerate until flavors meld, about 15 minutes.

RÉMOULADE
MAKES ABOUT 1 CUP

- ¾ cup mayonnaise
- ¼ cup chopped dill pickles
- 1 tablespoon whole-grain mustard
- 1 tablespoon lemon juice
- 1 scallion, sliced thin
- ¼ teaspoon cayenne pepper

Combine all ingredients in small bowl. Cover and refrigerate until flavors meld, about 15 minutes.

CALIFORNIA-STYLE FRIED FISH TACOS

SERVES 6 TOTAL TIME 1 HOUR 30 MINUTES

WHY THIS RECIPE WORKS It's easy to see the appeal of the fish taco: Crispy fried white fish, crunchy cabbage, and creamy white sauce come together on a corn tortilla to deliver an irresistible combination of flavors and textures. We were determined to come up with a tasty version that was easy enough to make for a weeknight dinner. We chose mild but sturdy white fish and coated it with an ultrathin beer batter to avoid a thick, bready coating. Cornstarch and baking powder in the batter ensured that the fish fried up golden brown and crisp. A quick pickle of red onions and jalapeños added color and spice, and we used a portion of the vinegary pickling liquid to dress the shredded cabbage. Our creamy white sauce got its tang from lime juice and sour cream, and a sprinkle of fresh cilantro provided the finishing touch. Although this recipe looks involved, all the components are easy to execute, and most can be prepared in advance. Cut the fish on a slight bias if your fillets aren't quite 4 inches wide. You should end up with about 24 pieces of fish.

Pickled Onions
- 1 cup white wine vinegar
- 2 tablespoons lime juice
- 1 tablespoon sugar
- 1 teaspoon salt
- 1 small red onion, halved and sliced thin
- 2 jalapeño chiles, stemmed and sliced into thin rings

White Sauce
- ½ cup mayonnaise
- ½ cup sour cream
- 2 tablespoons milk
- 2 tablespoons lime juice

Cabbage
- 3 cups shredded green cabbage
- ¼ cup pickling liquid from pickled onions
- ½ teaspoon salt
- ½ teaspoon pepper

Fish
- 2 pounds skinless cod fillets, cut crosswise into 4 by 1-inch strips
- Salt and pepper
- ¾ cup all-purpose flour
- ¼ cup cornstarch
- 1 teaspoon baking powder
- 1 cup mild lager, such as Budweiser
- 1 quart peanut or vegetable oil
- 24 (6-inch) corn tortillas, warmed
- 1 cup fresh cilantro leaves

1 For the pickled onions Microwave vinegar, lime juice, sugar, and salt in medium bowl until steaming, about 5 minutes. Stir in onion and jalapeños and let sit for at least 30 minutes. (Pickled onions can be refrigerated for up to 2 days.)

2 For the white sauce Whisk all ingredients together in second bowl and refrigerate until flavors meld, at least 15 minutes or up to 2 days.

3 For the cabbage Toss all ingredients together in third bowl; set aside for serving.

4 For the fish Adjust oven rack to middle position and heat oven to 200 degrees. Set wire rack in rimmed baking sheet. Pat fish dry with paper towels and season with salt and pepper. Whisk flour, cornstarch, baking powder, and 1 teaspoon salt together in large bowl. Whisk in beer until smooth. Transfer fish to batter and toss to evenly coat.

5 Add oil to Dutch oven until it measures about ¾ inch deep and heat over medium-high heat to 350 degrees. Using fork, remove 5 or 6 pieces of fish from batter, allowing excess batter to drip back into bowl, and add to hot oil, briefly dragging fish along surface of oil to prevent sticking. Fry fish, stirring gently to prevent pieces from sticking together, until golden brown and crispy, about 2 minutes per side. Adjust burner, if necessary, to maintain oil temperature between 325 and 350 degrees. Using wire skimmer or slotted spoon, transfer fish to prepared wire rack and keep warm in oven. Return oil to 350 degrees and repeat with remaining fish in 3 or 4 batches.

6 Divide fish evenly among tortillas. Top with cabbage, pickled onions, white sauce, and cilantro. Serve.

COCONUT SHRIMP WITH MANGO DIPPING SAUCE

SERVES 6 TO 8   TOTAL TIME 1 HOUR 30 MINUTES

WHY THIS RECIPE WORKS Making this bar food favorite at home is easy with our simple and flavorful recipe. To maximize coconut flavor in the shrimp, we added sweet shredded coconut to the panko coating and used creamy coconut milk as a binder to help it stick. Frying the shrimp in three small batches helped these quick-cooking morsels cook through evenly, since the Dutch oven could more easily maintain a consistent oil temperature. A dipping sauce of pureed mango, peach preserves, and fresh cilantro was the perfect bright accompaniment. Be sure to gently press the coconut mixture into the shrimp to help it adhere.

Dipping Sauce

- 6 ounces (¾ cup) frozen mango, thawed
- ¼ cup peach preserves
- 2 tablespoons lime juice
- Salt and pepper
- 2 teaspoons minced fresh cilantro
- 2 teaspoons minced shallot
- 2 teaspoons minced jalapeño chile

Shrimp

- 1⅓ cups all-purpose flour
- 2 cups sweetened shredded coconut
- 1 cup panko bread crumbs
- 2 teaspoons grated lime zest
- Salt and pepper
- 1½ teaspoons baking powder
- ¼ teaspoon cayenne pepper
- ½ cup mild lager, such as Budweiser
- ¼ cup canned coconut milk
- 1 large egg
- 1½ pounds extra-large shrimp (21 to 25 per pound), peeled and deveined
- 3 quarts peanut or vegetable oil

1 For the dipping sauce Process mango, preserves, lime juice, pinch salt, and pinch pepper in blender until completely smooth, about 1 minute, scraping down sides of blender jar as needed. Transfer to bowl and stir in cilantro, shallot, and jalapeño. Season with salt and pepper to taste; set aside for serving. (Dipping sauce can be refrigerated for up to 1 day.)

2 For the shrimp Adjust oven rack to middle position and heat oven to 200 degrees. Line rimmed baking sheet with parchment paper. Set wire rack in second rimmed baking sheet and line with triple layer of paper towels.

3 Spread ⅔ cup flour in shallow dish. Combine coconut, panko, lime zest, 1 teaspoon salt, and 1 teaspoon pepper in second shallow dish. Whisk baking powder, cayenne, and remaining ⅔ cup flour together in medium bowl. Whisk in beer, coconut milk, and egg until fully incorporated and smooth.

4 Pat shrimp dry with paper towels and season with salt and pepper. Working with 1 shrimp at a time, dredge in flour, dip into batter, letting excess drip back into bowl, and coat with coconut-panko mixture, pressing gently to adhere. Arrange breaded shrimp on parchment-lined sheet. Refrigerate for at least 20 minutes or up to 2 hours.

5 Add oil to Dutch oven until it measures about 2 inches deep and heat over medium-high heat to 350 degrees. Add one-third of shrimp, 1 at a time, to hot oil. Fry, stirring gently to prevent pieces from sticking together, until shrimp are golden brown, 1½ to 2 minutes. Adjust burner, if necessary, to maintain oil temperature between 325 and 350 degrees.

6 Using wire skimmer or slotted spoon, transfer shrimp to prepared wire rack and keep warm in oven. Return oil to 350 degrees and repeat with remaining shrimp in 2 batches. Serve with dipping sauce.

BEER-BATTERED ONION RINGS

SERVES 4 TO 6   TOTAL TIME 1 HOUR 15 MINUTES

WHY THIS RECIPE WORKS When making onion rings at home, many cooks resort to oven-baked versions—but nothing beats the crispy coating and sweet onion flavor of fried versions. Our simple recipe ensures that they don't turn out greasy, soggy, or heavy. Before frying, our onions required some pretreatment to tenderize them, since they needed to spend only a few minutes in the oil. Soaking the rings in a mixture of beer, malt vinegar, and salt softened them and boosted their flavor. As for the batter, tasters liked a combination of beer, flour, cornstarch, and baking powder: The beer contributed flavor and lift, the cornstarch upped the crispness, and baking powder yielded a light yet thick coating. To ensure that the rings didn't stick together, we added them to the oil one by one and fried them in 3 batches. In step 1, do not soak the onion rounds for longer than 2 hours or they will turn soft and become too saturated to crisp properly. We prefer to use sweet onions here, such as Vidalia, but ordinary large yellow onions will produce acceptable rings.

2 sweet onions, sliced into ½-inch-thick rounds
3 cups full-bodied lager, such as Sam Adams
2 teaspoons malt or cider vinegar
  Salt and pepper
2 quarts peanut or vegetable oil
¾ cup all-purpose flour
¾ cup cornstarch
1 teaspoon baking powder

1 Place onion rounds, 2 cups beer, vinegar, ½ teaspoon salt, and ½ teaspoon pepper in 1-gallon zipper-lock bag. Refrigerate for at least 30 minutes or up to 2 hours.

2 Adjust oven rack to middle position and heat oven to 200 degrees. Line rimmed baking sheet with triple layer of paper towels. Add oil to Dutch oven until it measures about 1½ inches deep and heat over medium-high heat to 350 degrees. Combine flour, cornstarch, baking powder, ½ teaspoon salt, and

¼ teaspoon pepper in large bowl. Whisk in ¾ cup beer until just combined (some lumps will remain). Whisk in remaining beer as needed, 1 tablespoon at a time, until batter falls from whisk in steady stream and leaves faint trail across surface of batter.

3 Remove onions from bag and discard liquid. Pat onion rounds dry with paper towels and separate into rings. Transfer one-third of rings to batter. Using fork, remove 1 ring at a time from batter, allowing excess batter to drip back into bowl, and add to hot oil, briefly dragging ring along surface of oil to prevent sticking. Fry until rings are golden brown and crisp, about 5 minutes, flipping halfway through frying. Using wire skimmer or slotted spoon, transfer rings to prepared sheet, season with salt and pepper to taste, and keep warm in oven. Return oil to 350 degrees and repeat with remaining onion rings and batter in 2 batches. Serve.

FRIED BRUSSELS SPROUTS

SERVES 4 TO 6   TOTAL TIME 40 MINUTES

WHY THIS RECIPE WORKS Fried Brussels sprouts at restaurants can be delightfully crispy, nutty, and salty. Yet when we first tried making them, the Brussels sprouts splattered every time they hit the hot oil. Instead, we tried submerging the sprouts in cold oil in our deep Dutch oven and heating the oil and the sprouts together over high heat. As long as we cooked the Brussels sprouts until they were deep brown, this method produced beautifully crisped sprouts. An easy stir-together lemon-chive sauce offered a vibrant creamy counterpoint, perfect for dipping. Be sure to choose Brussels sprouts that are similar in size to ensure even cooking. For this recipe, we prefer larger Brussels sprouts, about the size of golf balls, because they're easier to dip in the sauce. To keep the sprouts' leaves intact and attached to their cores, trim just a small amount from the stems before cutting the sprouts in half. If you choose to wash your sprouts before cooking, do so before trimming and halving them. Stir gently and not too often in step 2; excessive stirring will cause the leaves to separate from the sprouts.

Lemon-Chive Dipping Sauce
- ½ cup mayonnaise
- 2 tablespoons minced fresh chives
- 1 teaspoon grated lemon zest plus 1 tablespoon juice
- 1 teaspoon Worcestershire sauce
- 1 teaspoon Dijon mustard
- ¼ teaspoon garlic powder

Brussels Sprouts
- 2 pounds Brussels sprouts, trimmed and halved through stem
- 1 quart vegetable oil
- Kosher salt

1 For the lemon-chive dipping sauce Whisk all ingredients together in bowl. Cover and refrigerate until ready to serve.

2 For the Brussels sprouts Line rimmed baking sheet with triple layer of paper towels. Combine Brussels sprouts and oil in Dutch oven. Cook over high heat, occasionally stirring gently, until dark brown throughout and crispy, 20 to 25 minutes.

3 Using wire skimmer or slotted spoon, transfer Brussels sprouts to prepared sheet. Roll gently so paper towels absorb excess oil. Season with salt to taste. Serve immediately with sauce.

PREPPING BRUSSELS SPROUTS

1 Trim small amount from stem end of sprouts.

2 Halve sprouts through stem end so they stay intact during frying.

EASIER FRENCH FRIES

SERVES 4   TOTAL TIME 45 MINUTES

WHY THIS RECIPE WORKS Traditional methods of making French fries involve rinsing, soaking, double frying, and then draining and salting them—not an easy process. We wanted a recipe for crispy fries with a tender interior and lots of potato flavor, but without all the fuss. The key was to submerge the potatoes in room-temperature oil before frying them over high heat until browned. This gave the potatoes' interiors an opportunity to soften and cook through before the exteriors started to crisp. Starchy russets turned leathery with the longer cooking time. With lower-starch Yukon Golds, however, the result was a crisp exterior and a creamy interior. The fries stuck to the bottom of the pot at first, but letting the potatoes cook in the oil for 20 minutes before stirring gave them enough time to form a crust that would protect them. Thinner fries were also less likely to stick. We prefer peanut oil for frying, but vegetable or canola oil can be substituted. This recipe will not work with sweet potatoes or russets.

2½ pounds Yukon Gold potatoes, unpeeled
6 cups peanut or vegetable oil
   Kosher salt

1 Using chef's knife, square off sides of potatoes. Cut potatoes lengthwise into ¼-inch planks, then slice each plank into ¼-inch-thick fries.

2 Line rimmed baking sheet with triple layer of paper towels. Combine potatoes and oil in large Dutch oven. Cook over high heat until oil has reached rolling boil, about 5 minutes. Once boiling, continue to cook, without stirring, until potatoes are limp but exteriors are beginning to firm, about 15 minutes.

3 Using tongs, stir potatoes, gently scraping up any that stick, and continue to cook, stirring occasionally, until golden and crisp, 5 to 10 minutes. Using wire skimmer or slotted spoon, transfer fries to prepared sheet. Season with salt and serve.

CHIVE AND BLACK PEPPER DIPPING SAUCE
MAKES ABOUT ½ CUP

5 tablespoons mayonnaise
3 tablespoons sour cream
2 tablespoons minced fresh chives
1½ teaspoons lemon juice
¼ teaspoon salt
¼ teaspoon pepper

Whisk all ingredients together in small bowl. (Sauce can be refrigerated for up to 2 days.)

BELGIAN-STYLE DIPPING SAUCE
MAKES ABOUT ½ CUP

5 tablespoons mayonnaise
3 tablespoons ketchup
1 garlic clove, minced
½ teaspoon hot sauce
¼ teaspoon salt

Whisk all ingredients together in small bowl. (Sauce can be refrigerated for up to 2 days.)

SWEET POTATO FRIES

SERVES 4 TO 6   TOTAL TIME 1 HOUR 15 MINUTES

WHY THIS RECIPE WORKS Despite their name, sweet potatoes have little in common with russet potatoes—for one thing, they're much lower in starch, which means getting crispy exteriors can be a challenge. To make up for the sweet potatoes' lack of starch, we started by blanching them in our Dutch oven in water spiked with salt and baking soda. This seasoned the potatoes throughout and softened their exteriors. When we transferred the potatoes to a cornstarch slurry, the outer layer of the parcooked potatoes sloughed off, creating a substantial, pleasingly orange crust. Our Dutch oven then pulled double duty as our frying vessel, minimizing splatter and sticking. If your sweet potatoes are shorter than 4 inches in length, do not cut the wedges crosswise. We like these fries with our Spicy Fry Sauce (recipe follows), but they are also good served plain.

½ cup cornstarch
  Kosher salt
1 teaspoon baking soda
3 pounds sweet potatoes, peeled and cut into ¾-inch-thick wedges, wedges cut in half crosswise
1 quart peanut or vegetable oil

1 Adjust oven rack to middle position and heat oven to 200 degrees. Set wire rack in rimmed baking sheet. Whisk cornstarch and ½ cup cold water together in large bowl.

2 Bring 2 quarts water, ¼ cup salt, and baking soda to boil in Dutch oven. Add potatoes and return to boil. Reduce heat to simmer and cook until exteriors turn slightly mushy (centers will remain firm), 3 to 5 minutes. Whisk cornstarch slurry to recombine. Using wire skimmer or slotted spoon, transfer potatoes to bowl with slurry. Discard cooking water and wipe out Dutch oven with paper towels.

3 Using rubber spatula, fold potatoes with slurry until slurry turns light orange, thickens to paste, and clings to potatoes.

4 Add oil to Dutch oven until it measures ¾ inch deep and heat over high heat to 325 degrees. Using tongs, carefully add one-third of potatoes to oil, making sure that potatoes aren't touching one another. Fry until crispy and lightly browned, 7 to 10 minutes, using tongs to flip potatoes halfway through frying. Adjust burner, if necessary, to maintain oil temperature between 280 and 300 degrees. Using wire skimmer or slotted spoon, transfer fries to prepared wire rack (fries that stick together can be separated with tongs or forks). Season with salt to taste and keep warm in oven. Return oil to 325 degrees and repeat with remaining potatoes in 2 batches. Serve immediately.

SPICY FRY SAUCE
MAKES ABOUT ½ CUP
For a less-spicy version, use only 2 teaspoons of Asian chili-garlic sauce.

6 tablespoons mayonnaise
1 tablespoon Asian chili-garlic sauce
2 teaspoons distilled white vinegar

Whisk all ingredients together in small bowl. (Sauce can be refrigerated for up to 4 days.)

MOZZARELLA STICKS

SERVES 4 TO 6   TOTAL TIME 1 HOUR (PLUS CHILLING TIME)

WHY THIS RECIPE WORKS Making this restaurant dish at home doesn't require special equipment: just a freezer and a heavy Dutch oven. Sticks of mozzarella cut from a block tasted much better than string cheese and didn't take much time. We dredged the sticks in flour, dipped them in egg, and coated them with panko bread crumbs for the hallmark crunch. Letting the coated cheese chill in the freezer ensured that instead of exploding or leaking during frying, it became pleasantly gooey and stretchy. We heated the oil to 400 degrees—hotter than usual—so the cold mozzarella sticks could cook up with beautifully burnished exteriors in just 1 minute. Do not use fresh or part-skim mozzarella; their high moisture content can cause the sticks to rupture in the hot oil. This recipe was developed with Sorrento Galbani Whole Milk Mozzarella, which is the test kitchen's favorite. We do not recommend using string cheese.

1 pound whole-milk mozzarella cheese
½ cup all-purpose flour
2 large eggs
2 cups panko bread crumbs
½ teaspoon salt
½ teaspoon pepper
¼ teaspoon dried oregano
¼ teaspoon garlic powder
2 quarts peanut or vegetable oil
1 cup jarred marinara sauce, warmed

1 Set wire rack in rimmed baking sheet and line half of rack with triple layer of paper towels. Slice mozzarella crosswise into six ½-inch-wide planks. Cut each plank lengthwise into 3 equal sticks. (You will have 18 pieces.)

2 Spread flour in shallow dish. Beat eggs in second shallow dish. Pulse panko, salt, pepper, oregano, and garlic powder in food processor until finely ground, about 10 pulses; transfer to third shallow dish.

3 Working with 1 stick at a time, dredge in flour, dip in eggs, allowing excess to drip off, and coat with panko mixture, pressing gently to adhere. Transfer to plate and freeze until firm, at least 1 hour or up to 2 hours. (Chilled mozzarella sticks can be transferred to zipper-lock bag and frozen for up to 1 month; do not thaw before frying. Let fried sticks rest for 3 minutes before serving to allow residual heat to continue to melt centers.)

4 Add oil to Dutch oven until it measures about 1½ inches deep and heat over medium-high heat to 400 degrees. Add 6 sticks to hot oil and fry until deeply browned on all sides, about 1 minute. Adjust burner, if necessary, to maintain oil temperature between 375 and 400 degrees.

5 Using wire skimmer or slotted spoon, transfer sticks to paper towel–lined side of wire rack to drain for 30 seconds, then move to unlined side of rack. Return oil to 400 degrees and repeat with remaining 12 sticks in 2 batches. Serve with marinara.

HUSHPUPPIES

MAKES **ABOUT 25** TOTAL TIME **50 MINUTES**

WHY THIS RECIPE WORKS Hushpuppies, bite-size fried cornmeal dumplings, are a habit-forming treat served throughout the South with fried fish and barbecue. We wanted ours to boast a crisp crust, tender center, and strong corn taste without any cornmeal grit or extra effort. A combination of ¾ cup of cornmeal and ½ cup of flour struck the perfect balance of texture and flavor. Cayenne and finely chopped onion rounded out the corn flavor without overpowering it. Buttermilk contributed a nice tang, and baking soda provided a light texture and a golden-brown crust. Letting the batter sit allowed it to thicken nicely. No shaping was needed here—we simply dropped heaping tablespoonfuls of batter into the hot oil in our Dutch oven. Using a good amount of oil was necessary to allow the hushpuppies space to bob around without sticking together. Avoid coarsely ground cornmeal for this recipe, as it will make the hushpuppies gritty.

¾ cup cornmeal

½ cup all-purpose flour

1½ teaspoons baking powder

½ teaspoon baking soda

¾ teaspoon salt

¼ teaspoon cayenne pepper

¾ cup buttermilk

2 large eggs

¼ cup finely chopped onion

2 quarts peanut or vegetable oil

1 Combine cornmeal, flour, baking powder, baking soda, salt, and cayenne in large bowl. Whisk in buttermilk, eggs, and onion until combined. Let batter sit at room temperature for at least 10 minutes or up to 1 hour.

2 Set wire rack in rimmed baking sheet. Add oil to Dutch oven until it measures about 1½ inches deep and heat over medium-high heat to 350 degrees. Working with half of batter at a time, drop heaping tablespoonfuls into oil and fry until deep golden brown, 2 to 3 minutes, turning hushpuppies halfway through frying. Using wire skimmer or slotted spoon, transfer hushpuppies to prepared wire rack. Return oil to 350 degrees and repeat with remaining batter. Serve.

Weeknight Carrots and Parsnips with Dried Cranberries

SIMPLE SIDES

BRAISED ASPARAGUS, PEAS, AND RADISHES WITH TARRAGON

SERVES 4 TO 6   TOTAL TIME 45 MINUTES

WHY THIS RECIPE WORKS It's common to use your Dutch oven to braise large, hearty cuts of meat, but this technique is also a perfect way to create fresh, unique vegetable sides. We decided to take advantage of the Dutch oven's roomy interior and even heating to create a braise with our favorite spring vegetables. We started by softening a sliced shallot in olive oil with additional aromatics for a well-rounded flavor base. To keep the braise clean-tasting and fresh, we used water as the braising liquid and enhanced it with citrus zest and a bay leaf. Adding the vegetables in stages ensured that each cooked at its own rate and maintained a crisp texture. Peppery radishes, which turned soft and sweet with cooking, were nicely complemented by the more vegetal notes of asparagus and peas (frozen peas were reliably sweet, and adding them off the heat prevented over-cooking). In no time at all we had a simple side of radiant vegetables in an invigorating, complex broth, proof positive that Dutch oven–braising can bring out the best in even the most delicate flavors. A handful of chopped fresh tarragon gave a final nod to spring. Look for asparagus spears no thicker than ½ inch.

¼ cup extra-virgin olive oil
1 shallot, sliced into thin rounds
2 garlic cloves, sliced thin
3 sprigs fresh thyme
   Pinch red pepper flakes
10 radishes, trimmed and quartered lengthwise
1¼ cups water
2 teaspoons grated lemon zest
2 teaspoons grated orange zest
1 bay leaf
   Salt and pepper
1 pound asparagus, trimmed and cut into 2-inch lengths
2 cups frozen peas
4 teaspoons chopped fresh tarragon

1 Cook oil, shallot, garlic, thyme sprigs, and pepper flakes in Dutch oven over medium heat until shallot is just softened, about 2 minutes. Stir in radishes, water, lemon zest, orange zest, bay leaf, and 1 teaspoon salt and bring to simmer. Reduce heat to medium-low, cover, and cook until radishes can be easily pierced with tip of paring knife, 3 to 5 minutes. Stir in asparagus, cover, and cook until tender, 3 to 5 minutes.

2 Off heat, stir in peas, cover, and let sit until heated through, about 5 minutes. Discard thyme sprigs and bay leaf. Stir in tarragon and season with salt and pepper to taste. Serve.

TRIMMING ASPARAGUS

1 Remove 1 spear of asparagus from bunch and bend it at thicker end until it snaps.

2 With broken asparagus spear as guide, trim tough ends from remaining asparagus bunch using chef's knife.

WEEKNIGHT CARROTS AND PARSNIPS WITH DRIED CRANBERRIES

SERVES 4 TO 6   TOTAL TIME 45 MINUTES

WHY THIS RECIPE WORKS Root vegetables are often roasted, but braising offers a benefit that roasting can't—namely, a braising liquid that becomes an elegant serving sauce. We wanted our sauce to coat the vegetables and infuse them with flavor. Tasters liked the natural sweetness of carrots and parsnips; a mixture of chicken broth and apple cider offered both depth and complementary sweet-tart flavor. Reducing the liquid slightly before adding the vegetables concentrated its flavor, and because the pot was covered the vegetables cooked evenly and didn't dry out. Whisking in some butter and Dijon mustard at the end emulsified the sauce and gave it a silky texture and some body. Dried cranberries and fresh parsley lent color and bright, fresh flavor.

3 tablespoons unsalted butter, cut into
  ½-inch pieces
1 shallot, minced
1 cup chicken broth
1 cup apple cider
6 sprigs fresh thyme
2 bay leaves
  Salt and pepper
1 pound carrots, peeled and sliced on bias
  ¼ inch thick
1 pound parsnips, peeled and sliced on bias
  ¼ inch thick
½ cup dried cranberries
1 tablespoon Dijon mustard
2 tablespoons minced fresh parsley

1 Melt 1 tablespoon butter in Dutch oven over medium heat. Add shallot and cook until softened and lightly browned, about 3 minutes. Stir in broth, cider, thyme sprigs, bay leaves, 1½ teaspoons salt, and ½ teaspoon pepper. Bring to simmer and cook for 5 minutes. Stir in carrots and parsnips. Reduce heat to medium-low, cover, and cook, stirring occasionally, until vegetables are tender, 10 to 14 minutes.

2 Off heat, discard thyme sprigs and bay leaves and stir in cranberries. Push vegetable mixture to sides of pot. Add mustard, parsley, and remaining 2 tablespoons butter to center and whisk into cooking liquid. Stir to coat vegetable mixture with sauce. Serve.

Variations
WEEKNIGHT CARROTS AND CELERY ROOT WITH APPLE
Substitute 1½ pounds celery root, peeled, halved if medium or quartered if large, and sliced ¼ inch thick, for parsnips; 1 peeled and diced Fuji or Honeycrisp apple for dried cranberries; and 1 teaspoon minced fresh marjoram or thyme for parsley. In step 1, cook celery root in braising liquid by itself for 15 minutes before adding carrots and proceeding with recipe as directed.

WEEKNIGHT CARROTS AND SWEET POTATOES WITH CANDIED GINGER
Substitute sweet potatoes, peeled, halved lengthwise, and sliced ¼ inch thick, for parsnips; ¼ cup coarsely chopped candied ginger for dried cranberries; and 3 tablespoons minced fresh cilantro for parsley.

WHOLE POT-ROASTED CAULIFLOWER WITH TOMATOES AND OLIVES

SERVES 4 TO 6   TOTAL TIME 1 HOUR 20 MINUTES

WHY THIS RECIPE WORKS Eaten as a hearty side or a light vegetarian main, whole braised cauliflower is becoming increasingly popular, and for good reason: Not only is the dish a showstopper, it's also healthy and tastes great. We opted for an aromatic, tomato-based sauce for our version. Most recipes start by searing the whole cauliflower in a Dutch oven, but we found this task unwieldy, and the browning was spotty at best. Luckily, once the cauliflower was coated in our tangy, piquant sauce of bright tomatoes, sweet golden raisins, savory anchovies, and briny capers and olives, we couldn't taste or see the difference between browned and unbrowned cauliflower, so we skipped the hassle of browning altogether. To ensure all the rich flavors of our sauce penetrated the dense vegetable, we started by cooking it upside down and spooned some of the sauce into the crevices between the stalk and florets. Partway through cooking, we flipped the cauliflower right side up, spooned more sauce over the top, and left the Dutch oven uncovered as it finished cooking. This allowed the sauce to thicken and the flavors to intensify as the cauliflower cooked to tenderness. This recipe makes a generous amount of sauce that we recommend using to top other elements of your meal: You can serve the cauliflower as a light entrée with rice, grains, or beans, or as a side for simply prepared meat, poultry, or fish.

2 (28-ounce) cans whole peeled tomatoes
2 tablespoons extra-virgin olive oil, plus extra for drizzling
6 anchovy fillets, rinsed and minced
6 garlic cloves, minced
¼ teaspoon red pepper flakes
¼ teaspoon salt
¼ cup golden raisins
¼ cup pitted kalamata olives, chopped coarse
3 tablespoons capers, rinsed
1 head cauliflower (2 pounds), outer leaves discarded and stem trimmed flush with bottom florets
1 ounce Parmesan cheese, grated (½ cup)
¼ cup minced fresh parsley

1 Adjust oven rack to middle position and heat oven to 450 degrees. Pulse tomatoes and their juice in food processor until coarsely chopped, 6 to 8 pulses.

2 Cook oil, anchovies, garlic, and pepper flakes in Dutch oven over medium heat, stirring constantly, until fragrant, about 2 minutes. Stir in tomatoes and salt, bring to simmer, and cook until slightly thickened, about 10 minutes.

3 Stir in raisins, olives, and capers. Nestle cauliflower, stemmed side up, into sauce and spoon some of sauce over top. Cover, transfer pot to oven, and roast until cauliflower is just tender (paring knife can be slipped in and out of cauliflower core with some resistance), 30 to 35 minutes.

4 Uncover pot and, using tongs, flip cauliflower over. Spoon some of sauce over cauliflower, then scrape down sides of pot. Continue to roast, uncovered, until cauliflower is tender, 10 to 15 minutes.

5 Remove pot from oven. Sprinkle cauliflower with Parmesan and parsley, and drizzle with extra oil. Cut cauliflower into wedges and serve, spooning sauce over individual portions.

EGGPLANT WITH GARLIC AND BASIL SAUCE

SERVES 6   TOTAL TIME 1 HOUR

WHY THIS RECIPE WORKS Eggplant shines in this dish, where its melt-in-your mouth consistency and ability to soak up a flavor-packed sauce are on full display. But its excess moisture can be a serious liability, leading many recipes to require time-consuming salting, draining, and drying. We wanted to use our Dutch oven to bring this versatile vegetable to its full potential without all the extra work. By cutting the eggplant into cubes and cooking it in two batches, we found we could take advantage of the Dutch oven's heat to drive away moisture and brown the eggplant at the same time. To complement its earthy flavor, we also added sweet red bell peppers to the pot, along with a generous dose of aromatic garlic and ginger. A bold Thai-style sauce, flavored with potent ingredients like fish sauce, brown sugar, lime, and red pepper flakes, completed the dish. Basil and scallions added freshness and a pop of color. Do not peel the eggplant; leaving the skin on helps it hold together during cooking.

Sauce

- 1 cup water
- ⅓ cup fish sauce
- ¼ cup packed brown sugar
- 4 teaspoons grated lime zest plus 1 tablespoon juice (2 limes)
- 4 teaspoons cornstarch
- ¼ teaspoon red pepper flakes

Vegetables

- 7 tablespoons vegetable oil
- 12 garlic cloves, minced
- 2 tablespoons grated fresh ginger
- 2 pounds eggplant, cut into ¾-inch pieces
- 2 red bell peppers, stemmed, seeded, and cut into ¼-inch pieces
- 1 cup fresh basil leaves, torn into rough ½-inch pieces
- 4 scallions, sliced thin

1 For the sauce Whisk all ingredients together in bowl.

2 For the vegetables Combine 1 tablespoon oil, garlic, and ginger in bowl; set aside. Heat 3 tablespoons oil in Dutch oven over medium-high heat until shimmering. Add half of eggplant and half of bell peppers and cook, stirring often and scraping bottom of pan to loosen any browned bits, until tender, about 12 minutes; transfer to separate bowl. Repeat with remaining 3 tablespoons oil, eggplant, and bell pepper; transfer to bowl.

3 Scrape away any remaining browned bits from now-empty pot. Return cooked vegetables to pot and push to sides. Add garlic mixture to center and cook over medium-high heat until fragrant, about 1 minute. Stir garlic mixture into vegetables. Whisk sauce to recombine, then add to pot. Cook, stirring constantly, until sauce is thickened, about 1 minute. Off heat, stir in basil and scallions. Serve.

CUTTING UP EGGPLANT

1 To cut eggplant into tidy pieces, first cut eggplant crosswise into 1-inch-thick rounds.

2 Then cut each round into pieces as directed in recipe.

BRAISED GREEN BEANS WITH POTATOES AND BASIL

SERVES 6　TOTAL TIME　1 HOUR 30 MINUTES

WHY THIS RECIPE WORKS Unlike crisp-tender green beans that have been steamed or sautéed, Greece's traditional braised green beans boast a uniquely soft, velvety texture without being mushy. Unfortunately, achieving this can require upwards of 2 hours of simmering. To get ultratender braised green beans with less cooking time, we first simmered them with a pinch of baking soda to weaken their cell walls. Once the beans were partially softened, we stirred in canned diced tomatoes to add sweet flavor; their acid also neutralized the baking soda and prevented the beans from oversoftening. The beans turned meltingly tender after less than an hour in a low oven. Sautéed garlic and onion plus some lemon juice, basil, and a drizzle of olive oil delivered bright flavor and richness. Finally, to make the dish more substantial, we added chunks of potatoes; 1-inch pieces turned tender in the same amount of time as the beans.

5　tablespoons extra-virgin olive oil

1　onion, chopped fine

2　tablespoons minced fresh oregano or
　　2 teaspoons dried

4　garlic cloves, minced

1½　cups water

1½　pounds green beans, trimmed and cut into
　　2-inch lengths

1　pound Yukon Gold potatoes, peeled and cut
　　into 1-inch pieces

½　teaspoon baking soda

1　(14.5-ounce) can diced tomatoes, drained
　　with juice reserved, chopped

1　tablespoon tomato paste
　　Salt and pepper

3　tablespoons chopped fresh basil
　　Lemon juice

1 Adjust oven rack to lower-middle position and heat oven to 275 degrees. Heat 3 tablespoons oil in Dutch oven over medium heat until shimmering. Add onion and cook until softened, about 5 minutes. Stir in oregano and garlic and cook until fragrant, about 30 seconds. Stir in water, green beans, potatoes, and baking soda, bring to simmer, and cook, stirring occasionally, for 10 minutes.

2 Stir in tomatoes and their juice, tomato paste, 2 teaspoons salt, and ¼ teaspoon pepper. Cover, transfer pot to oven, and cook until sauce is slightly thickened and green beans can be cut easily with side of fork, 40 to 50 minutes.

3 Remove pot from oven. Stir in basil and season with salt, pepper, and lemon juice to taste. Transfer green beans to serving bowl and drizzle with remaining 2 tablespoons oil. Serve.

CREAMY MASHED POTATOES

SERVES 8 TO 10   TOTAL TIME 1 HOUR

WHY THIS RECIPE WORKS We wanted lush, creamy mashed potatoes with enough richness and flavor that they could stand on their own—no gravy necessary. But when it comes to mashed potatoes, there's a fine line between creamy and gluey. For a substantial mash, we found that Yukon Golds were perfect—less fluffy than russets but not as heavy as red potatoes. Slicing the peeled and quartered potatoes and starting them in cold (not boiling) water helped them cook evenly, intensifying their creamy texture without making them gluey. Returning the boiled and drained potatoes to the Dutch oven for a brief cook over a low flame helped further evaporate any excess moisture. Using 1½ sticks of butter and 1½ cups of heavy cream gave the potatoes luxurious flavor and richness without making the mash too thin. If you prefer an absolutely smooth puree, you can use a food mill or ricer rather than a potato masher in step 2.

4 pounds Yukon Gold potatoes, peeled, quartered, and sliced ¾ inch thick
Salt and pepper
1½ cups warm heavy cream
12 tablespoons unsalted butter, melted

1 Place potatoes in Dutch oven, add water to cover by 1 inch and 1 tablespoon salt. Bring to boil, then reduce to simmer and cook until potatoes are fall-apart tender (potatoes break apart when paring knife is inserted and gently wiggled), 20 to 25 minutes.

2 Drain potatoes and return to now-empty pot. Stir over low heat until potatoes are thoroughly dried, 1 to 2 minutes. Using potato masher, mash potatoes until few small lumps remain. Combine warm cream and melted butter in bowl, then gently fold mixture into potatoes with rubber spatula until combined and potatoes are thick and creamy. Season with salt and pepper to taste. Serve.

Variations

CREAMY MASHED POTATOES WITH SCALLIONS AND HORSERADISH
Buy refrigerated prepared horseradish, not the shelf-stable kind, which contains preservatives and additives.

Stir ½ cup drained prepared horseradish and 6 minced scallions into cream mixture before folding into potatoes.

CREAMY MASHED POTATOES WITH PARMESAN AND LEMON
Fold 2 cups grated Parmesan cheese and ¼ cup grated lemon zest (4 lemons) into potatoes with cream mixture.

SCALLOPED POTATOES

SERVES 10 TO 12   TOTAL TIME 1 HOUR 30 MINUTES

WHY THIS RECIPE WORKS Scalloped potatoes—thinly sliced potatoes layered with cream and baked until they are bubbling and browned—are a classic accompaniment to holiday roasts. But this rich side dish can occupy the oven for over 2 hours, dirty a slew of pots and baking dishes, and still produce unevenly cooked potatoes in a heavy, curdled sauce. We wanted to minimize the oven time and cleanup while turning out layers of tender potatoes and creamy sauce with a nicely browned, cheesy crust. We found the answer to many of these problems in our Dutch oven. We simmered the potatoes briefly in cream on the stovetop to cut down on the baking time; covering the pot held in moisture so the potatoes cooked evenly. Then, instead of transferring the mixture to a baking dish, we simply transferred the Dutch oven to the oven; the pot's well-insulated walls and bottom, along with the dry heat of the oven, ensured that the sauce thickened without curdling and the top began to brown nicely. To finish off the casserole, we put the pot under the broiler to get a bronzed, crisp lid on the potatoes. Prep and assemble all of the other ingredients before slicing the potatoes or they will begin to brown (do not store them in water or the gratin will be bland and watery). If the potato slices do start to discolor, put them in a bowl and cover with the cream and milk. Slicing the potatoes ⅛ inch thick is crucial for the success of this dish; use a mandoline, a V-slicer, or a food processor fitted with a slicing disk.

2   tablespoons unsalted butter
1   small onion, chopped fine
2   garlic cloves, minced
3   cups heavy cream
1   cup whole milk
4   sprigs fresh thyme
2   bay leaves
2   teaspoons salt
½   teaspoon pepper
4   pounds russet potatoes, peeled and sliced
     ⅛ inch thick
4   ounces cheddar cheese, shredded (1 cup)
2   tablespoons minced fresh chives

1 Adjust oven rack to lower-middle position and heat oven to 350 degrees. Melt butter in Dutch oven over medium heat. Add onion and cook until softened and lightly browned, 5 to 7 minutes. Stir in garlic and cook until fragrant, about 30 seconds. Stir in cream, milk, thyme sprigs, bay leaves, salt, and pepper. Stir in potatoes and bring to simmer. Reduce heat to low, cover, and cook, stirring occasionally, until potatoes are almost tender (paring knife can be slipped in and out of potato slice with some resistance), 15 to 20 minutes.

2 Discard thyme sprigs and bay leaves. Smooth surface of potatoes, then sprinkle with cheddar. Transfer pot to oven and bake, uncovered, until sauce is thickened and potatoes are tender, about 15 minutes.

3 Remove pot from oven and heat broiler element. Return pot to oven and broil until bubbling around edges and top is spotty brown, 5 to 10 minutes. Let cool for 15 minutes. Sprinkle with chives and serve.

CREAMY MASHED SWEET POTATOES

SERVES 8 TO 10   TOTAL TIME 1 HOUR 15 MINUTES TO 1 HOUR 45 MINUTES

WHY THIS RECIPE WORKS Mashed sweet potatoes can offer earthy counterbalance to any number of rich roasts. But simply boiling sweet potatoes like regular russets produced bland, washed-out flavors. The better solution? Ditch the water, and use the right pot. Cooking the potatoes right in the liquid we would already be mixing in—heavy cream and butter—allowed the sweet potatoes' flavor to stay in the pot where it belonged. A small amount of liquid was enough; thanks to the Dutch oven's high sides, heat retention, and heavy lid, all of which helped hold in moisture, we could simply cook the potatoes until they were fall-apart tender and then mash them right in the pot. A bit of extra cream stirred in at the end offered a little boost of richness without clouding the sweet potatoes' flavor.

4 pounds sweet potatoes, peeled, quartered lengthwise, and sliced ¼ inch thick

8 tablespoons unsalted butter, cut into 8 pieces

6 tablespoons heavy cream

2 teaspoons sugar

Salt and pepper

1 Combine potatoes, butter, 4 tablespoons cream, sugar, 1 teaspoon salt, and ½ teaspoon pepper in Dutch oven. Cover and cook over low heat until potatoes are fall-apart tender (potatoes break apart when paring knife is inserted and gently wiggled), 1 to 1½ hours.

2 Off heat, use potato masher to mash potatoes until few small lumps remain. Gently fold in remaining 2 tablespoons cream and season with salt and pepper to taste. Serve.

Variations

MAPLE-ORANGE MASHED SWEET POTATOES

Fold ¼ cup maple syrup and 1 teaspoon grated orange zest into mashed potatoes with cream in step 2.

INDIAN-SPICED MASHED SWEET POTATOES WITH RAISINS AND CASHEWS

Substitute dark brown sugar for granulated sugar and add 1½ teaspoons garam masala to pot along with sweet potatoes in step 1. Stir ¼ cup golden raisins and ¼ cup roasted unsalted cashews, chopped coarse, into mashed sweet potatoes with cream in step 2.

GARLIC MASHED SWEET POTATOES WITH COCONUT AND CILANTRO

Substitute ¾ cup coconut milk for butter and cream in step 1, and add 1 minced garlic clove and ½ teaspoon red pepper flakes to pot with potatoes. Substitute ¼ cup coconut milk for cream in step 2, and fold 2 tablespoons minced fresh cilantro into mashed sweet potatoes with coconut milk.

WALK-AWAY RATATOUILLE

SERVES 6 TO 8 TOTAL TIME 1 HOUR 45 MINUTES

WHY THIS RECIPE WORKS Ratatouille is a rustic Provençal specialty that transforms fresh late-summer produce into a rich stew. But many recipes are labor-intensive, and the vegetables' moisture content often results in a waterlogged dish. We found that adding each ingredient to the Dutch oven at the right time was the key to solving both issues. First, we sautéed onions and aromatics on the stovetop. We then added chunks of eggplant and tomatoes before transferring the pot to the oven, where the dry, ambient heat thoroughly evaporated moisture, concentrated flavors, and caramelized some of the vegetables. After 45 minutes, the tomatoes and eggplant became meltingly soft and could be mashed into a thick, silky sauce. Zucchini and bell peppers went into the pot last so that they retained some texture. This dish is best prepared using ripe, in-season tomatoes. To quickly peel tomatoes, score a small X in the bottom of cored tomatoes and lower them into boiling water; cook until the skins loosen, about 1 minute. Remove the tomatoes from the water and peel off strips of loosened skin with a paring knife. If good tomatoes are not available, substitute one 28-ounce can of whole peeled tomatoes that have been drained and chopped coarse. Serve ratatouille as an accompaniment to meat or fish or on its own with crusty bread, topped with an egg, or over pasta or rice. This dish can be served warm, at room temperature, or chilled.

⅓ cup plus 1 tablespoon extra-virgin olive oil
2 large onions, cut into 1-inch pieces
8 large garlic cloves, peeled and smashed
  Salt and pepper
1½ teaspoons herbes de Provence
¼ teaspoon red pepper flakes
1 bay leaf
1½ pounds eggplant, peeled and cut into 1-inch pieces
2 pounds plum tomatoes, cored, peeled, and chopped coarse
2 small zucchini, halved lengthwise and sliced 1 inch thick
2 red or yellow bell peppers, stemmed, seeded, and cut into 1-inch pieces
2 tablespoons chopped fresh basil
1 tablespoon minced fresh parsley
1 tablespoon sherry vinegar

1 Adjust oven rack to middle position and heat oven to 400 degrees. Heat ⅓ cup oil in Dutch oven over medium-high heat until shimmering. Add onions, garlic, 1 teaspoon salt, and ¼ teaspoon pepper and cook, stirring occasionally, until onions are translucent and starting to soften, about 10 minutes.

Add herbes de Provence, pepper flakes, and bay leaf and cook, stirring frequently, for 1 minute. Add eggplant, tomatoes, ¾ teaspoon salt, and ½ teaspoon pepper and stir to combine. Transfer pot to oven and cook, uncovered, until vegetables are very tender and spotty brown, 40 to 45 minutes.

2 Remove pot from oven and, using potato masher or heavy wooden spoon, smash and stir eggplant mixture until broken down to sauce-like consistency. Stir in zucchini and bell peppers and return to oven. Cook, uncovered, until zucchini and bell peppers are just tender, 20 to 25 minutes.

3 Remove pot from oven, cover, and let sit until zucchini is translucent and easily pierced with tip of paring knife, 10 to 15 minutes. Using wooden spoon, scrape any browned bits from sides of pot and stir back into ratatouille. Discard bay leaf. Stir in 1 tablespoon basil, parsley, and vinegar. Season with salt and pepper to taste. Transfer to large platter, drizzle with remaining 1 tablespoon oil, and sprinkle with remaining 1 tablespoon basil. Serve.

GARLICKY SWISS CHARD WITH GOAT CHEESE AND GOLDEN RAISINS

SERVES 4 TO 6   TOTAL TIME 25 MINUTES

WHY THIS RECIPE WORKS Making enough greens to serve four to six people can be a challenge—the greens start out so voluminous that they won't fit in a small pot or skillet and must be wilted down in batches. Using our Dutch oven solved this problem, and relying on a hybrid steam-sauté method gave the greens (Swiss chard, in this case) the best flavor and texture. We started by blooming garlic in oil, then added a full 2 pounds of chard and covered the pot so the steam could wilt the chard enough for us to be able to stir it easily. Cutting the sturdy stems smaller than the tender leaves meant that we could throw them in the pot at the same time, keeping the recipe streamlined. To avoid a watery dish, we finished cooking the chard uncovered to evaporate the liquid. Adding golden raisins to the pot with the chard hydrated the fruit and offered pops of sweetness. Finishing the dish with a splash of balsamic vinegar added brightness, and a sprinkle of toasted hazelnuts and crumbled goat cheese offered crunchy, creamy contrast.

2 tablespoons plus 1 teaspoon extra-virgin olive oil
6 garlic cloves, minced
2 pounds Swiss chard, stems chopped, leaves sliced into ½-inch-wide strips
¼ cup golden raisins
   Salt and pepper
⅛ teaspoon red pepper flakes
1 teaspoon balsamic vinegar
1½ ounces goat cheese, crumbled (⅓ cup)
¼ cup hazelnuts, toasted, skinned, and chopped

1 Heat 2 tablespoons oil and garlic in Dutch oven over medium-low heat, stirring occasionally, until garlic is light golden, about 3 minutes. Add chard, raisins, ¼ teaspoon salt, and pepper flakes and toss to combine. Increase heat to high, cover, and cook, stirring occasionally, until chard is wilted but still bright green, 2 to 4 minutes.

2 Uncover and continue to cook, stirring frequently, until liquid evaporates, 4 to 6 minutes. Add vinegar and remaining 1 teaspoon oil and toss to combine. Season with salt and pepper to taste. Transfer to serving platter and sprinkle with goat cheese and hazelnuts. Serve.

Variation

GARLICKY SWISS CHARD WITH FETA AND WALNUTS
Omit raisins. Substitute white wine vinegar for balsamic vinegar, crumbled feta cheese for goat cheese, and toasted and chopped walnuts for hazelnuts.

PREPPING SWISS CHARD

1 Cut leaves away from stems and chop stems into small pieces.

2 Slice leaves into ½-inch-wide strips.

BRAISED WINTER GREENS WITH CHORIZO

SERVES **4 TO 6**   TOTAL TIME **1 HOUR**

WHY THIS RECIPE WORKS   Recipes for braising sturdy greens like kale often call for hours of cooking and result in lifeless greens. We wanted a one-pot recipe that would maintain some of the kale's firm texture and cabbage-like flavor. We started by browning some chorizo in the Dutch oven, then set it aside while we cooked the kale; the rendered fat made for an ultraflavorful base. While we didn't want to wash out the greens' flavor with tons of liquid, we still needed to add enough to cook them evenly; we settled on a cup of water and a cup of chicken broth for depth. Once the kale was tender, we uncovered the pot and cooked off the remaining liquid so that no flavor was poured down the drain. A bit of lemon juice, stirred in at the end with the browned chorizo, brought liveliness. You can substitute collard greens for the kale; increase the covered cooking time to 35 to 45 minutes in step 2.

3 tablespoons extra-virgin olive oil

8 ounces Spanish-style chorizo sausage, halved lengthwise and sliced ¼ inch thick

1 onion, chopped fine

5 garlic cloves, minced

1½ teaspoons ground cumin

2 pounds kale, ribs removed, leaves chopped into 3-inch pieces and rinsed

1 cup chicken broth

1 cup water

Salt and pepper

2 teaspoons lemon juice, plus extra for seasoning

1 Heat 2 tablespoons oil in Dutch oven over medium heat until shimmering. Add chorizo and cook until lightly browned, 4 to 6 minutes. Using slotted spoon, transfer chorizo to paper towel–lined plate; set aside.

2 Add onion to fat left in pot and cook, stirring frequently, until softened and lightly browned, 4 to 5 minutes. Stir in garlic and cumin and cook until fragrant, about 1 minute. Stir in kale and cook until beginning to wilt, about 1 minute. Add broth, water, and ¼ teaspoon salt. Quickly cover pot and reduce heat to medium-low. Cook, stirring occasionally, until greens are tender, 25 to 35 minutes.

3 Remove lid and increase heat to medium-high. Cook, stirring occasionally, until most of liquid has evaporated (bottom of pot will be almost dry and kale will begin to sizzle), 8 to 12 minutes. Off heat, stir in chorizo, lemon juice, and remaining 1 tablespoon oil. Season with salt, pepper, and extra lemon juice to taste. Serve.

HERBED RICE PILAF WITH ALMONDS

SERVES 4 TO 6   TOTAL TIME 1 HOUR

WHY THIS RECIPE WORKS Rice pilaf is one of the simplest sides you can make—which means there's no hiding flaws like under- or overcooked rice. For perfect rice every time, we first rinsed long-grain rice to remove excess starch and then toasted the grains in butter until they started to turn translucent around the edges. This helped develop rich, nutty flavors and also began to set the starches in the grains, providing extra insurance against clumping. Next, we added broth to give the pilaf savory back-bone; while most recipes call for a 2:1 ratio of liquid to rice, we found that using less liquid gave our rice a better texture. The Dutch oven's ability to heat evenly was key here, since the rice needed to steam without being stirred. An off-heat rest with a dish towel under the lid absorbed excess moisture and resulted in distinct, separate grains. To give our pilaf some layers of flavor as well as textural interest, we stirred in some garlic and thyme when toasting the rice; lemon zest with the broth; and chopped almonds and fresh, delicate herbs just before serving. Allow the rice to cook for the full 15 minutes before lifting the lid to check it.

1½ cups long-grain white rice, rinsed
3 tablespoons unsalted butter
1 small onion, chopped fine
Salt and pepper
2 garlic cloves, minced
1 teaspoon minced fresh thyme or ¼ teaspoon dried
2¼ cups chicken broth
2 teaspoons grated lemon zest
¼ cup whole almonds, toasted and chopped coarse
¼ cup chopped fresh basil, parsley, or tarragon, or any combination thereof

1 Melt butter in Dutch oven over medium-high heat. Add onion and ¾ teaspoon salt and cook until onion is just softened, about 3 minutes. Add rice and cook, stirring frequently, until edges begin to turn translucent, about 2 minutes. Stir in garlic and thyme and cook until fragrant, about 30 seconds.

2 Stir in broth and lemon zest and bring to boil. Reduce heat to low, cover, and cook until liquid is absorbed and rice is tender, 15 to 20 minutes. Off heat, lay clean dish towel underneath lid and let pilaf sit 10 minutes.

3 Add almonds and basil to rice and gently fluff with fork to combine. Season with salt and pepper to taste. Serve.

Variation
CURRIED RICE PILAF WITH APPLE
Omit thyme and lemon zest. Add 1 tablespoon curry powder to pot with garlic. Substitute 1 peeled and finely chopped apple for almonds and chopped fresh cilantro for basil.

BROWN RICE PILAF WITH PEAS, FETA, AND MINT

SERVES 4 TO 6   TOTAL TIME 1 HOUR 45 MINUTES

WHY THIS RECIPE WORKS Brown rice can be difficult to cook well: All too often, it is underseasoned and turns starchy and mushy. Plus, it takes a long time to cook, so stovetop recipes run the risk of scorching on the bottom. While rice cookers can turn out perfect rice every time, most American home cooks don't own one, so we hoped to use our Dutch oven and a moderate oven to approximate the controlled, indirect heat of these specialty appliances. The thick, heavy cast-iron pot and enveloping heat of the oven promoted even cooking and eliminated scorching. A bit of sautéed onion offered an aromatic flavor boost as the rice cooked, and incorporating chicken broth into the cooking liquid provided savory notes. We decided to brighten up the brown rice's nutty flavor by adding frozen peas (we didn't need to cook them; simply adding them to the pot while the rice rested was enough to warm them through) along with some fresh mint, lemon zest, and feta.

1 tablespoon extra-virgin olive oil
1 onion, chopped fine
1 cup chicken broth
2¼ cups water
1½ cups long-grain brown rice
1 teaspoon salt
1 cup frozen peas, thawed
¼ cup chopped fresh mint
½ teaspoon grated lemon zest
2 ounces feta cheese, crumbled (½ cup)

1 Adjust oven rack to middle position and heat oven to 375 degrees. Heat oil in Dutch oven over medium heat until shimmering. Add onion and cook, stirring occasionally, until softened and well browned, 12 to 14 minutes.

2 Stir in broth and water and bring to boil. Off heat, stir in rice and salt. Cover, transfer pot to oven, and bake until liquid is absorbed and rice is tender, 65 to 70 minutes.

3 Remove pot from oven and sprinkle peas over rice. Cover, laying clean dish towel underneath lid, and let sit for 5 minutes. Add mint and lemon zest and gently fluff with fork to combine. Sprinkle with feta and serve.

Variation
BROWN RICE PILAF WITH ONIONS AND ROASTED RED PEPPERS
Increase oil to 4 teaspoons and onion to 2 onions. Substitute ¾ cup chopped jarred roasted red peppers for peas, ½ cup chopped fresh parsley for mint, ¼ teaspoon pepper for lemon zest, and ½ cup grated Parmesan cheese for feta.

MEXICAN RICE

SERVES 6 TO 8   TOTAL TIME 1 HOUR 15 MINUTES

WHY THIS RECIPE WORKS Traditional Mexican rice is a cornerstone of Mexican cuisine, and it's easy to understand why: Nutty, tender rice is perfectly complemented by plenty of aromatic ingredients, and the dish has an appealing grassy spice from fresh chiles. The rice is usually fried until golden, which gives it its signature nutty flavor; tomatoes, onions, garlic, and chicken broth add complexity and savory flavors. But many versions we tried turned out soupy, oily, or one-note. We wanted a version with clean, balanced flavor and tender rice that wasn't greasy or watery. Traditionally, the liquid component in this dish is a mix of chicken broth and pureed fresh tomatoes; we settled on equal parts of each for the most balanced flavor. For an appealing red color we added tomato paste, which, although nontraditional, boosted flavor as well. Rather than deep-frying the rice, as some recipes suggested, we sautéed it in a smaller amount of oil; cooking the rice until golden helped develop deep, toasty notes. Moving the Dutch oven from the stovetop to the even heat of the oven ensured that the rice cooked uniformly. A bit of fresh cilantro, jalapeño, and a squeeze of lime juice provided brightness and complemented the rich rice. To make this dish vegetarian, substitute vegetable broth for the chicken broth.

2   tomatoes, cored and quartered
1   onion, chopped coarse
3   jalapeño chiles, stemmed and halved
⅓   cup vegetable oil
2   cups long-grain white rice, rinsed
4   garlic cloves, minced
2   cups chicken broth
1   tablespoon tomato paste
1½ teaspoons salt
½   cup minced fresh cilantro
    Lime wedges

1 Adjust oven rack to middle position and heat oven to 350 degrees. Process tomatoes and onion in food processor until smooth, about 15 seconds, scraping down sides of bowl as needed. Measure out and reserve 2 cups tomato mixture; discard remaining mixture. Remove ribs and seeds from 2 jalapeños and discard; mince flesh and set aside. Mince remaining 1 jalapeño, including ribs and seeds; set aside.

2 Place rice in fine-mesh strainer and rinse under cold running water, swishing with your hands, until water runs clear. Drain thoroughly.

3 Heat oil in Dutch oven over medium-high heat until shimmering. Add rice and cook, stirring frequently, until light golden and translucent, 6 to 8 minutes.

4 Reduce heat to medium. Add garlic and reserved seeded jalapeños and cook, stirring constantly, until fragrant, about 1½ minutes. Stir in reserved tomato mixture, broth, tomato paste, and salt and bring to boil. Cover, transfer pot to oven, and bake until liquid is absorbed and rice is tender, 30 to 35 minutes, stirring well after 15 minutes.

4 Remove pot from oven and fold in cilantro, adding reserved jalapeño with seeds to taste. Serve with lime wedges.

SEEDING JALAPEÑOS

To remove seeds from jalapeños, cut pepper in half lengthwise, then use melon baller or small spoon to scoop along inside of each half.

PARMESAN FARROTTO

SERVES 6   TOTAL TIME 1 HOUR

WHY THIS RECIPE WORKS Farrotto, a twist on classic Italian risotto, is made with farro, an ancient form of wheat that boasts a nutty flavor and a tender chew. Using this whole grain instead of rice yields a more robust dish that still cooks relatively quickly. But since farro retains most of its bran, much of the valuable starch is trapped inside the grains. To ensure that some of the starch could escape and create the creamy, velvety farrotto we were after, we cracked about half of the grains in a blender. To make our recipe more hands-off than traditional risotto (which can require near-constant stirring), a Dutch oven was key: By adding all of the cooking liquid at once and covering the pot, we could trap and distribute the heat throughout the grains, cutting back on the need to stir to ensure even cooking. A brief period of vigorous stirring at the end of cooking gave the farrotto a creamy consistency. Seasoned with Parmesan, parsley, and lemon juice, our farrotto was hearty, satisfying, and flavorful. We prefer the flavor and texture of whole farro. Do not use quick-cooking or pearled farro. The consistency of farrotto is a matter of personal taste; if you prefer a looser texture, add extra hot broth in step 4.

1½ cups whole farro

4 tablespoons unsalted butter

½ onion, chopped fine

1 garlic clove, minced

2½ cups chicken broth, plus extra as needed

2½ cups water

2 teaspoons minced fresh thyme or ½ teaspoon dried
   Salt and pepper

2 ounces Parmesan cheese, grated (1 cup)

2 tablespoons minced fresh parsley

2 teaspoons lemon juice

1 Pulse farro in blender until about half of grains are broken into smaller pieces, about 6 pulses.

2 Melt 2 tablespoons butter in Dutch oven over medium-low heat. Add onion and cook until softened, about 4 minutes. Stir in garlic and cook until fragrant, about 30 seconds. Add farro and cook, stirring frequently, until grains are lightly toasted, about 3 minutes.

3 Meanwhile, bring broth and water to boil in medium saucepan over medium-high heat. Stir broth mixture into farro mixture, reduce heat to low, cover, and cook until almost all liquid has been absorbed and farro is just al dente, about 25 minutes, stirring twice during cooking.

4 Add thyme, 1 teaspoon salt, and ¾ teaspoon pepper and cook, stirring constantly, until farro becomes creamy, about 5 minutes. Off heat, stir in Parmesan, parsley, lemon juice, and remaining 2 tablespoons butter. Season with salt and pepper to taste. Adjust consistency with extra hot broth as needed. Serve.

NEW ENGLAND BAKED BEANS

SERVES 6 TO 8   TOTAL TIME 3 HOURS 45 MINUTES (PLUS SOAKING TIME)

WHY THIS RECIPE WORKS Traditionally, New England baked beans were cooked in crocks in dying ovens or ember-filled holes in the ground, where the beans could slowly turn tender overnight. To re-create this gentle cooking environment, we turned to our heavy Dutch oven and a low oven, which surrounded the beans with even, ambient heat. Brining the beans overnight helped jump-start hydration and also softened their skins so they cooked up tender, with few blowouts. Uncovering the pot for the last hour of cooking ensured that the liquid reduced sufficiently to coat the beans in a thick sauce. Molasses, brown sugar, dry mustard, bay leaf, onion, and salt pork, plus one nontraditional ingredient (soy sauce), gave the beans rich flavor. You'll get fewer blowouts if you soak the beans overnight, but if you're pressed for time, you can quick-salt-soak your beans: In step 1, bring the salt, water, and beans to a boil in the Dutch oven. Remove the pot from the heat, cover, and let sit for 1 hour. Drain and rinse the beans and proceed with step 2.

Salt and pepper
1 pound (2½ cups) dried navy beans, picked over and rinsed
6 ounces salt pork, rinsed, cut into 3 pieces
1 onion, halved
½ cup molasses
2 tablespoons packed dark brown sugar
1 tablespoon soy sauce
2 teaspoons dry mustard
1 bay leaf

1 Dissolve 3 tablespoons salt in 4 quarts cold water in large container. Add beans and let soak at room temperature for at least 8 hours or up to 24 hours. Drain and rinse well.

2 Adjust oven rack to lower-middle position and heat oven to 300 degrees. Combine beans, salt pork, onion, molasses, sugar, soy sauce, mustard, ½ teaspoon pepper, bay leaf, ¼ teaspoon salt, and 4 cups water in Dutch oven. (Liquid should cover beans by about ½ inch. Add more water if necessary.) Bring to boil over high heat. Cover, transfer pot to oven, and cook until beans are softened and bean skins curl up and split when you blow on them, about 2 hours. (After 1 hour, stir beans and check amount of liquid. Liquid should just cover beans. Add water if necessary.)

3 Uncover and continue to cook until beans are fully tender, browned, and slightly crusty on top, about 1 hour. (Liquid will reduce slightly below top layer of beans.)

4 Remove pot from oven, cover, and let sit for 5 minutes. Using wooden spoon or rubber spatula, scrape any browned bits from sides of pot and stir into beans. Discard onion and bay leaf. Let beans sit, uncovered, until liquid has thickened slightly and clings to beans, 10 to 15 minutes, stirring once halfway through. Season with salt and pepper to taste. Serve.

PICKING OVER DRIED BEANS

Before cooking dried beans, pick them over for any small stones or debris and then rinse them. To check for small stones, spread beans out over large plate or rimmed baking sheet.

COWBOY BEANS

SERVES 6 TO 8   **TOTAL TIME** 3 HOURS 45 MINUTES TO 4 HOURS 45 MINUTES
(PLUS SOAKING TIME)

WHY THIS RECIPE WORKS Most barbecue joints serve ladlefuls of smoky, deep-flavored cowboy beans alongside slabs of ribs and mounds of pulled pork. We wanted to make those creamy-textured, saucy beans at home to accompany our own barbecue. To get there, we used navy beans. We found that bacon was a convenient substitute for smoky barbecued meat. We blended mustard, barbecue sauce, and brown sugar for sweet-spicy, deep flavor—a fair amount of garlic and onion helped, too. But the real secret ingredient in this recipe: coffee. The roasted, slightly bitter flavor tied all the flavors together. Using a Dutch oven ensured that the sugars in our saucy beans didn't scorch and that the beans themselves cooked evenly and consistently. You'll get fewer blowouts if you soak the beans overnight, but if you're pressed for time, you can quick-salt-soak your beans: In step 1, bring the salt, water, and beans to a boil in the Dutch oven. Remove the pot from the heat, cover, and let sit for 1 hour. Drain and rinse the beans and proceed with step 2.

Salt and pepper
1 pound (2½ cups) dried navy beans, picked over and rinsed
4 slices bacon, chopped fine
1 onion, chopped fine
4 garlic cloves, minced
1 cup brewed coffee
½ cup plus 2 tablespoons barbecue sauce
⅓ cup packed dark brown sugar
2 tablespoons spicy brown mustard
½ teaspoon hot sauce

1 Dissolve 3 tablespoons salt in 4 quarts cold water in large container. Add beans and let soak at room temperature for at least 8 hours or up to 24 hours. Drain and rinse well.

2 Adjust oven rack to lower-middle position and heat oven to 300 degrees. Cook bacon in Dutch oven over medium heat until crisp, 5 to 7 minutes. Stir in onion and cook until softened and lightly browned, 6 to 8 minutes. Stir in garlic and cook until fragrant, about 30 seconds. Stir in beans, 4½ cups water, coffee, ½ cup barbecue sauce, sugar, mustard, hot sauce, and 2 teaspoons salt and bring to boil. Cover, transfer pot to oven, and cook until beans are just tender, 2 to 2½ hours.

3 Uncover and continue to cook, stirring occasionally, until beans are fully tender, 1 to 1½ hours.

4 Remove pot from oven and let beans sit until liquid has thickened slightly and clings to beans, 10 to 15 minutes, stirring once halfway through. Stir in remaining 2 tablespoons barbecue sauce and season with salt and pepper to taste. Serve.

DRUNKEN BEANS

SERVES 6 TO 8   TOTAL TIME 2 HOURS (PLUS SOAKING TIME)

WHY THIS RECIPE WORKS Soupy beans are a staple at Mexican tables; the cooking liquid thickens slightly from the beans' starches and the dish is as satisfying as any rich stew. One such iteration, known as drunken beans, cooks pinto beans in beer or tequila, which lends subtle, complex flavor to the pot. To make sure the alcohol didn't make our beans boozy or bitter, we added tequila at the beginning of cooking (evaporating it to mellow its flavor) and beer partway through (so that its malty notes would be present in the finished dish). Brining the beans ensured they stayed tender, creamy, and intact. Sautéing onion, garlic, and poblano chiles in rendered bacon fat created a flavorful base, and we reserved the crisp bacon to sprinkle on at the end. Cilantro leaves are a classic garnish for drunken beans, and we decided to use the aromatic stems to add more flavor to the cooking liquid. A vigorous simmer to finish jostled the beans, causing them to release starches that gave the cooking liquid pleasant body. You'll get fewer blowouts if you soak the beans overnight, but if you're pressed for time, you can quick-salt-soak your beans: In step 1, bring the salt, water, and beans to a boil in the Dutch oven. Remove the pot from the heat, cover, and let sit for 1 hour. Drain and rinse the beans and proceed with step 2. Serve with rice.

Salt
1 pound (2½ cups) dried pinto beans, picked over and rinsed
30 sprigs fresh cilantro (1 bunch)
4 slices bacon, cut into ¼-inch pieces
1 onion, chopped fine
2 poblano chiles, stemmed, seeded, and chopped fine
3 garlic cloves, minced
½ cup tequila
2 bay leaves
1 cup Mexican lager
¼ cup tomato paste
2 limes, quartered
2 ounces cotija cheese, crumbled (½ cup)

1 Dissolve 3 tablespoons salt in 4 quarts cold water in large container. Add beans and let soak at room temperature for at least 8 hours or up to 24 hours. Drain and rinse well.

2 Adjust oven rack to lower-middle position and heat oven to 300 degrees. Pick leaves from 20 cilantro sprigs (reserve stems), mince, and refrigerate until needed. Using kitchen twine, tie remaining 10 cilantro sprigs and reserved stems into bundle.

3 Cook bacon in Dutch oven over medium heat, stirring occasionally, until crisp, 5 to 7 minutes. Using slotted spoon, transfer bacon to paper towel–lined bowl and set aside. Add onion, poblanos, and garlic to fat left in pot and cook until vegetables are softened, 6 to 8 minutes. Off heat, add tequila and cook until evaporated, 3 to 4 minutes.

4 Stir in 3½ cups water, bay leaves, 1 teaspoon salt, beans, and cilantro bundle and bring to boil over high heat. Cover, transfer pot to oven, and cook until beans are just tender, 45 to 60 minutes.

5 Remove pot from oven. Discard bay leaves and cilantro bundle. Stir in beer and tomato paste and bring to simmer over medium-low heat. Cook, stirring frequently, until liquid is thick and beans are fully tender, about 30 minutes. Season with salt to taste. Serve, passing minced cilantro, lime wedges, cotija, and reserved bacon separately.

CRANBERRY BEANS WITH WARM SPICES

SERVES 6 TO 8   TOTAL TIME 2 HOURS TO 2 HOURS 30 MINUTES (PLUS SOAKING TIME)

WHY THIS RECIPE WORKS Cranberry beans have a delicate flavor and a creamy texture similar to that of pinto and cannellini beans. We wanted to create a dish that would highlight these beans using a gently spiced flavor profile. Since cranberry beans are rarely canned, we knew we'd have to start with dried beans. We sautéed aromatic vegetables along with tomato paste for depth of flavor; just a touch of cinnamon imparted a subtle yet distinct warmth. White wine offered acidity, and broth gave the dish a hearty backbone. Letting the beans cook through in the Dutch oven in a moderate oven ensured that they were perfectly cooked without the need for constant monitoring. We completed our comforting side dish with lemon juice and fresh mint, which nicely balanced the warm, rich flavors of the beans. If cranberry beans are unavailable, you can substitute pinto beans. You'll get fewer blowouts if you soak the beans overnight, but if you're pressed for time, you can quick-salt-soak your beans: In step 1, bring the salt, water, and beans to a boil in the Dutch oven. Remove the pot from the heat, cover, and let sit for 1 hour. Drain and rinse the beans and proceed with step 2.

Salt and pepper
1 pound (2½ cups) dried cranberry beans, picked over and rinsed
¼ cup extra-virgin olive oil
1 onion, chopped fine
2 carrots, peeled and chopped fine
4 garlic cloves, sliced thin
1 tablespoon tomato paste
½ teaspoon ground cinnamon
½ cup dry white wine
4 cups chicken broth
2 tablespoons lemon juice, plus extra for seasoning
2 tablespoons minced fresh mint

1 Dissolve 3 tablespoons salt in 4 quarts cold water in large container. Add beans and let soak at room temperature for at least 8 hours or up to 24 hours. Drain and rinse well.

2 Adjust oven rack to lower-middle position and heat oven to 300 degrees. Heat oil in Dutch oven over medium heat until shimmering. Add onion and carrots and cook until softened, about 5 minutes. Stir in garlic, tomato paste, cinnamon, and ¼ teaspoon pepper and cook until fragrant, about 1 minute. Stir in wine, scraping up any browned bits. Stir in broth, ½ cup water, and beans and bring to boil. Cover, transfer pot to oven, and cook, stirring occasionally, until beans are tender, about 1½ to 2 hours.

3 Remove pot from oven. Stir in lemon juice and mint and season with salt, pepper, and extra lemon juice to taste. Adjust consistency with extra hot water as needed. Serve.

BAKERY-STYLE BREADS

Braided Chocolate Babka

ALMOST NO-KNEAD BREAD

MAKES 1 LOAF   TOTAL TIME 3 HOURS TO 3 HOURS 30 MINUTES
(PLUS 8 HOURS RESTING TIME AND 3 HOURS COOLING TIME)

WHY THIS RECIPE WORKS A Dutch oven and an almost-no-knead method make artisan-style bread achievable for any home cook. Our technique skirted most of the usual kneading by making a wet dough and using a long resting period. This allowed the flour to fully hydrate, and the proteins to break down, so that the dough required only a brief, 1-minute knead to develop good structure. Vinegar and mild beer gave the loaf the yeasty tang of good bakery breads. Baking the bread in a Dutch oven was key to success here: The moisture and steam trapped under the heavy lid encouraged the air bubbles inside the bread to expand much faster, leading to a more open crumb structure. The steam also condensed onto the surface of the baking bread, causing the starches to form a thin sheath that dried out and gave the loaf a shatteringly crisp crust. We found that preheating the oven was unnecessary; putting the pot right into a cold oven still encouraged enough rise. Uncovering the bread for the second half of baking crisped the crust. We prefer to use a mild American lager, such as Budweiser, here; strongly flavored beers will make the bread taste bitter.

3 cups (15 ounces) all-purpose flour
1½ teaspoons salt
¼ teaspoon instant or rapid-rise yeast
¾ cup (6 ounces) water, room temperature
½ cup (4 ounces) mild lager such as Budweiser, room temperature
1 tablespoon distilled white vinegar

1 Whisk flour, salt, and yeast together in large bowl. Whisk water, beer, and vinegar together in 2-cup liquid measuring cup. Using rubber spatula, gently fold water mixture into flour mixture, scraping up dry flour from bottom of bowl, until dough starts to form and no dry flour remains. Cover bowl tightly with plastic wrap and let sit at room temperature for at least 8 hours or up to 18 hours.

2 Lay 18 by 12-inch sheet of parchment paper on counter and lightly spray with vegetable oil spray. Transfer dough to lightly floured counter and knead by hand until smooth and elastic, about 1 minute.

3 Shape dough into ball by pulling edges into middle, then transfer, seam side down, to center of prepared parchment.

4 Using parchment as sling, gently lower loaf into Dutch oven. Cover, tucking any excess parchment into pot, and let rise until loaf has doubled in size and dough springs back minimally when poked gently with your knuckle, 1½ to 2 hours.

5 Adjust oven rack to middle position. Holding sharp paring knife or single-edge razor blade at 30-degree angle to loaf, make two 5-inch-long, ½-inch-deep slashes with swift, fluid motion along top of loaf to form cross. Cover pot and transfer to oven. Turn oven to 425 degrees and bake loaf for 30 minutes while oven heats.

6 Uncover and continue to bake until loaf is deep golden brown and registers 205 to 210 degrees, 25 to 30 minutes. Using parchment sling, remove loaf from pot and transfer to wire rack; discard parchment. Let cool completely, about 3 hours, before serving.

Variation

ALMOST NO-KNEAD WHOLE-WHEAT BREAD
Substitute 1 cup (5½ ounces) whole-wheat flour for 1 cup all-purpose flour. Whisk 2 tablespoons honey into water mixture before adding to dry ingredients in step 1.

SEEDED SEVEN-GRAIN BREAD

MAKES 1 LOAF   TOTAL TIME 3 HOURS 45 MINUTES TO 4 HOURS 45 MINUTES
(PLUS 3 HOURS COOLING TIME)

WHY THIS RECIPE WORKS This hearty loaf is chock-full of whole grains and seeds that give it an appealingly rustic flavor and texture. We used our Dutch oven to give this loaf a crackly crust and even crumb. First, we focused on the dough itself: Rather than call for a laundry list of grains to get the right flavor, we turned to seven-grain hot cereal mix. Pepitas, sunflower seeds, sesame seeds, and poppy seeds, both incorporated into to the dough and sprinkled on top, offered a range of textures. To encourage the loaf to rise high, we used a hot oven to aid "oven spring," a term for the fast expansion of bread dough in the first few minutes of baking. We prevented the crust from setting too quickly in the intense heat by covering the Dutch oven for the first part of baking; the humidity in the closed pot kept the dough moist and allowed it to rise high before the crust set. To get a browned exterior, we finished the bread uncovered, lowering the oven temperature to avoid burning the seeds on top. Be sure to use hot cereal mix, not boxed cold breakfast cereals, which may also be labeled "seven-grain."

2 cups (16 ounces) warm tap water (110 degrees)
1½ cups (7½ ounces) seven-grain hot cereal mix
2 tablespoons honey
2 tablespoons vegetable oil
3½ cups (19¼ ounces) bread flour
1¾ teaspoons salt
1 teaspoon instant or rapid-rise yeast
3 tablespoons raw, unsalted pepitas
3 tablespoons raw, unsalted sunflower seeds
1 teaspoon sesame seeds
1 teaspoon poppy seeds
1 large egg, lightly beaten with 1 tablespoon water and pinch salt

1 Whisk water, cereal, honey, and oil in bowl of stand mixer until honey has completely dissolved; let sit for 10 minutes.

2 Add flour, salt, and yeast to cereal mixture. Using dough hook on low speed, mix until cohesive dough starts to form and no dry flour remains, about 2 minutes, scraping down bowl as needed. Increase speed to medium-low and knead until dough is smooth and elastic and clears sides of bowl, 6 to 8 minutes. Reduce speed to low, slowly add 2 tablespoons pepitas and 2 tablespoons sunflower seeds, and mix until mostly incorporated, about 1 minute.

3 Transfer dough to lightly floured counter and knead by hand until smooth, round ball forms and any loose seeds are evenly distributed, about 2 minutes. Place dough, seam side down, in lightly greased large bowl or container, cover tightly with plastic wrap, and let rise until doubled in size, 1½ to 2 hours.

4 Lay 18 by 12-inch sheet of parchment paper on counter and lightly spray with vegetable oil spray. Transfer dough to lightly floured counter. Using lightly floured hands, press and stretch dough into 10-inch round, deflating any gas pockets larger than 1 inch.

5 Working around circumference of dough, fold edges toward center until ball forms. Flip dough ball seam side down and, using your cupped hands, drag in small circles on counter until dough feels taut and round and all seams are secured on underside of loaf.

6 Place loaf, seam side down, in center of prepared parchment. Using parchment as sling, gently lower loaf into Dutch oven. Cover, tucking any excess parchment into pot, and let rise until loaf increases in size by about half and dough springs back minimally when poked gently with your knuckle, 30 minutes to 1 hour.

7 Adjust oven rack to middle position and heat oven to 450 degrees. Combine remaining 1 tablespoon pepitas, remaining 1 tablespoon sunflower seeds, sesame seeds, and poppy seeds in small bowl. Holding sharp paring knife or single-edge razor blade at 30-degree angle to loaf, make two 5-inch-long, ½-inch-deep slashes with swift, fluid motion along top of loaf to form cross. Brush loaf with egg mixture and sprinkle seed mixture evenly over top.

8 Cover pot, transfer to oven, and bake loaf for 30 minutes. Uncover, reduce oven temperature to 375 degrees, and continue to bake until loaf is deep golden brown and registers 205 to 210 degrees, about 25 minutes.

9 Using parchment sling, remove loaf from pot and transfer to wire rack; discard parchment. Let cool completely, about 3 hours, before serving.

SPICY OLIVE BREAD

MAKES 1 LOAF   TOTAL TIME 3 HOURS 30 MINUTES TO 4 HOURS 30 MINUTES
(PLUS 3 HOURS COOLING TIME)

WHY THIS RECIPE WORKS In pursuit of the ideal artisanal sandwich bread, perfect for a piquant Italian salumi sandwich, we turned to olives, garlic, and red pepper flakes. Because we intended this bread to be a vehicle for sandwiches, we wanted a tight crumb rather than an open one. To get there, we minimized air pockets by pressing the risen dough into a 10-inch round and deflating any large bubbles. Beyond folding the dough into a taut ball, we didn't incorporate additional folds, a technique often used in artisanal breads to add more air to the loaf. Slashing a shallow X in the top of the shaped dough ensured that the loaf expanded evenly, making it easy to slice into uniform pieces for sandwiches. The steam trapped in the covered Dutch oven during baking converted the starches on the bread's surface to a thin layer of gel that crisped up beautifully once we uncovered the Dutch oven. Almost any variety of brined or oil-cured olive works in this recipe, although we prefer a mix of green and black.

¾ cup pitted olives, rinsed, patted dry, and chopped coarse

2 garlic cloves, minced

3 cups (16½ ounces) bread flour

2 teaspoons instant or rapid-rise yeast

2 teaspoons salt

2 teaspoons red pepper flakes

1⅓ cups (10⅔ ounces) water, room temperature

2 tablespoons sugar

1 tablespoon extra-virgin olive oil

1 Combine olives and garlic in bowl. Whisk flour, yeast, salt, and pepper flakes together in bowl of stand mixer. Whisk water, sugar, and oil in 2-cup liquid measuring cup until sugar has dissolved. Using dough hook on low speed, slowly add water mixture to flour mixture and mix until cohesive dough starts to form and no dry flour remains, about 2 minutes, scraping down bowl as needed.

2 Increase speed to medium-low and knead until dough is smooth and elastic and clears sides of bowl, about 8 minutes. Reduce speed to low, slowly add olive mixture, ¼ cup at a time, and mix until mostly incorporated, about 1 minute.

3 Transfer dough and any loose olives to lightly floured counter and knead by hand to form smooth, round ball, about 30 seconds. Place dough, seam side down, in lightly greased large bowl or container, cover tightly with plastic wrap, and let rise until nearly doubled in size, 1½ to 2 hours.

4 Lay 18 by 12-inch sheet of parchment paper on counter and lightly spray with vegetable oil spray. Transfer dough to lightly floured counter. Using lightly floured hands, press and stretch dough into 10-inch round, deflating any gas pockets larger than 1 inch.

5 Working around circumference of dough, fold edges toward center until ball forms. Flip dough ball seam side down and, using your cupped hands, drag in small circles on counter until dough feels taut and round and all seams are secured on underside of loaf.

6 Place loaf, seam side down, in center of prepared parchment and cover loosely with greased plastic wrap. Let rise until loaf increases in size by about half and dough springs back minimally when poked gently with your knuckle, 30 minutes to 1 hour.

7 Thirty minutes before baking, adjust oven rack to lower-middle position, place Dutch oven (with lid) on rack, and heat oven to 500 degrees. Holding sharp paring knife or single-edge razor blade at 30-degree angle to loaf, make two 5-inch-long, ½-inch-deep slashes with swift, fluid motion along top of loaf to form cross.

8 Carefully transfer pot to wire rack and uncover. Using parchment as sling, gently lower dough into Dutch oven. Cover pot, tucking any excess parchment into

pot, and return to oven. Reduce oven temperature to 425 degrees and bake loaf for 15 minutes. Uncover and continue to bake until loaf is deep golden brown and registers 205 to 210 degrees, about 20 minutes.

9 Using parchment sling, remove loaf from pot and transfer to wire rack; discard parchment. Let cool completely, about 3 hours, before serving.

FIG AND FENNEL BREAD

MAKES 1 LOAF   TOTAL TIME 4 HOURS TO 4 HOURS 30 MINUTES
(PLUS 6 HOURS SPONGE RISING TIME AND 3 HOURS COOLING TIME)

WHY THIS RECIPE WORKS This sophisticated loaf calls on the elegant combination of sweet figs and earthy fennel seeds for a bread that's perfect with cheese and charcuterie plates. We wanted our loaf to have the rustic and open crumb of great bakery breads, so we turned to our Dutch oven. Often, artisanal-style breads are baked on preheated baking stones and lava rocks are placed in the oven to create a moist environment; together, the hot stone and the steam produce an open, airy crumb, a good lift, and a nicely browned, crisp crust. We found that we could do away with both of these specialty items and achieve the same effects by preheating our (empty) Dutch oven. The Dutch oven's heavy cast-iron construction helps it retain heat effectively, similar to a baking stone. Putting the loaf in the hot Dutch oven and covering the pot created a humid, moist environment reminiscent of that created by lava rocks. Thrilled that we didn't need to buy additional equipment to make perfect bread, we turned our attention to building flavor in the dough. Swapping out some of the bread flour for rye flour added interest and depth. We also used a sponge, a mixture of a portion of the dough's flour, water, and yeast that is allowed to ferment for around 6 hours to develop more complex flavor. Introducing a series of folds as the dough rose incorporated air, which gave it better structure and a more open crumb. Gently pressing the dough into a round before shaping it into a ball relaxed the gluten network for better extensibility and redistributed the yeast so it could continue to work. Finally, to give the finished loaf an even more rustic appearance and a unique crunch, we dusted it with cornmeal. While any variety of dried figs will work, we especially like the flavor of Calimyrna figs. Use light or medium rye flour; dark rye flour is overpowering.

Sponge

- 1 cup (5½ ounces) bread flour
- ¾ cup (6 ounces) water, room temperature
- ⅛ teaspoon instant or rapid-rise yeast

Dough

- 1 cup plus 2 tablespoons (6¼ ounces) bread flour
- 1 cup (5½ ounces) light or medium rye flour
- 1 tablespoon fennel seeds, toasted
- 2 teaspoons salt
- 1½ teaspoons instant or rapid-rise yeast
- 1 cup water (8 ounces), room temperature
- 1 cup dried figs, stemmed and chopped coarse
  Cornmeal

1 For the sponge Stir all ingredients in 4-cup liquid measuring cup with wooden spoon until well combined. Cover tightly with plastic wrap and let sit at room temperature until sponge has risen and begins to collapse, about 6 hours (sponge can sit at room temperature for up to 24 hours).

2 For the dough Whisk bread flour, rye flour, fennel seeds, salt, and yeast together in bowl of stand mixer. Stir water into sponge with wooden spoon until well combined. Using dough hook on low speed, slowly add sponge mixture to flour mixture and mix until cohesive dough starts to form and no dry flour remains, about 2 minutes, scraping down bowl as needed.

3 Increase speed to medium-low and continue to knead until dough is smooth, elastic, and slightly sticky, about 5 minutes. Reduce speed to low, slowly add figs, ¼ cup at a time, and mix until mostly incorporated, about 1 minute. Transfer dough to lightly greased large bowl or container, cover tightly with plastic, and let rise for 30 minutes.

4 Using greased bowl scraper (or your fingertips), fold dough over itself by gently lifting and folding edge of dough toward middle. Turn bowl 45 degrees and fold dough again; repeat turning bowl and folding dough 6 more times (total of 8 folds). Cover tightly with plastic; let rise for 30 minutes. Repeat folding and rising every 30 minutes, 2 more times. After third set of folds, cover bowl tightly with plastic and let rise until nearly doubled in size, 45 minutes to 1¼ hours.

5 Lay 18 by 12-inch sheet of parchment paper on counter, lightly spray with vegetable oil spray, and dust evenly with cornmeal. Transfer dough to lightly floured counter. Using lightly floured hands, press and stretch dough into 10-inch round, deflating any gas pockets larger than 1 inch.

6 Working around circumference of dough, fold edges toward center until ball forms. Flip dough ball seam side down and, using your cupped hands, drag in small circles on counter until dough feels taut and round and all seams are secured on underside of loaf.

7 Place loaf, seam side down, in center of prepared parchment and cover loosely with greased plastic wrap. Let rise until loaf increases in size by about half and dough springs back minimally when poked gently with your knuckle, about 30 minutes.

8 Thirty minutes before baking, adjust oven rack to lower-middle position, place Dutch oven (with lid) on rack, and heat oven to 500 degrees. Holding sharp paring knife or single-edge razor blade at 30-degree angle to loaf, make two 5-inch-long, ½-inch-deep slashes with swift, fluid motion along top of loaf to form cross. Dust top of loaf with cornmeal.

9 Carefully transfer pot to wire rack and uncover. Using parchment as sling, gently lower dough into Dutch oven. Cover pot, tucking any excess parchment into pot, and return to oven. Reduce oven temperature to 425 degrees and bake loaf for 15 minutes. Uncover and continue to bake until loaf is deep golden brown and registers 205 to 210 degrees, about 20 minutes.

10 Using parchment sling, remove loaf from pot and transfer to wire rack; discard parchment. Let cool completely, about 3 hours, before serving.

SHAPING AND SLASHING FIG AND FENNEL BREAD

1 Once dough has completed first rise, transfer dough to lightly floured counter. Press and stretch dough into 10-inch round, deflating any gas pockets larger than 1 inch.

2 Working around circumference of dough, fold edges toward center until ball forms.

3 Flip dough ball seam side down and, using your cupped hands, drag in small circles on counter until dough feels taut and round and all seams are secured on underside of loaf.

4 Once loaf is fully risen, hold sharp paring knife at 30-degree angle to loaf and make two 5-inch-long, ½-inch-deep slashes with swift, fluid motion along top to form cross.

Fig and Fennel Bread

Oatmeal-Raisin Bread

OATMEAL-RAISIN BREAD

MAKES 1 LOAF   TOTAL TIME 4 HOURS 15 MINUTES TO 4 HOURS 45 MINUTES
(PLUS 3 HOURS COOLING TIME)

WHY THIS RECIPE WORKS This bread, flavored with oatmeal, sweet raisins, and just a touch of brown sugar, is great toasted up for breakfast or perfect with coffee for an afternoon snack. As with our Fig and Fennel Bread (page 270), we found that baking the bread in a preheated Dutch oven created a beautifully even crumb and a bronzed crust without the need for specialty equipment. Since this bread was a bit sweeter than the Fig and Fennel, a prefermented sponge was unnecessary; we focused instead on getting the oat flavor to really shine. Mixing the oatmeal into the dough toward the end of kneading proved the perfect way to incorporate it without creating big clumps of oats. We tried incorporating oat flour into the dough in addition to the oatmeal, but the flour absorbed so much water that the loaf turned out dry. We found instead that replacing a small amount of the bread flour with whole-wheat flour complemented the earthy flavor of the oats and ensured that the crumb stayed light and moist. To give the loaf a pretty finish, we misted it with water and then sprinkled more oats on top. Do not substitute quick or instant oats in this recipe.

 1 cup (3 ounces) old-fashioned rolled oats
¾ cup (6 ounces) water, room temperature
 2 cups (11 ounces) bread flour
½ cup (2¾ ounces) whole-wheat flour
 2 teaspoons instant or rapid-rise yeast
1½ teaspoons salt
 1 cup (8 ounces) whole milk, room temperature
 3 tablespoons unsalted butter, melted
½ cup raisins

1 Microwave ¾ cup oats and water in large covered bowl, stirring occasionally, until oats are softened and water is completely absorbed, about 5 minutes; let cool completely before using.

2 Whisk bread flour, whole-wheat flour, yeast, and salt together in bowl of stand mixer. Whisk milk and melted butter together in 2-cup liquid measuring cup. Using dough hook on low speed, slowly add milk mixture to flour mixture and mix until cohesive dough starts to form and no dry flour remains, about 2 minutes, scraping down bowl as needed.

3 Increase speed to medium-low and knead until dough is smooth and elastic and clears sides of bowl, about 6 minutes. Reduce speed to low, slowly add raisins, then slowly add oatmeal, 2 tablespoons at a time, and mix until mostly incorporated, about 3 minutes. Transfer dough to lightly greased large bowl or container, cover tightly with plastic, and let rise for 30 minutes.

4 Using greased bowl scraper (or your fingertips), fold dough over itself by gently lifting and folding edge of dough toward middle. Turn bowl 45 degrees and fold dough again; repeat turning bowl and folding dough 6 more times (total of 8 folds). Cover tightly with plastic and let rise for 30 minutes. Repeat folding and rising every 30 minutes, 2 more times. After third set of folds, cover bowl tightly with plastic and let dough rise until nearly doubled in size, 45 minutes to 1¼ hours.

5 Lay 18 by 12-inch sheet of parchment paper on counter; spray with vegetable oil spray. Transfer dough to lightly floured counter. Using lightly floured hands, press and stretch dough into 10-inch round; deflate any gas pockets larger than 1 inch.

6 Working around circumference of dough, fold edges toward center until ball forms. Flip dough ball seam side down and, using your cupped hands, drag in small circles on counter until dough feels taut and round and all seams are secured on underside of loaf. Mist loaf with water on all sides and sprinkle with remaining ¼ cup oats, pressing gently on sides of loaf to adhere.

7 Place loaf, seam side down, in center of prepared parchment and cover loosely with greased plastic wrap. Let rise until loaf increases in size by about half and dough springs back minimally when poked gently with your knuckle, 30 minutes to 1 hour.

8 Thirty minutes before baking, adjust oven rack to lower-middle position, place Dutch oven (with lid) on rack, and heat oven to 500 degrees. Holding sharp paring knife or single-edge razor blade at 30-degree angle to loaf, make two 5-inch-long, ½-inch-deep slashes with swift, fluid motion along top of loaf to form cross. Discard any exposed raisins on top of loaf.

9 Carefully transfer pot to wire rack and uncover. Using parchment as sling, gently lower dough into Dutch oven. Cover pot, tucking any excess parchment into pot, and return to oven. Reduce oven temperature to 425 degrees and bake loaf for 15 minutes. Uncover and continue to bake until loaf is deep golden brown and registers 205 to 210 degrees, about 20 minutes.

10 Using parchment sling, remove loaf from pot and transfer to wire rack; discard parchment. Let cool completely, about 3 hours, before serving.

MIXING AND KNEADING DOUGH FOR OATMEAL-RAISIN BREAD

1 Whisk dry ingredients together in bowl of stand mixer. Whisk wet ingredients in 2-cup liquid measuring cup until sugar has dissolved.

2 Using dough hook on low speed, slowly add wet ingredients to dry ingredients and mix until cohesive dough starts to form and no dry flour remains.

3 Increase speed to medium-low and knead until dough is smooth and elastic. Add raisins, then add oatmeal and mix until incorporated. Transfer to lightly greased large bowl or container and cover with plastic wrap.

4 After dough has risen for 30 minutes, use greased bowl scraper to fold dough over itself by gently lifting and folding edge of dough toward middle. Turn bowl 45 degrees and repeat folding 7 more times.

PULL-APART DINNER ROLLS

MAKES 15 ROLLS   TOTAL TIME 4 TO 5 HOURS

WHY THIS RECIPE WORKS Soft, buttery homemade dinner rolls are the perfect complement to just about any meal, and they don't have to be hard to make. Using our Dutch oven to bake the rolls offered two benefits: First, we could easily fit enough rolls in the pot to feed a crowd; second, the Dutch oven's high sides were able to support the dough as it rose into beautifully dramatic, tall rolls. We were surprised to find that a combination of butter and vegetable shortening in the dough offered good buttery flavor without making the rolls greasy; because shortening coats the gluten strands in the flour more effectively than does butter, a small amount ensured tenderness and prevented the rolls from drying out. Whole milk provided our rolls with just the right level of moisture and richness, and one egg contributed structure and flavor. For a hint of sweetness, tasters preferred honey to sugar. Lining the Dutch oven with a foil sling on which we placed the shaped dough balls made it easy to get the baked rolls out of the pot. Finally, brushing the dough with an egg wash before baking gave the rolls a golden color. As a bonus, this dough can be shaped into rolls and then refrigerated overnight, making our rolls not only easy but convenient, too.

5 cups (25 ounces) all-purpose flour
2¼ teaspoons instant or rapid-rise yeast
  Salt
1½ cups (12 ounces) whole milk, room temperature
⅓ cup honey
2 large eggs, room temperature
4 tablespoons vegetable shortening, melted
3 tablespoons unsalted butter, melted
1 tablespoon water

1 Whisk flour, yeast, and 2 teaspoons salt together in bowl of stand mixer. Whisk milk, honey, 1 egg, melted shortening, and melted butter in 4-cup liquid measuring cup until honey has dissolved.

2 Using dough hook on low speed, slowly add milk mixture to flour mixture and mix until shaggy dough forms and no dry flour remains, about 2 minutes, scraping down bowl as needed. Increase speed to medium-low and knead until dough is smooth and elastic and clears sides of bowl, 6 to 8 minutes.

3 Transfer dough to lightly floured counter and knead by hand to form smooth, round ball, about 30 seconds. Place dough seam side down in lightly greased large bowl or container, cover tightly with plastic wrap, and let rise until doubled in size, 1½ to 2 hours.

4 Make foil sling for Dutch oven by folding 2 long sheets of aluminum foil so each is 7 inches wide. Lay sheets of foil in pot perpendicular to each other, with extra foil hanging over edges of pot. Push foil into bottom and up sides of pot, smoothing foil flush to bottom of pot, then spray with vegetable oil spray.

5 Press down on dough to deflate. Transfer dough to clean counter and roll into even 15-inch log. Cut log into 15 equal pieces (about 3 ounces each) and cover loosely with greased plastic wrap.

6 Working with 1 piece of dough at a time (keep remaining pieces covered), form into rough ball by stretching dough around your thumbs and pinching edges together so that top is smooth. Place ball, seam side down, on clean counter and, using your cupped hand, drag in small circles until dough feels taut and round.

7 Evenly space 10 balls, seam side down, around edge of pot. Place remaining 5 balls in center, staggering them between seams of balls around edge. Cover and let rise until nearly doubled in size and dough springs back minimally when poked gently with your knuckle, 1 to 1½ hours. (Unrisen rolls can be refrigerated for at least 8 hours or up to 16 hours; let rolls sit at room temperature for 1 hour before baking.)

8 Adjust oven rack to lower-middle position and heat oven to 350 degrees. Lightly beat remaining 1 egg, water, and pinch salt together in bowl, then gently brush rolls with egg mixture. Transfer pot to oven and bake, uncovered, until rolls are golden brown, 35 to 40 minutes, rotating pot halfway through baking. Let rolls cool in pot for 15 minutes. Using foil overhang, lift rolls out of pot and transfer to wire rack. Serve warm or at room temperature.

Variations

PULL-APART PARMESAN AND BLACK PEPPER DINNER ROLLS

Add 1 teaspoon coarsely ground pepper to flour mixture. After kneading dough in step 2, reduce mixer speed to low and slowly add ¾ cup grated Parmesan; mix until incorporated, about 2 minutes. Proceed with recipe as directed, sprinkling rolls with additional ¼ cup grated Parmesan after brushing with egg mixture.

PULL-APART CRANBERRY-PECAN DINNER ROLLS

After kneading dough in step 2, reduce mixer speed to low and slowly add ¾ cup pecans, toasted and chopped, and ½ cup dried cranberries; mix until incorporated, about 2 minutes. Transfer dough to counter and knead by hand until round ball forms and any loose pecans and cranberries are evenly distributed, about 2 minutes. Proceed with recipe as directed.

SHAPING AND ASSEMBLING DINNER ROLLS

1 Cut dough log into equal pieces and cover them loosely with greased plastic wrap.

2 Working with 1 piece of dough at a time, form dough into rough ball, stretching it around your thumbs as though you're turning it inside out, and pinching ends together so that top is smooth.

3 Place ball, seam side down, on counter and, using your cupped hand, drag dough in small circles until it feels taut and round.

4 Evenly space 10 balls, seam side down, around edge of pot. Place remaining 5 balls in center, staggering them between seams of balls around edge.

Pull-Apart Dinner Rolls

Braided Chocolate Babka

BRAIDED CHOCOLATE BABKA

MAKES 1 LOAF   TOTAL TIME 6 HOURS 45 MINUTES TO 7 HOURS 45 MINUTES
(PLUS 3 HOURS COOLING TIME)

WHY THIS RECIPE WORKS Elegant and decadent chocolate babka is always a treat, but we wanted to take this dramatic loaf one step further and create a statuesque braided version with stunning spirals of deep, rich chocolate that would be worthy of a holiday breakfast table. For a dark, fudgy filling, we used a combination of bittersweet chocolate and cocoa powder mixed with confectioners' sugar and egg whites, which helped make the filling sticky and stable enough that it wouldn't ooze out of the dough as we shaped and baked it. We found that we needed to double our usual dough recipe in order to achieve the spiral effect we were after. The Dutch oven enabled us to bake this larger loaf with ease; its high sides and large capacity guided the loaf as it rose and baked. Because the hefty loaf needed a good amount of time in the oven to bake through, we baked it on the middle rack and created a foil sling for the Dutch oven, which insulated the bottom crust and prevented it from burning. The foil also made it easier to remove our finished masterpiece from the pot. We covered the pot for the first 20 minutes of baking; the extra insulation and steam trapped in the pot kept the top crust moist while the dense mass of dough gently baked through. We do not recommend mixing this dough by hand.

Dough

- 4 cups (20 ounces) all-purpose flour
- 1 tablespoon instant or rapid-rise yeast
- 1 teaspoon salt
- 1 cup (8 ounces) whole milk, room temperature
- ½ cup (3½ ounces) granulated sugar
- 4 large egg yolks, room temperature
- 2 teaspoons vanilla extract
- 16 tablespoons unsalted butter, softened

Filling

- 4 ounces bittersweet chocolate, chopped
- 8 tablespoons unsalted butter
- 6 tablespoons (1⅛ ounces) unsweetened cocoa powder
- ½ cup (2 ounces) confectioners' sugar
- 2 large egg whites

- 1 large egg, lightly beaten with 1 tablespoon water and pinch salt

1 For the dough Whisk flour, yeast, and salt together in bowl of stand mixer. Whisk milk, sugar, egg yolks, and vanilla in 4-cup liquid measuring cup until sugar has dissolved. Using dough hook on low speed, slowly add milk mixture to flour mixture and mix until cohesive dough starts to form and no dry flour remains, about 2 minutes, scraping down bowl as needed.

2 Increase speed to medium-low, add butter, 1 tablespoon at a time, and knead until butter is fully incorporated, about 4 minutes, scraping down bowl as needed. Continue to knead until dough is smooth and elastic and clears sides of bowl, 10 to 12 minutes.

3 Transfer dough to lightly floured counter and knead by hand to form smooth, round ball, about 30 seconds. Place dough, seam side down, in lightly greased large bowl or container, cover tightly with plastic wrap, and let rise until increased in size by about half, 1½ to 2 hours. Place in refrigerator until dough is firm, at least 1 hour or up to 24 hours. (If dough is chilled longer than 1 hour, let rest at room temperature for 15 minutes before rolling out in step 5.)

4 For the filling Microwave chocolate, butter, and cocoa together in medium bowl at 50 percent power, stirring occasionally, until melted, about 3 minutes. Stir in sugar until combined and let cool completely, about 30 minutes. Whisk in egg whites until fully combined and mixture turns glossy.

5 Press down on dough to deflate, then transfer to lightly floured counter. Press and roll dough into 18 by 24-inch rectangle, with short side parallel to counter edge. Spread filling over dough, leaving ½-inch border around edges.

6 Roll dough away from you into firm, taut cylinder. Pinch seam closed, then reshape cylinder as needed to be 18 inches in length with uniform thickness. Wrap in plastic, transfer to rimmed baking sheet, and refrigerate until firm but still supple, about 30 minutes.

7 Make foil sling for Dutch oven by folding 2 long sheets of aluminum foil so each is 7 inches wide. Lay sheets of foil in pot perpendicular to each other, with extra foil hanging over edges of pot. Push foil into bottom and up sides of pot, smoothing foil flush to bottom of pot, then spray with vegetable oil spray.

8 Transfer dough log to lightly floured counter, with short side facing you. Using bench scraper or sharp knife, cut log in half lengthwise. Turn dough halves cut sides up and arrange side by side. Pinch top ends together. Lift and place 1 dough half on opposite side of second half. Repeat, keeping cut sides up, until dough halves are tightly braided. Pinch remaining ends together. Twist braided dough into spiral and tuck end underneath. Transfer loaf to prepared pot, cover with lid, and let rise until increased in size by about half, 1½ to 2 hours.

9 Adjust oven rack to middle position and heat oven to 350 degrees. Gently brush loaf with egg mixture. Cover pot, transfer to oven, and bake loaf for 20 minutes. Uncover, rotate pot, and continue to bake until loaf is deep golden brown and registers 190 to 195 degrees, 40 to 50 minutes.

10 Using foil overhang, lift loaf out of pot and let cool completely on wire rack, about 3 hours.

SHAPING CHOCOLATE BABKA

1 Press and roll dough into 18 by 24-inch rectangle, with short side parallel to counter edge. Spread filling over dough, then roll dough away from you into cylinder. Pinch seam closed.

2 Using bench scraper, cut log in half lengthwise. Turn dough halves cut sides up and arrange side by side. Pinch top ends together.

3 Lift and place 1 dough half on opposite side of second half. Repeat, keeping cut sides up, until dough halves are tightly braided. Pinch remaining ends together.

4 Twist braided dough into spiral and tuck end underneath.

DESSERTS

Pear-Ginger Crisp

APPLE PANDOWDY

SERVES 6 TO 8   TOTAL TIME 2 HOURS 15 MINUTES (PLUS 1 HOUR 30 MINUTES DOUGH CHILLING TIME)

WHY THIS RECIPE WORKS More rustic than an apple pie, this comforting dessert features just one pastry crust placed on top of a spiced apple filling. During baking, the crust is pressed into the filling so the juices flood over the top and caramelize in the oven. Although pandowdies are often baked in a skillet, we found that our Dutch oven had two advantages: We could use it as a mixing bowl for our apples, cutting down on dishes, and the "dowdying" process was easier and neater, since the Dutch oven's high sides kept the juices in the pot. We started the filling on the stovetop to encourage even cooking, then topped the apples with squares of dough to allow steam to escape during baking and prevent the apples from overcooking. Do not use store-bought pie dough in this recipe; it yields gummy results.

Dough

- 3 tablespoons ice water
- 1 tablespoon sour cream
- ⅔ cup (3⅓ ounces) all-purpose flour
- 1 teaspoon granulated sugar
- ½ teaspoon salt
- 6 tablespoons unsalted butter, cut into ½-inch pieces and frozen for 15 minutes

Filling

- 6 tablespoons unsalted butter
- 5 pounds Golden Delicious apples, peeled, cored, halved, and cut into ½-inch-thick wedges
- ½ cup packed (3½ ounces) light brown sugar
- 1 teaspoon ground cinnamon
- ½ teaspoon salt
- 1½ cups apple cider
- 2 tablespoons cornstarch
- 4 teaspoons lemon juice

Topping

- 1 tablespoon granulated sugar
- ¼ teaspoon ground cinnamon
- 1 large egg, lightly beaten

    Vanilla ice cream

1 For the dough Combine ice water and sour cream in bowl. Process flour, sugar, and salt in food processor until combined, about 3 seconds. Scatter butter over top and pulse until size of large peas, 6 to 8 pulses. Add sour cream mixture and pulse until dough forms large clumps and no dry flour remains, 3 to 6 pulses, scraping down sides of bowl as needed.

2 Form dough into 4-inch disk, wrap tightly in plastic wrap, and refrigerate for 1 hour. (Wrapped dough can be refrigerated for up to 2 days or frozen for up to 1 month. If frozen, let dough thaw completely on counter before rolling.)

3 Adjust oven rack to middle position and heat oven to 400 degrees. Let chilled dough sit at room temperature to soften slightly, about 5 minutes. Roll dough into 10-inch circle on lightly floured counter. Using pizza cutter, cut dough into four 2½-inch-wide strips, then make four 2½-inch-wide perpendicular cuts to form squares. (Pieces around edges of dough will be smaller.) Transfer dough pieces to parchment paper–lined baking sheet, cover with plastic, and refrigerate until firm, at least 30 minutes.

4 For the filling Melt butter in Dutch oven over medium heat. Add apples, sugar, cinnamon, and salt and toss to coat. Cover and cook, stirring occasionally, until apples become slightly pliable and release their juice, about 10 minutes.

5 Whisk cider, cornstarch, and lemon juice in bowl until no lumps remain, then stir mixture into apples. Bring to simmer and cook, uncovered, stirring occasionally, until sauce is thickened, about 2 minutes. Off heat, press apples into even layer.

6 For the topping Combine sugar and cinnamon in small bowl. Working quickly, shingle dough pieces over filling until mostly covered, overlapping as needed. Brush dough pieces with egg and sprinkle with cinnamon-sugar mixture. Transfer pot to oven and bake, uncovered, until crust is slightly puffed and beginning to brown, 15 to 20 minutes.

7 Remove pot from oven. Using back of large spoon, press down in center of crust until juices come up over top of crust. Repeat 4 more times around pot. Make sure all apples are submerged and return pot to oven. Bake, uncovered, until crust is golden brown, 35 to 40 minutes.

8 Remove pot from oven and transfer to wire rack. Let pandowdy cool for 20 minutes. Serve with ice cream, drizzling extra sauce over top.

PEAR-GINGER CRISP

SERVES 6 TO 8   TOTAL TIME 1 HOUR 15 MINUTES

WHY THIS RECIPE WORKS We wanted a simple pear crisp that would allow the fruit's subtle floral flavor to shine against the sweet topping and spice. Our spacious Dutch oven allowed us to easily increase the amount of pears from the usual 3 pounds to a generous 5 pounds for a more fruit-forward crisp. To keep the pears' ample moisture in check, we added some cornstarch to the filling. For a topping, we first prepared a standard streusel but found the liquid-y pears washed out the loose mixture. The solution was to replace the cold butter with melted, which soaked up the flour for a more cohesive streusel that stayed crunchy atop the juicy pears. Adding almonds to the topping provided more texture and an extrabuttery note that tasters liked. To give the crisp more character, we traded the typical warm spices for a triple hit of ginger—using fresh ginger in the pear filling, and a mix of ground and crystallized in the topping. We prefer a crisp made with Bartlett pears, but Bosc pears can also be used. Select pears that yield slightly when pressed. Serve with ice cream.

Topping

- ¾ cup slivered almonds
- ½ cup (2½ ounces) all-purpose flour
- ¼ cup packed (1¾ ounces) light brown sugar
- 2 tablespoons chopped crystallized ginger
- 2 tablespoons granulated sugar
- ¾ teaspoon ground ginger
- ⅛ teaspoon salt
- 5 tablespoons unsalted butter, melted and cooled

Filling

- 4 tablespoons unsalted butter
- 3 tablespoons granulated sugar
- 1½ teaspoons cornstarch
- 1½ teaspoons lemon juice
- 1 teaspoon grated fresh ginger
  Pinch salt
- 5 pounds ripe but firm Bartlett pears, peeled, halved, cored, and cut into 1½-inch pieces

1 For the topping Adjust oven rack to lower-middle position and heat oven to 425 degrees. Pulse almonds, flour, brown sugar, crystallized ginger, granulated sugar, ground ginger, and salt in food processor until nuts are finely chopped, about 10 pulses. Drizzle melted butter over flour mixture and pulse until mixture resembles wet sand, about 5 pulses, scraping down sides of bowl as needed.

2 For the filling Melt butter in Dutch oven over medium heat. Off heat, whisk in sugar, cornstarch, lemon juice, ginger, and salt. Add pears and toss to coat.

3 Sprinkle topping evenly over fruit, breaking up any large chunks. Scrape down exposed sides of pot, then transfer to oven. Bake, uncovered, until pears are bubbling around edges and topping is deep golden brown, 25 to 30 minutes, rotating pot halfway through baking.

4 Remove pot from oven and transfer to wire rack. Let crisp cool for 20 minutes before serving.

PEACH COBBLER

SERVES 6 TO 8   TOTAL TIME 1 HOUR 30 MINUTES

WHY THIS RECIPE WORKS Fresh peach cobbler should be the epitome of summer, with plenty of sweet peaches topped with tender biscuits. But peaches' biggest asset—their sweet, flavorful juice—can be a big liability in baking. To avoid a watery filling, we first sautéed a portion of the peaches in our Dutch oven, starting them covered to encourage them to release their liquid, then uncovering the pot to allow the juices to evaporate and the fruit to lightly caramelize, deepening its flavor. To keep the filling from becoming too mushy in the oven, we reserved some peaches to add after sautéing. A cornstarch–lemon juice slurry thickened the filling just enough without making it sludgy or bouncy. Tasters liked the rich flavor of buttermilk biscuits, but the usual method—cutting cold butter into the dry ingredients to give the biscuits a flaky texture—resulted in overly delicate biscuits that fell apart when baked on the juicy filling. To fix this, we swapped out the cold butter for melted butter, which made for sturdier biscuits that stayed crisp through baking. You can substitute 4 pounds of frozen sliced peaches for fresh; there is no need to defrost them.

Filling

- 4 tablespoons unsalted butter
- 5 pounds peaches, peeled, halved, pitted, and cut into ½-inch wedges
- 6 tablespoons (2⅔ ounces) sugar
- ⅛ teaspoon salt
- 1 tablespoon lemon juice
- 1½ teaspoons cornstarch

Topping

- 1½ cups (7½ ounces) all-purpose flour
- 6 tablespoons (2⅔ ounces) sugar
- 1½ teaspoons baking powder
- ¼ teaspoon baking soda
- ¼ teaspoon salt
- ¾ cup buttermilk
- 4 tablespoons unsalted butter, melted and cooled
- 1 teaspoon ground cinnamon

1 For the filling Adjust oven rack to middle position and heat oven to 425 degrees. Melt butter in Dutch oven over medium-high heat. Add two-thirds of peaches, sugar, and salt and cook, covered, until peaches release their juices, about 5 minutes. Uncover and continue to cook until all liquid has evaporated and peaches begin to caramelize, 15 to 20 minutes. Stir in remaining peaches and cook until heated through, about 5 minutes. Whisk lemon juice and cornstarch in small bowl until combined, then stir into peach mixture. Remove pot from heat and cover to keep warm.

2 For the topping Whisk flour, 5 tablespoons sugar, baking powder, baking soda, and salt together in medium bowl. Using wooden spoon, stir in buttermilk and melted butter until dough forms and no dry flour remains; do not overmix.

3 Combine remaining 1 tablespoon sugar and cinnamon in bowl. Pinch off dough into rough 1-inch pieces and space them about ½ inch apart on top of hot peach mixture. Sprinkle with cinnamon sugar and bake, uncovered, until topping is golden brown and filling is thickened, 18 to 22 minutes.

4 Remove pot from oven and transfer to wire rack. Let cobbler cool for 20 minutes before serving.

BLUEBERRY GRUNT

SERVES 12   TOTAL TIME 1 HOUR

WHY THIS RECIPE WORKS This old-fashioned fruit dessert boasts sweetened stewed berries covered with drop biscuit dough that is steamed on the stovetop, rather than baked. A Dutch oven was the perfect vessel here; the heavy bottom prevented the fruit from burning, and the heavy lid held in steam nicely. To avoid the downfalls of many recipes, including washed-out fruit and a soggy topping, we cooked down half of the berries until jammy, and then stirred in the remaining berries to maintain a fresh fruit flavor. A little bit of cornstarch further thickened the filling. For a fluffy biscuit topping, we placed a dish towel under the lid during cooking to absorb condensation that would turn the biscuits soggy. A sprinkle of cinnamon sugar over the finished dessert provided sweet crunch. Do not use frozen blueberries here, as they will make the filling watery.

Filling

2½ pounds (8 cups) blueberries
½   cup (3½ ounces) sugar
½   teaspoon ground cinnamon
2   tablespoons water
1   teaspoon grated lemon zest plus 1 tablespoon juice
1   teaspoon cornstarch

Topping

¾   cup buttermilk
6   tablespoons unsalted butter, melted and
    cooled slightly
1   teaspoon vanilla extract
2¼ cups (11¼ ounces) all-purpose flour
1½ teaspoons baking powder
½   teaspoon baking soda
½   teaspoon salt
½   cup (3½ ounces) sugar
½   teaspoon ground cinnamon

1 For the filling Cook 4 cups blueberries, sugar, cinnamon, water, and lemon zest in Dutch oven over medium-high heat, stirring occasionally, until mixture is thick and jamlike, 10 to 12 minutes. Whisk lemon juice and cornstarch in small bowl until combined, then stir into blueberry mixture. Add remaining 4 cups blueberries and cook until heated through, about 1 minute. Remove pot from heat and cover to keep warm.

2 For the topping Combine buttermilk, melted butter, and vanilla in 2-cup liquid measuring cup. Whisk flour, baking powder, baking soda, salt, and 6 tablespoons sugar together in large bowl. Slowly stir buttermilk mixture into flour mixture until dough forms.

3 Using small ice cream scoop or 2 large spoons, spoon golf ball–size dough pieces on top of warm berry mixture (you should have 14 pieces). Wrap lid of Dutch oven with clean dish towel (keeping towel away from heat source) and cover pot. Simmer gently until biscuits have doubled in size and toothpick inserted in center comes out clean, 16 to 22 minutes.

4 Combine remaining 2 tablespoons sugar and cinnamon in bowl. Remove lid and sprinkle biscuit topping with cinnamon sugar. Serve immediately.

WHITE WINE–POACHED PEARS WITH LEMON AND HERBS

SERVES 6 TO 8   TOTAL TIME 1 HOUR (PLUS CHILLING TIME)

WHY THIS RECIPE WORKS A classic French dessert, poached pears are surprisingly simple to make at home. We wanted a recipe for meltingly tender pears that we could serve chilled, using the poaching liquid as an aromatic sauce. We discovered that not all varieties of pears worked equally well; Bosc and Bartlett won tasters over with their honeyed sweetness and clean appearance. Cutting the pears in half ensured that they cooked evenly from base to stem end. We tested poaching the fruit in water, fruit juice, and wine and found that white wine offered a nuanced flavor that tasters loved, especially when enhanced with bright, fresh additions like lemon zest, mint, and thyme. To poach six pears at once, we found it was necessary to use a full bottle of wine and turn the pears several times as they cooked. We then removed them from the pot and reduced the cooking liquid to a syrupy consistency before pouring it back over the fruit. Letting the pears cool in the syrup prevented them from drying out; it also allowed them to absorb some of the syrup, giving them a candied translucency and making them plump, sweet, and pleasantly spiced. Select pears that yield slightly when pressed. Use a medium-bodied dry white wine such as Sauvignon Blanc or Chardonnay here. The fruit can be served as is or with crème fraîche.

1 vanilla bean
1 (750-ml) bottle dry white wine
¾ cup sugar
6 (2-inch) strips lemon zest
5 sprigs fresh mint, plus extra leaves for serving
3 sprigs fresh thyme
½ cinnamon stick
⅛ teaspoon salt
6 ripe but firm Bosc or Bartlett pears (8 ounces each), peeled, halved, and cored

1 Cut vanilla bean in half lengthwise. Using tip of paring knife, scrape out seeds. Bring wine, sugar, lemon zest, mint sprigs, thyme sprigs, cinnamon stick, salt, and vanilla seeds and pod to boil in Dutch oven over high heat and cook, stirring occasionally, until sugar has dissolved, about 5 minutes.

2 Add pears and return to boil. Reduce heat to medium-low, cover, and simmer until pears are tender and toothpick slips easily in and out of pears, 10 to 20 minutes, gently turning pears over every 5 minutes.

3 Using slotted spoon, transfer pears to shallow casserole dish. Bring syrup to simmer over medium heat and cook, stirring occasionally, until slightly thickened and measures 1¼ to 1½ cups, about 15 minutes. Strain syrup through fine-mesh strainer over pears; discard solids. Let pears cool to room temperature, then cover and refrigerate until well chilled, at least 2 hours or up to 3 days. Serve with extra mint leaves.

CHOCOLATE LAVA CAKE FOR A CROWD

SERVES 12   TOTAL TIME 2 HOURS

WHY THIS RECIPE WORKS Individual-size chocolate lava cakes are a classic restaurant dessert: Moist chocolate cake surrounds a fudgy, molten center that acts like a sauce when the cake is cut open. But this irresistibly chocolaty dessert can be fussy to make at home, especially when serving a crowd—the timing has to be just so to avoid over-baking, and the cakes must be served quickly, before the molten centers cool. We wondered if we could use our Dutch oven to make a large-scale lava cake that would maintain the magic of the originals. First we mixed the batter right in the Dutch oven, and then, taking a cue from a classic pudding cake method, we sprinkled the batter with a mixture of granulated sugar, brown sugar, and cocoa powder and finished the assembly by pouring a combination of water and coffee (to enhance the chocolate flavor) over the top. During baking, the sugar-cocoa mixture sank to the bottom and the cake rose to the top, creating just the fudgy layers we were looking for. We removed the cake from the oven and let it cool slightly; the Dutch oven's heat-retaining walls effectively kept the cake's center gooey and warm even as we went back for seconds. Serve with whipped cream.

12 tablespoons unsalted butter, cut into 12 pieces

4 ounces bittersweet chocolate, chopped coarse

1⅓ cups (4 ounces) unsweetened cocoa powder

⅔ cup packed (4⅔ ounces) light brown sugar

2 cups (14 ounces) granulated sugar

1½ cups brewed coffee

1½ cups water

⅔ cup whole milk

2 tablespoons vanilla extract

2 large egg yolks

4 teaspoons baking powder

½ teaspoon salt

1½ cups (7½ ounces) all-purpose flour

1 Adjust oven rack to middle position and heat oven to 325 degrees. Melt butter, chocolate, and ⅔ cup cocoa in Dutch oven over low heat, stirring frequently, until smooth, 2 to 4 minutes. Remove pot from heat and let cool slightly.

2 Whisk brown sugar, ⅔ cup granulated sugar, and remaining ⅔ cup cocoa together in bowl, breaking up any large clumps of brown sugar with fingers. In separate bowl, combine coffee and water.

3 Whisk milk, vanilla, egg yolks, baking powder, salt, and remaining 1⅓ cups granulated sugar into cooled chocolate mixture. Whisk in flour until just combined. Sprinkle brown sugar mixture evenly over top, covering entire surface of batter. Pour water mixture gently over brown sugar mixture.

4 Scrape down exposed sides of pot, then transfer to oven. Bake, uncovered, until cake begins to pull away from sides of pot and top is just firm to touch, 1¼ to 1½ hours, rotating pot halfway through baking. Remove pot from oven and transfer to wire rack. Let cake cool for 15 minutes before serving.

Variation

CHOCOLATE-ORANGE LAVA CAKE FOR A CROWD
Substitute 1 cup orange juice and ½ cup Grand Marnier for coffee.

BOURBON-PECAN BREAD PUDDING

SERVES 8 TO 10   TOTAL TIME 2 HOURS

WHY THIS RECIPE WORKS We wanted to make a refined bread pudding with a moist, creamy interior and a crisp, sweet top crust. We used our Dutch oven as both mixing bowl and baking dish, which not only was convenient but also allowed us to accommodate a full pound of cubed challah (our top choice for its rich flavor). To make our custard, we whisked the ingredients together in the Dutch oven—no parcooking or tempering required. Heavy cream, milk, and egg yolks (instead of whole eggs) ensured that the custard was rich and not eggy. Brown sugar offered caramel notes, and ⅓ cup of bourbon gave the custard distinctive character without making it boozy. Cardamom and vanilla brought aromatic flavor. We stirred in the bread and let the mixture sit for about half an hour so the cubes could soak up the custard, then sprinkled the pudding with brown sugar and pecans for a nutty-sweet, crunchy top. Baking in a moderate oven prevented the custard from curdling. As an elegant finishing touch, we made a sweet bourbon sauce to pour over the finished pudding. Challah is an egg-enriched bread that can be found in most bakeries and supermarkets. Hearty white sandwich bread can be substituted for the challah. If you don't have time to stale the bread overnight, you can dry fresh bread pieces by baking them on a rimmed baking sheet in a 225-degree oven for about 40 minutes, stirring occasionally. Serve with Bourbon–Brown Sugar Sauce if desired.

2½ cups heavy cream
2½ cups whole milk
 9 large egg yolks
 ¾ cup packed (5¼ ounces) plus 2 tablespoons
    brown sugar
 ⅓ cup bourbon
 1 tablespoon vanilla extract
 ¾ teaspoon salt
 ¼ teaspoon ground cardamom
 1 pound challah, cut into 1-inch pieces (12 cups),
    staled overnight
 ½ cup pecans, chopped

1 Adjust oven rack to middle position and heat oven to 325 degrees. Whisk cream, milk, egg yolks, ¾ cup sugar, bourbon, vanilla, salt, and cardamom in Dutch oven until sugar has dissolved and mixture is well combined. Fold in challah and let sit until custard is mostly absorbed, about 30 minutes, folding again halfway through sitting.

2 Sprinkle pudding with pecans and remaining 2 tablespoons sugar. Transfer pot to oven and bake, uncovered, until center of bread pudding is set, 50 to 70 minutes.

3 Remove pot from oven and transfer to wire rack. Let bread pudding cool for 15 minutes before serving.

BOURBON–BROWN SUGAR SAUCE
MAKES ABOUT 1 CUP

 ½ cup packed (3½ ounces) light brown sugar
 7 tablespoons heavy cream
2½ tablespoons unsalted butter
1½ tablespoons bourbon

Bring sugar and cream to boil in small saucepan over medium heat and cook, whisking frequently, until sugar is fully dissolved. Off heat, whisk in butter and bourbon. Let cool slightly. (Sauce can be refrigerated for up to 2 weeks; gently warm in microwave, stirring every 10 seconds, until pourable, before using.)

DROP DOUGHNUTS

MAKES **24 DOUGHNUTS**   TOTAL TIME **1 HOUR**

WHY THIS RECIPE WORKS For quick, tender cake-style doughnuts, we first did away with rolling and stamping out the dough into rings. Instead, we merely dropped generous spoonfuls of batter into hot oil, creating round doughnut "holes." The perfect ratio of flour to baking powder produced a light, airy batter. All-purpose flour gave these doughnuts the right amount of structure, and just 2 tablespoons of butter and some milk added richness and tenderness without weighing the batter down. The most important factor in preventing greasy doughnuts was making sure we fried them at the right temperature; we were careful to keep the oil between 325 and 350 degrees while cooking each batch. The excellent heat retention of a Dutch oven made it the ideal vessel for frying, since it was able to keep the oil nice and hot. A dusting of confectioners' sugar made a nice final touch.

2 cups (10 ounces) all-purpose flour
2 teaspoons baking powder
¼ teaspoon salt
½ cup (3½ ounces) granulated sugar
2 large eggs
1 teaspoon ground nutmeg
½ cup whole milk
2 tablespoons unsalted butter, melted and cooled
½ teaspoon vanilla extract
2 quarts peanut or vegetable oil
   Confectioners' sugar, for dusting

1 Whisk flour, baking powder, and salt together in medium bowl. In separate bowl, whisk granulated sugar, eggs, and nutmeg together until smooth, then whisk in milk, melted butter, and vanilla. Stir egg mixture into flour mixture with wooden spoon until evenly combined. (Batter can be refrigerated for up to 12 hours.)

2 Add oil to Dutch oven until it measures about 1½ inches deep and heat over medium-high heat to 350 degrees. Line rimmed baking sheet with paper towels. Using small ice cream scoop or 2 large spoons, carefully spoon 6 golf ball–size batter portions into hot oil. Fry doughnuts until crisp and deeply browned on all sides, 3 to 6 minutes. Adjust burner, if necessary, to maintain oil temperature between 325 and 350 degrees.

3 Using wire skimmer or slotted spoon, transfer doughnuts to prepared sheet and let drain. Repeat with remaining batter in 3 batches. Dust with confectioners' sugar and serve warm.

Variations
SPICE DROP DOUGHNUTS
Add 1½ teaspoons ground cinnamon and ¼ teaspoon ground allspice to batter with nutmeg. In medium bowl, combine ½ cup granulated sugar, 1 tablespoon ground cinnamon, ¾ teaspoon ground nutmeg, and ½ teaspoon ground allspice; set aside. Let fried doughnuts drain for 2 minutes, then roll in spiced sugar to coat.

BANANA DROP DOUGHNUTS
Add 1 mashed ripe banana to batter and substitute cinnamon for nutmeg. In medium bowl, combine ½ cup granulated sugar and 1 tablespoon ground cinnamon; set aside. Let fried doughnuts drain for 2 minutes, then roll in cinnamon sugar to coat.

ORANGE DROP DOUGHNUTS
Substitute 1 tablespoon grated orange zest for nutmeg, and ½ cup orange juice for milk. Process ½ cup granulated sugar and 1 teaspoon grated orange zest in food processor until fragrant, about 20 seconds; transfer to medium bowl and set aside. Let fried doughnuts drain for 2 minutes, then roll in orange sugar to coat.

CONVERSIONS AND EQUIVALENTS

Some say cooking is a science and an art. We would say that geography has a hand in it, too. Flours and sugars manufactured in the United Kingdom and elsewhere will feel and taste different from those manufactured in the United States. So we cannot promise that the loaf of bread you bake in Canada or England will taste the same as a loaf baked in the United States, but we can offer guidelines for converting weights and measures. We also recommend that you rely on your instincts when making our recipes. Refer to the visual cues provided. If the dough hasn't "come together in a ball" as described, you may need to add more flour—even if the recipe doesn't tell you to. You be the judge.

The recipes in this book were developed using standard U.S. measures following U.S. government guidelines. The charts below offer equivalents for U.S. and metric measures. All conversions are approximate and have been rounded up or down to the nearest whole number.

example

1 teaspoon = 4.9292 milliliters,
rounded up to 5 milliliters
1 ounce = 28.3495 grams,
rounded down to 28 grams

VOLUME CONVERSIONS

U.S.	Metric
1 teaspoon	5 milliliters
2 teaspoons	10 milliliters
1 tablespoon	15 milliliters
2 tablespoons	30 milliliters
¼ cup	59 milliliters
⅓ cup	79 milliliters
½ cup	118 milliliters
¾ cup	177 milliliters
1 cup	237 milliliters
1¼ cups	296 milliliters
1½ cups	355 milliliters
2 cups (1 pint)	473 milliliters
2½ cups	591 milliliters
3 cups	710 milliliters
4 cups (1 quart)	0.946 liter
1.06 quarts	1 liter
4 quarts (1 gallon)	3.8 liters

WEIGHT CONVERSIONS

Ounces	Grams
½	14
¾	21
1	28
1½	43
2	57
2½	71
3	85
3½	99
4	113
4½	128
5	142
6	170
7	198
8	227
9	255
10	283
12	340
16 (1 pound)	454

CONVERSION FOR COMMON BAKING INGREDIENTS

Baking is an exacting science. Because measuring by weight is far more accurate than measuring by volume, and thus more likely to produce reliable results, in our recipes we provide ounce measures in addition to cup measures for many ingredients. Refer to the chart below to convert these measures into grams.

Ingredient	Ounces	Grams
Flour		
1 cup all–purpose flour*	5	142
1 cup cake flour	4	113
1 cup whole–wheat flour	5½	156
Sugar		
1 cup granulated (white) sugar	7	198
1 cup packed brown sugar (light or dark)	7	198
1 cup confectioners' sugar	4	113
Cocoa Powder		
1 cup cocoa powder	3	85
Butter†		
4 tablespoons (½ stick, or ¼ cup)	2	57
8 tablespoons (1 stick, or ½ cup)	4	113
16 tablespoons (2 sticks, or 1 cup)	8	227

* U.S. all-purpose flour, the most frequently used flour in this book, does not contain leaveners, as some European flours do. These leavened flours are called self-rising or self-raising. If you are using self-rising flour, take this into consideration before adding leavening to a recipe.

† In the United States, butter is sold both salted and unsalted. We generally recommend unsalted butter. If you are using salted butter, take this into consideration before adding salt to a recipe.

OVEN TEMPERATURES

Fahrenheit	Celsius	Gas Mark
225	105	¼
250	120	½
275	135	1
300	150	2
325	165	3
350	180	4
375	190	5
400	200	6
425	220	7
450	230	8
475	245	9

CONVERTING TEMPERATURES FROM AN INSTANT-READ THERMOMETER

We include doneness temperatures in many of the recipes in this book. We recommend an instant-read thermometer for the job. Refer to the above table to convert Fahrenheit degrees to Celsius. Or, for temperatures not represented in the chart, use this simple formula:

Subtract 32 degrees from the Fahrenheit reading, then divide the result by 1.8 to find the Celsius reading.

example
"Roast chicken until thighs register 175 degrees."

to convert
175°F − 32 = 143°
143° ÷ 1.8 = 79.44°C, rounded down to 79°C

INDEX

Note: Page references in *italics* indicate photographs.

P